The Pink Panther

ALSO BY HOWARD MAXFORD
AND FROM McFARLAND

*Hammer Complete: The Films, the Personnel,
the Company* (2023 [2018])

TV Gothic: The Golden Age of Small Screen Horror (2022)

The Pink Panther
A Complete History

HOWARD MAXFORD

McFarland & Company, Inc., Publishers
Jefferson, North Carolina

Library of Congress Cataloging-in-Publication Data

Names: Maxford, Howard author
Title: The Pink Panther : a complete history / Howard Maxford.
Description: Jefferson, North Carolina : McFarland & Company, Inc., Publishers, 2025. | Includes bibliographical references and index.
Identifiers: LCCN 2025023107 | ISBN 9781476696348 paperback ∞
    ISBN 9781476655604 ebook
Subjects: LCSH: Pink Panther films | BISAC: PERFORMING ARTS / Film / Genres / Comedy | LCGFT: Film criticism
Classification: LCC PN1997.P511925 M38 2025 | DDC 791.43/75—dc23/eng/20250514
LC record available at https://lccn.loc.gov/2025023107

ISBN (print) 978-1-4766-9634-8
ISBN (ebook) 978-1-4766-5560-4

© 2025 Howard Maxford. All rights reserved

No part of this book may be reproduced or transmitted in any form or by any means, electronic or mechanical, including photocopying or recording, or by any information storage and retrieval system, without permission in writing from the publisher.

Front cover image: Peter Sellers as Inspector Clouseau in the 1982 film *Trail of the Pink Panther* (MGM/Photofest)

Printed in the United States of America

McFarland & Company, Inc., Publishers
  Box 611, Jefferson, North Carolina 28640
    www.mcfarlandpub.com

Table of Contents

Introduction   1

1. Hollywood B.C. (Before Clouseau)   5
2. Send in the Clowns   15
3. Getting Animated   44
4. A Second Shot   52
5. The Interloper   75
6. The Panther Returns   87
7. Lightning Strikes Twice   109
8. Revenge Is Sweet   126
9. The Trail Goes Cold   142
10. Panther Resurrectus   165

Filmography (Movies, Theatrical Cartoons, TV Shows, Computer Games)   177
Chapter Notes   185
Bibliography   191
Index   193

Introduction

When I sat down in late 2023 to start work on this examination of the phenomenally successful series of comedies starring Peter Sellers as the bumbling Inspector Jacques Clouseau, the inaugural film, *The Pink Panther* (1963), had just reached its 60th anniversary. Still popular on TV, Blu-ray and various streaming platforms, the films have remained firm favorites with audiences around the world down the decades, and as I write, plans are already afoot to reboot the franchise (again). However, while other actors have played the role of Clouseau (Alan Arkin, Roger Moore and Steve Martin), it is Sellers' portrayal that remains the one cherished by fans. Of the eleven features made to date, he appears in six of them (including *Trail of the Pink Panther* [1982], which was made after his death using previously unseen footage), and the character, with his absurd French accent, pompous self-regard and capacity to produce mayhem wherever he goes, remains one of the silver screen's most beloved comic creations. But it wasn't Sellers alone who was responsible for the series' continued success. This belongs in equal measure to the admired writer-director Blake Edwards and his long-standing composer Henry Mancini, whose slinky title music remains, like the James Bond theme, one of the cinema's most enduring and instantly recognizable pieces of music.

As a youngster, I'd watched the first three Clouseau films on TV at home, along with the cartoons and the Saturday morning show derived from the animated credits of the first movie, but seeing *The Return of the Pink Panther* (1975) on the big screen with a packed audience was a revelation. I'd never heard people erupt with laughter like that, especially during the sequence in which Clouseau manages to drive not one but *two* small trucks into the same swimming pool, the second just as the first is being lifted out. People were literally helpless with laughter at the sheer absurdity of it all, and you couldn't hear the film for a good minute afterward, as the noise was so loud and sustained. The two follow-ups, *The Pink Panther Strikes Again* (1976), with its floating

Quasimodo sequence, and *Revenge of the Pink Panther* (1978), with its various explosions and calamities, provoked equal hilarity, and it was as much a pleasure to hear that laughter and be a part of it as it was to watch the movies. And like the Bond films, the Panthers became an event to look forward to for their increasingly elaborate sight gags and stunts, as well as for Sellers' absurd disguises and progressively strangulated vowel sounds (no one could say "meunky" or "reum" or "beumb" or "sol-ved" the way he did).

Fast forward a decade or so, and I was working as a freelance entertainment journalist, contributing to a variety of British magazines, including *Film Review*, *What's On in London* and *Gold*. This saw me interview many of my movie heroes, either for articles promoting their latest films or for retrospectives about their past triumphs, among them writers, directors, producers, composers and stars, including the likes of (name dropping alert) Peter Jackson, Christopher Lee, John Barry, Ray Harryhausen, Christian Bale, Susannah York, George Sidney, Lewis Gilbert, John Mills, Ken Adam, Vangelis, Ann Miller, William Goldman and Joel and Ethan Coen. And looking back, I can't believe how lucky I was to have been able to talk to them all. I also had the pleasure of speaking to Blake Edwards and Henry Mancini, as well as several other Panther alumni, including Herbert Lom (Chief Inspector Charles Dreyfus), Burt Kwouk (Cato), Graham Stark (Hercule LaJoy and Auguste Balls, among others), Tony Adams (producer) and Christopher Challis (cinematographer), as well as Peter Ustinov, the original choice to play Clouseau, whom I briefly questioned about his involvement in the first Panther while preparing a retrospective about *Death on the Nile* (1978).

I first interviewed Mancini back in 1991 in London in his suite at the Four Seasons' Inn on the Park, where he regularly stayed while in the UK. On this occasion, he was here for a concert tour, as well as to promote his latest film venture with Blake Edwards, *Switch* (1991). However, he was happy to talk about his past glories as well as upcoming projects, among them *Tom and Jerry: The Movie* (1992). In fact, during our interview, his lyricist Leslie Bricusse called to quickly discuss one of the songs they were writing together for the cartoon. Mancini, whom I was lucky enough to interview a second time on the phone in 1992 about the upcoming *Son of the Pink Panther* (1993) on which he was then working, is clearly one of the cinema's great composers with his own distinctive sound, and deserves to be ranked alongside the likes of Bernard Herrmann, John Barry, Ennio Morricone, Jerry Goldsmith and John Williams (who played the piano on some of Mancini's early film and TV scores before his own career took off). Consequently, as a lifelong soundtrack aficionado, to be sat opposite someone whose music I had been listening to from an early age was a real thrill, especially as I got to ask him about his work for such personal favorites as *Breakfast at Tiffany's* (1961), *Hatari!* (1962, known for the catchy "Baby Elephant Walk"), *Charade* (1963) and *Arabesque* (1966), and such evergreen songs as "Moon River" about the writing of which he revealed, "It was a struggle for a long time.... But once I hit upon those first three notes, it was like a month and a half hour, something like that, to write it."[1]

I interviewed Edwards, whom I equally revered as one of Hollywood's most polished comedy directors, just once on the phone in 1999 for a couple of retrospectives. A class act, he was under no obligation to speak to me (he wasn't promoting a film at the time), yet couldn't have been more pleasant and accommodating, and to be in conversation with the man who had given us such extravaganzas as *The Great Race* (1965), with its hilarious scenes of catastrophe; *The Party* (1968), which reduced my father and me to paroxysms of laughter when we caught on TV; *10* (1979), which introduced Ravel's "Boléro" to a whole new audience; and *Victor/Victoria* (1982), easily his most sophisticated work, was something of a head-spinner, especially as the interview lasted well over an hour. "Keep going,"[2] he enthused at one point when it looked like we might be interrupted, and when our time together was finally getting close to its end he said, "I'm gonna have to say goodbye in five minutes,"[3] quickly adding, "I can't let the potatoes burn,"[4] which conjured up a delightful image of him getting dinner ready for himself and the missus, who of course just happened to be Julie Andrews. During our call, he spoke in detail about the Panthers, and even agreed with me when I said I thought that *The Return of the Pink Panther* was the best of them ("Yes, *I do*,"[5] he said). He also spoke with candor and good humor about his increasingly tense relationship with Sellers, and even inadvertently let slip that his wife might never perform again following a botched throat operation in 1997. "We don't even know whether the lady's ever gonna sing again. She certainly can't sing now,"[6] he told me. The story broke soon after and subsequently became world news, but not having a tabloid mentality, in my naïveté, I didn't use the quote.

When I forwarded the published articles to those I'd spoken to, along with my thanks for their time (a courtesy I always extended to interviewees), each of them took the trouble to reply. Wrote Mancini: "You were very kind to send me your article which appeared in *What's On in London*. I really appreciate your professionalism. The quotes were spot on. I hope we can do it again. Kindest regards...." I couldn't believe it; Hank Mancini thanking *me* for *my* professionalism *and* hoping that we might do it again some time. Wow! Wrote Graham Stark: "Thank you for the Pink Panther feature you sent. Very well written and it's nice to read something which gets every fact right. Congratulations, and again my thanks. Sincerely...." Julie Andrews' personal assistant Francine Taylor, meanwhile, wrote to me on behalf of Blake and Julie (who I'd also interviewed via written correspondence following that fateful operation). "Thank you for your kindness in sending copies of the features you wrote on *The Pink Panther* and *Victor/Victoria*. They were most enjoyable, and I have passed on your thanks to Ms. Andrews and Mr. Edwards. Sincerely...."

Between Edwards and Mancini and the other Panther veterans I spoke to, I'd recorded much more material than I was ever likely to use for the features I was going to write, and thought there might be more than enough for a book about the films and cartoons. Yet despite my writing up some notes in the early 2000s, the project didn't take off for a number of reasons, and after various distractions (other books, my main job as a stage manager, life in general), it was put on the back burner ... until now. Incredibly, the Mancini tape sat in box for thirty-two years and the Edwards one for twenty-four. Listening to their voices answer my questions again was a genuine journey back in time, and it was a real pleasure to be in their company once more (though hearing my 27-year-old self talking to Mancini felt a bit odd). Even now I can't believe that I got to speak to them both so intimately. So here at last, rescued from dusty obscurity, are the reminiscences of Blake Edwards, Henry Mancini and all those other Panther legends about the making of the silver screen's most successful comedy franchise, from those glory days in the sixties and seventies through to the present and beyond. So spin that globe, mount those parallel bars and practice your karate chops—it's time for the Pink Panther to strike again, you kneuw.

A Note on the Text

As well as quotes from my own interviews, for the sake of narrative clarity, the book is occasionally augmented by comments from a variety of other sources, including autobiographies, biographies, talk shows, newspapers, magazines and DVD commentaries. All quotations are annotated, with the sources provided at the back of the book. All stills, posters and album covers, etc., are credited to their respective companies.

1

Hollywood B.C. (Before Clouseau)

When the trio of director Blake Edwards, composer Henry Mancini and comedy actor Peter Sellers joined forces to make *The Pink Panther* (1963), none of them could have imagined that their destinies would be so closely entwined for the remainder of their careers, for the success of the film not only helped Sellers become a front rank star but also launched a number of sequels that would go on to conquer the box office around the world and become firm favorites with comedy fans everywhere, resulting in some of the cinema's most hilarious scenes of mishap and mayhem.

Of the three protagonists, Edwards was the one with the most established track record at this point. Hailing from a family of moviemakers, he was born William Blake Crump on 26 July 1922 in Tulsa, Oklahoma. He never knew his real father, Donald Crump, who abandoned his mother Lillian before he was born, and when she subsequently relocated to Los Angeles and remarried in 1926, the young Blake was adopted by his stepfather, Jack McEdward (sometimes McEdwards), a former theater director who was by then working as a production manager and assistant director at Fox in Hollywood. Despite the security the marriage brought, it apparently wasn't all wine and roses, as Blake later recalled. "I had a very insecure childhood, and not a particularly family-oriented childhood."[1] McEdward's own father, J. Gordon Edwards, had also been in the movies, his major contribution to screen history being several vehicles starring the noted silent screen vamp Theda Bara, among them *Cleopatra* (1917), *Salome* (1918) and *A Woman There Was* (1919), each of which had been hugely popular at the time. All but forgotten now, he was one of the most commercially successful directors of his day, an achievement his step-grandson would eventually go on to emulate. Recalled Edwards, "My grandfather was a very prominent filmmaker.... He was considered one of the really top directors of his time."[2]

J. Gordon Edwards pulled a few strings to get his son Jack a job at Fox (initially in the prop department), and Blake likewise ended up at Fox when, having graduated from Beverly Hills High School, he decided to turn his attention toward acting, making his screen debut as one of several cadets in the studio's *Ten Gentlemen from West Point* (1942). His role may have been minor, but it led to a contract worth $150 a week, a not insubstantial sum in the early forties. As well as appearing in Fox productions, Edwards was often loaned out to other studios as a supporting actor under the terms of his contract, and consequently got to work for a number of top-drawer filmmakers over the following few years, among them Victor Fleming, Otto Preminger, Mervyn LeRoy, William Wellman, John Ford and William Wyler, appearing in the likes of *A Guy Named Joe* (1944), *They Were Expendable* (1945) and *The Best Years of Our Lives* (1946). Unfortunately, not all of the films he appeared in were of such a high quality, among them *Marshal of Reno* (1944) and *Strangler of the Swamp* (1945), which he made for the Poverty Row outfits Republic and PRC respectively, and though he had a substantial role in the latter, with so many loan outs, it must have seemed clear even to him that his career as an actor was going nowhere. Recalled Edwards, "I was never a very good actor, but I wasn't bad. I don't think I would have had a great career, but you never know."[3] So following experience in the Coast Guard and a couple more minor roles, this time over at Columbia, he looked toward changing his career path and becoming a screenwriter.

He subsequently teamed up with another budding young scribe, John C. Champion, and together they wrote a low-budget western, *Panhandle* (1948), which went before the cameras in late 1947 at Allied Artists under the direction of second feature veteran Lesley Selander. In addition to writing the script, the duo managed to persuade the studio into letting them produce the film, in which Edwards also appears (not entirely convincingly, it must be said) as a black-clad bad guy named Floyd Schofield, who at one point is poised to attack leading man Rod Cameron (who describes him as a "cheap, tinhorn gunslinger") in a bar with a broken bottle. The resultant movie, "Filmed in glorious Sepia Tone!" as the poster has it, is a fairly cliché-ridden affair, and may not have blazed any trails, yet it was noticed by the trade paper *Variety* ("As a first production for two newcomers, *Panhandle* registers well," it commented), and Edwards at least now had a precious writer-producer credit under his belt. He may have been on the bottom rung of the ladder, but at least he was actually *on* the ladder. Consequently, having hit upon a mildly successful formula, Edwards and Champion stuck to their guns and turned out another B western script, *Stampede* (1949),

1. Hollywood B.C. (Before Clouseau)

this time taken from a novel by Edward Beverly Mann, which also found a home at Allied Artists, with Selander and Cameron returning as director and star, and the writers retaining their status as producers (Edwards also acted for the last time in the film, appearing briefly as a bank teller).

Having now established himself in his hyphenated role as a writer-producer, Edwards sought to widen his range, and while Champion doggedly remained on the sagebrush trail churning out western scripts, he instead turned to other genres. Radio was hugely popular in the forties, and it was to this medium that Edwards next turned his attention, creating the popular series *Richard Diamond, Private Detective* (1949–1953) for NBC, which starred Hollywood favorite Dick Powell (it was later turned into a TV show [1957–1960] starring David

Bottling it. A bequiffed Blake Edwards loses his rag in *Panhandle* (1948) (Champion-Edwards Productions/Monogram/Allied Artists).

Janssen). Meanwhile, back at the movies, he entered into a new partnership with writer-director Richard Quine, with whom he would go on to make a number of light musicals and comedies. Like Edwards, Quine had had started his career as an actor. Similarly, he yearned for more, perhaps realizing that he'd never make it to the front ranks of stardom either, and so turned to direction instead, making his debut with *Leather Gloves* (1948, aka *Loser Take All*) for Columbia, which featured Edwards in his penultimate performance (it was released between his two westerns). The studio put Quine under contract, and it was here that he and Edwards went to work on their first film together, a service farce with music titled *Sound Off* (1952), one of several they would make for producer Jonie Taps.

Comedy seemed to suit Edwards' style, and he and Quine decided to stick with the mix of laughs and music with their successive three collaborations, *Rainbow 'Round My Shoulder* (1952), *All Ashore* (1953) and *Cruisin' Down the River* (1953), which made for a busy period both on screen and off, as Edwards also married his first wife, Patricia Walker, in 1953, with whom he would go on to have two children, Geoffrey (after whom he would name one of his production companies) and Jennifer. Quine and Edwards briefly turned to thrills next with *Drive a Crooked Road* (1954), following which they had their greatest success with a musical version of *My Sister Eileen* (1955), which was choreographed by Bob Fosse (Quine had appeared as a drugstore clerk in the 1942 version). Commented *Variety* of the results: "Even those well-acquainted with all of the material will find a freshness here that assures acceptance."

Edwards' own ambition to direct was realized next, albeit on television, where he made his debut with *Knockout* (1953, TV), the first of five episodes he helmed for *Four Star Playhouse* (1952–1956, TV), for which he'd already written a couple of installments. The episode, which he also wrote with Robert Wells, was made via Four Star Television, whose founders included Dick Powell (the lead in Edwards' *Richard Diamond* radio series) and David Niven, whom he also directed for the first time in another *Playhouse* story titled *The Bomb* (1954, TV). As a consequence of this, along with further episode work on such series as *The Pepsi-Cola Playhouse* (1953–1955, TV), *City Detective* (1953–1955, TV) and *The Star and the Story* (1955–1956, TV), plus an unsold pilot for *Mike Hammer!* (1954, TV), Columbia allowed him to have a stab at a feature with the comedy musical *Bring Your Smile Along* (1955), which he also scripted from a story by himself and Quine. The results, again produced by Jonie Taps, didn't quite set the world alight, but he had at least successfully steered a modestly effective movie from script to screen.

1. Hollywood B.C. (Before Clouseau)

Quine went on to work with Judy Holliday next on *The Solid Gold Cadillac* (1956) and *Full of Life* (1956), yet found time to co-script Edwards' following film as a director, *He Laughed Last* (1956), a nightclub comedy with music, while Edwards in turn helped to co-script Quine's *Operation Mad Ball* (1957), another army comedy which proved to be another hit, after which their careers inevitably began to diverge as Edwards further established himself as a director, though the two remained on friendly terms (he later helped to co-script *The Notorious Landlady* [1962] for Quine). Edwards went on to make the gangster comedy-drama *Mister Cory* (1957), the first of four films he made under a new contract with Universal, and though the picture is all but forgotten today, it proved important to him in one respect, given that it marked his first association with the composer Henry Mancini who, working under the supervision of Universal's resident music director, Joseph Gershenson, supplied a couple of cues for the film. Neither could have known that this would lead to a thirty-seven-year working relationship, during which Mancini would score the majority of Edwards' movies, along with several television series and a Broadway musical.

Recalled Mancini of that original encounter, "The first time I met Blake was at Universal in 1957 when I did part of the score, though not the whole score, for *Mister Cory*. Then I did some work on *This Happy Feeling* and several other things for him. He was a contract director and I was under contract too, and we were just thrown together. Then, in the early part of 1958, the studio system began to break down and theaters began to close all over the country because of television coming in. As a consequence, the music department was disbanded, and I think the last picture I did at Universal was a James Cagney picture called *Never Steal Anything Small*. After that I was without a job. That summer, Blake came up with the idea for the *Peter Gunn* TV show, for which I wrote the theme. I was just happy to get something to do, but as things turned out, it was a very good move, because without it I don't know what turn my career would have taken. In fact that *was* the turning point. But I had no idea, and neither did Blake, that it would lead on to twenty-six films! It was success followed by success, and he wasn't about to change it—and I was happy he wasn't!"[4]

Born in Cleveland on 16 April 1924, Enrico Nicola Mancini developed an interest in music at the age of eight when his steelworker father, who'd immigrated to America from Abruzzi in Italy with his wife, taught him to play the flute and piccolo. At twelve, he took up the piano, while at thirteen he was named principal flutist in the Pennsylvania All-State Band, all of which led to his studying music at the Carnegie Tech Music School and, from the age of eighteen, Juilliard. Following military service in the Army Air Corps during World War II, Mancini began his professional career as a pianist and arranger with The Glenn Miller Orchestra (by then led by Tex Beneke), having met several members of the band in the army. It was during this time that Mancini also met his future wife, singer Ginny O'Connor, whom he married in 1947. As well as singing for The Glenn Miller Orchestra, O'Connor was also a member of a vocal group called The Mel-Tones (formed by singer Mel Tormé), which caught the eye of a Universal talent spotter. Subsequently, O'Connor and her colleagues found themselves signed to a contract with the studio in 1952. More importantly, Mancini was also signed as an arranger, initially to work on the Abbott and Costello comedy *Lost in Alaska* (1952). However, while The Mel-Tones were soon forgotten, Mancini's initial two-week contract was continually extended, and he went on to work (often uncredited) on dozens of films before he left the studio in 1958, providing cues and arrangements for the likes of *It Came from Outer Space* (1953), *The Creature from the Black Lagoon* (1954) and *Abbott and Costello Meet the Mummy* (1955).

Recalled Mancini of this period, "Joe Gershenson was the head of the music department at Universal. In those days the studio system was still very much in existence, and every studio had a staff orchestra as well as staff composers, arrangers and copyists. It was a full-time operation. I began there as an arranger, but within a couple of days of starting they gave me various scenes to compose, to sort of ease me into it. So I started doing everything immediately—arranging, composing—though I ended up mostly composing. But it was Joe who conducted all the pictures. He was a very, very accomplished musician and conductor. He knew *exactly* what was needed."[5] Ironically, one of the biggest pictures Mancini worked on while he was at Universal was *The Glenn Miller Story* (1954), which earned him his first Oscar nomination (shared with Gershenson) for his arrangements, which accurately re-produced the distinctive Miller sound. Mancini performed similar duties on *The Benny Goodman Story* (1956), after which he began to score entire movies, among them *Man Afraid* (1957) and *A Touch of Evil* (1958), the latter directed by Orson Welles. Unfortunately, Mancini's contract was terminated soon after as part of the severe economic cut backs at the studio. Luckily, Edwards remembered the composer when he was setting up *Peter Gunn* (1958–1961, TV), and the rest, as the cliché has it, is history.

The TV show, which Edwards also produced and occasionally wrote and directed, was an affable blend of comedy and crime revolving round the adventures of a big city private eye, and notched up 114 half-hour episodes during its hugely successful run. Contributing to that success was Mancini's jazzy title theme, with its pounding piano

1. Hollywood B.C. (Before Clouseau)

baseline (played by John Williams). It was an instant hit, and a recording of it arranged by Mancini for trumpeter Ray Anthony (a bandleader formerly with The Glenn Miller Orchestra) reached number eight on the Billboard Hot 100 chart, while Mancini's own LP of music from the series reached the coveted number-one spot, where it remained for an astonishing ten weeks, becoming a million seller. It also went on to earn him the very first Grammy for best album of the year in 1959, as well as a long-standing contract with RCA, through which he subsequently released many of his movie scores and easy listening albums, among them the follow-up *More Music from* Peter Gunn (1959). In fact, so cool was the theme considered, it was later featured in *The Blues Brothers* (1980), not once but *twice*.

Just for the record. The original LP release of Henry Mancini's groundbreaking music for the TV series *Peter Gunn* (1958–1961, TV) (RCA/NBC/Spartan).

A proto panther? The cool cat featured in the credits for the Blake Edwards series *Mr. Lucky* (1959–1960, TV) (CBS/Spartan).

Peter Gunn wasn't Edwards' only foray into television during this period. He also created *Mr. Lucky* (1959–1960, TV), about a professional gambler, which Mancini also scored, and the nightclub drama *Dante* (1960–1961, TV), which was based upon an episode he'd penned for *Four Star Playhouse* (1952–1956, TV), by which time he'd concluded his Universal contract with two service comedies, *The Perfect Furlough* (1958, aka *Strictly for Pleasure*) and *Operation Petticoat* (1959), the latter of which starred Cary Grant, and which went on to become Edwards' biggest box office success to date, coming in at number four in the year's box office rankings with a take of $23,300,000 in the U.S. and Canada alone ("The film is directed by Blake Edwards with a slam-bang pace," enthused *Variety*).

Edwards and Mancini were now clearly on the map, and next collaborated on the Bing Crosby vehicle *High Time* (1960), a cheerful college comedy which contains the composer's first full (and first fully acknowledged) big-screen score for Edwards, whose direction *Variety* found to be "light and fluid." The film wasn't exactly groundbreaking, and while Edwards had established himself as a director of breezy, likeable comedies, and had created several hit TV shows, he hadn't quite hit

1. Hollywood B.C. (Before Clouseau)

his stride yet. All that changed with his next film, the beloved *Breakfast at Tiffany's* (1961), a glossy (if bowdlerized) adaptation of Truman Capote's 1958 novella, which follows the adventures of Holly Golightly, a kooky high-class call girl. With its expert blend of eye-catching New York locations and smart Hollywood interiors, and its scenes of wild cocktail parties and madcap antics, capped by a career-defining performance by Audrey Hepburn (who is nothing short of iconic in her sunglasses and little black Givenchy dress), the film, which *Variety* described as "a sleek, artistic piece of craftsmanship," delighted audiences and went on to be a sizeable commercial and critical success, grossing $9,551,904, coming in at number eighteen in the annual charts, all of which helped to catapult Edwards onto Hollywood's A-list.

For Mancini, the movie's hit song "Moon River" made him the music world's golden boy (the soundtrack LP went to number one in the Billboard charts) and led to opportunities he could only previously have dreamed of, among them assignments to work with such high ranking directors as Stanley Donen, Howard Hawks, Terence Young, Norman Jewison and Vittorio de Sica. The film, which was nominated for five Oscars, including best actress for Hepburn, went on to win two for Mancini, for best score and best song, the latter shared with Johnny Mercer, who provided the enchanting "Huckleberry friend" lyrics (Mancini was also nominated for a *third* Oscar that year for the title song for *Bachelor in Paradise* [1961], which had lyrics by Mack David). Said the composer upon accepting his award for best score: "I'm deeply grateful to the members of the Academy, [and] to my good friend Blake Edwards."[6] The song also won Mancini two further Grammys, for best song

Smiling "wider than a mile," Johnny Mercer (left) and Henry Mancini proudly hold their Oscars for the song "Moon River" from *Breakfast at Tiffany's* (1961) (AMPAS/ABC).

and best record, and has since been covered over 500 times, though like "Over the Rainbow" in *The Wizard of Oz* (1939), one studio executive wanted to cut it from the movie. Recalled the composer of his double Oscar win, "It really made me feel like I'd arrived. But that's what happens with Oscars—all of a sudden people have something to relate to as far as what you've done."[7]

Instead of coming out of the same trap again, Edwards next made two black and white films starring Lee Remick: *Experiment in Terror* (1962, aka *The Grip of Fear*), a nerve-jangling thriller which he also produced and for which Mancini provided an unsettling score, and *Days of Wine and Roses* (1962), an adult drama about alcoholism, which was nominated for five Oscars, and led to Mancini winning a third statuette for his title song (with lyrics again by Johnny Mercer), as well as Grammys for best song and best record. Having successfully dealt with two heavily dramatic subjects, Edwards, in a bid to prove his versatility, as well as further display his eye for projects with box office appeal, next decided to return to comedy. The move was fortuitous, as the film was *The Pink Panther* (1963), and it would become one of the defining moments of his career, but it would be a difficult birth (note that the Pink Panther wasn't the first alliterative animal to be found in an Edwards production; his unsold pilot for *Mike Hammer!* [1954, TV] features a restaurant called The Purple Peacock, while the credits for *Mr. Lucky* [1959–1960, TV] contain an elongated black cat that winks).

2

Send in the Clowns

As was by now his custom, Blake Edwards assembled a crew of familiar talents to assist him with his latest project, whose focus is the attempted theft of a priceless diamond, a flaw in which looks like a springing panther—and a pink one at that. In addition to Mancini and his lyricist Johnny Mercer, the production team also included cinematographer Philip Lathrop, who had photographed *Experiment in Terror* (1962) and *Days of Wine and Roses* (1962) along with multiple episodes of *Peter Gunn* (1958–1961, TV) and *Mr. Lucky* (1959–1960, TV) for Edwards; script supervisor Betty Abbott (later Abbott Griffin), who'd also worked on *Experiment in Terror* and *Days of Wine and Roses*, as well as a dialogue director on *Peter Gunn*; stunt arranger and bit player Dick Crockett, whose association with Edwards went all the way back to *Panhandle* (1948), and who here also did double duty as the film's associate producer; screenwriter Maurice Richlin, who'd been Oscar nominated for co-writing *Operation Petticoat* (1959) and had co-written the Ralph Nelson-directed *Soldier in the Rain* (1963) with Edwards, who had also produced it with Martin Jurow, his producer on *Breakfast at Tiffany's* (1961); and editor, Ralph E. Winters, who had cut *Soldier in the Rain*, and would go on to work on a number of other films for him. Keeping things in the family, Edwards' stepfather Jack was the film's production supervisor (he'd previously worked with his stepson as an assistant director on *Detective's Holiday* [1954, TV], the fifth of his episodes for *Four Star Playhouse* [1952–1956, TV], as an associate producer on both *Peter Gunn* and *Mr. Lucky*, and as the unit manager on *Days of Wine and Roses*), while his uncle, Owen Crump (brother of his actual father, Donald), was the film's second unit director (he'd go on to produce or executive produce three of his nephew's later films). Said Edwards of his habit of surrounding himself by familiar talent, "I've always been that way. I'm really searching for that extended family experience."[1]

This time the production company was Mirisch, which had been founded by brothers Walter, Marvin and Harold in 1957, and which had already known major success with such films as *Some Like It Hot* (1959), *The Apartment* (1960), *The Magnificent Seven* (1960) and *West Side Story* (1961), with *The Apartment* and *West Side Story* having bagged an astonishing fifteen Oscars between them, including two Best Picture nods. Each had been released by United Artists, with whom the siblings had a multi-picture deal (UA, which was also involved with the Bond films, went on to acquire the company in 1963). Edwards' own company, G-E Productions, formed with Martin Jurow, was also involved with the film.

It was clear from the outset that *The Pink Panther* was to going be a major, star-studded enterprise, yet despite the high hopes of all concerned, the movie, whose production cost was estimated to be $3m, almost derailed just days before the start of filming. By this point, Edwards and Maurice Richlin had concocted a crisp and lively screenplay that revolves round a unique jewel belonging to Dala, a beautiful young Middle Eastern princess who, while vacationing at the chic Italian ski resort of Cortina d'Ampezzo (host of the 1956 Winter Olympics), is romanced by the raffish Sir Charles Lytton, who is none other than the notorious jewel thief known as the Phantom. As well as stealing the princess's heart, Sir Charles also has designs on her bauble, said to be worth half a million pounds sterling, which he plans to nab while romancing her. Meanwhile, the law, in the guise of French Inspector Jacques Clouseau, is hot on the trail of Sir Charles, but little does Clouseau know that his wife Simone is also Sir Charles' lover and accomplice, which allows her to alert her cohort whenever her husband is about to pounce. Throw into this brew Sir Charles' handsome American nephew George Lytton, who also has designs on both Simone and the princess, not to mention the diamond, and you have a pretty complex caper of cross and double-cross peppered with plenty of farcical bedroom door slamming.

Recalled Edwards of the writing of the screenplay, "I was under contract to the Mirisch Company. One day, Maurice Richlin, the writer—a friend of mine, we had worked together before—came to me with a notion about a French inspector of police who was determined to catch this notorious jewel thief, and didn't know that his own wife was sleeping with this jewel thief. It was a good notion, so he and I sat down and developed it. I took it to Harold Mirisch of the Mirisch Company and said, 'This is the first film I'd like to make for you,' and Harold gave me the go-ahead.... We finished it [the script], presented it to various actors who agreed to do it. We were shooting maybe four of five months later in Europe."[2] In fact Edwards and Richlin polished the screenplay as they sailed to Europe on the SS *France* (Mancini and his wife were also onboard).

The film, whose production was first announced in the 16 May

2. Send in the Clowns

1962 edition of *Variety*, was to be made in Italy (where Edwards' step-grandfather had shot the silent epic *Nero* [1922]), and was based at Rome's famous Cinecittà Studios (or Hollywood-on-the-Tiber as it was affectionately known), which was the home of the world-renowned director Federico Fellini, as well as such international productions as *Helen of Troy* (1956) and *Cleopatra* (1963). Filming was set to begin on 5 November 1962 on locations in both the city and the Dolomites, as well as at the studios, where carpenters and plasterers realized the eye-catching set designs by Fernando Carrere, among them several luxurious hotel and chalet suites (Carrere, who had recently worked on *The Great Escape* [1963] for Mirisch, would go on to become another member of Edwards' coterie). Additional filming was also set to take place in Paris and Burbank. Casting was well underway by this point, and for the leading role of Sir Charles Lytton—who was deemed to be the central character at this stage—Edwards had chosen his old *Four Star Playhouse* boss, the debonair David Niven, who would bring a touch of Raffles to his part (the star had already played E.W. Hornung's gentleman thief in the 1939 film of the book). Lined up to support him were the Italian beauty Claudia Cardinale as Princess Dala (Edwards had hoped to sign Audrey Hepburn for the role, for which Nancy Kwan was also considered) and the handsome American leading man Robert Wagner as Sir Charles' playboy nephew George. Other casting considerations included Cyd Charisse and Janet Leigh, while as the cuckolded Inspector

Eyes and teeth. Claudia Cardinale and David Niven pose with a certain diamond in this publicity shot for *The Pink Panther* (1963) (Mirisch/G-E/United Artists/MGM).

Clouseau, under whose nose the Phantom has been operating undetected for so long, Edwards chose ... Peter Ustinov.

The part of Clouseau, as originally written, was very much a supporting one. This obviously didn't bother Ustinov, who had made his mark in a number of eye-catching secondary roles, among them Nero in *Quo Vadis* (1951), George IV in *Beau Brummell* (1954) and the slave trader Batiatus in *Spartacus* (1960), the latter of which had earned him a best supporting actor Oscar. Indeed, he must have been enticed by the scene-stealing opportunities that playing Clouseau offered. Another inducement was the actress Ustinov had been promised to play the role of Madame Clouseau, Hollywood legend Ava Gardner. Unfortunately, when her demands became excessive (among them an allowance for a secretary, chauffeur, make-up artist and hairdresser, etc.) she was replaced by model-turned-actress Capucine (real name Germaine Lefebvre). Following Gardner's departure, Ustinov himself left the production. As the actor explained, "I pulled out of it because they told me who was going to be cast, and they said it was going to be Ava Gardner. I was rather looking forward to that! Then it turned out to be Capucine, and I didn't think she had enough weight for the role."[3]

Instead, Ustinov took the role of con artist Arthur Simpson in another caper comedy, Jules Dassin's *Topkapi* (1964), a role that originally belonged to Peter Sellers, who had in turn walked away from the film over fears of a personality clash with co-star Maximilian Schell. "Peter Sellers and I swapped parts,"[4] said Ustinov. "He was going to do *Topkapi* and I was supposed to do *The Pink Panther*. They sued me for some reason, but they hadn't got a leg to stand on because there was no contract. Nothing at all! They'd probably agreed to a fee, but they hadn't got any closer than that. And so I did *Topkapi* instead and got another Oscar for it!"[5] Remembered Sellers of his casting, "In a matter of fact, Peter Ustinov was playing the role at that time and I was going to go into *Topkapi* for Jules Dassin. I successfully talked my way out of that in an interview at The Dorchester and Peter left the film because of some problems. We crossed over. He went in to *Topkapi* as the taxi driver and I went into *The Pink Panther* and it all worked out."[6] So did Ustinov ever regret about walking away from Clouseau? "Not at all,"[7] though he did admit that he would have played it differently than Sellers. "He would inevitably have borne some resemblance to Poirot, except he would have made more mistakes. He wouldn't have been infallible."[8] Of course, Ustinov later went on to play Hercule Poirot in six films (three for the large screen, three for the small), about which he said, "I didn't want to end my life only doing Poirot. Peter lived, unfortunately, not a very long time, and he did Pink Panthers right to the end."[9]

2. Send in the Clowns

As Ustinov stated, a lawsuit was indeed filed against him, given that his departure had thrown the film's production schedule into disarray, with the Mirisch Company announcing on 9 December 1963 that they were seeking $175,000 in damages for the violation of a contract. In the meantime, Edwards had to find a new Clouseau, at which point Peter Sellers fortuitously entered stage right. Commented the director of his loss of Ustinov, "It was a very complicated situation and I will forever be ambivalent about it. On the one hand I was greatly pissed off that he was as unprofessional as he was being. The Clouseau character that we know would never have happened had Ustinov played him as planned. The clumsiness and things like that were not a part of it. He was much more sophisticated. He was a very serious inspector who was looking for this notorious jewel thief called the Phantom, but he was totally unaware that his wife was having an affair with the Phantom! Then, at the last moment, Ustinov left. I was truly pissed off. We then found out that Sellers was available."[10]

As a consequence of the re-casting of the role and the adjusting of the shooting schedule, a number of other supporting roles were reassigned, with Brenda de Banzi now onboard as society party-giver Angela Dunning, a role previously mooted to have been offered to both Kay Thompson and Hermione Gingold, while other performers added to the cast included John Le Mesurier, Colin Gordon, Guy Thomajan and, last but by no means least, James Lanphier, who had played minor roles in several of Edwards' previous outings, from *The Perfect Furlough* (1958) onward, and who would also work as the film's dialogue coach, as he had done previously for the director on *Days of Wine and Roses* (1962), in which he'd also appeared.

At the time of being approached to play Clouseau, Sellers' star was very much in the ascent. In the year prior to working on *The Pink Panther* he'd already made *Lolita* (1962) for Stanley Kubrick and *Heavens Above!* (1963) for the Boulting Brothers, prior to which he'd dazzled critics and audiences alike with a series of showy performances in such diverse films as *The Mouse That Roared* (1959), in which he'd played three roles (among them a grand duchess), *I'm Alright Jack* (1959), which had earned him a best actor BAFTA as the bolshie trade union leader Fred Kite, *Only Two Can Play* (1962) and *Waltz of the Toreadors* (1962). Like Alec Guinness, with whom he'd co-starred in the Ealing classic *The Ladykillers* (1955), Sellers was regarded as much a character actor and master of disguise as he was a comedy performer (in fact his first major claim to fame came via his ability to provide a wide variety of voices, dialects and impersonations on radio). However, while he was very much a big fish in the comparatively small pond of the British film

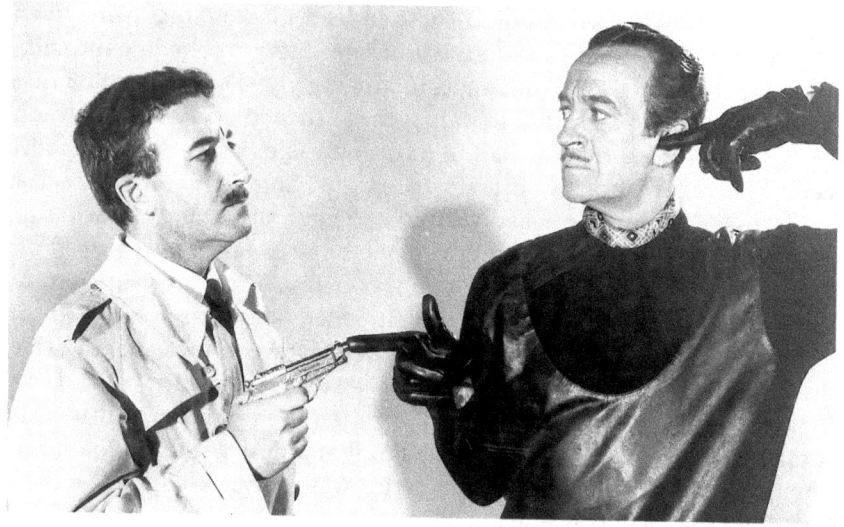

Star wars. Peter Sellers (left) and David Niven in a gag publicity shot for *The Pink Panther* (1963). Niven may have been the leading man, but it was Sellers audiences remembered (Mirisch/G-E/United Artists/MGM).

industry, albeit one with an increasingly visible profile abroad, Clouseau would give him that final push and catapult him to international stardom.

Richard Henry Sellers, to give him his real name, was born in Southsea, England, on 8 September 1925 into a family already firmly established in show business. Sellers' great-grandfather was the pugilist and sometime actor Daniel Mendoza, while his maternal grandmother was Welcome Mendoza, known theatrically as Belle Ray, who ran a touring variety company, whose productions included a number of pioneering aqua shows. Sellers' mother Agnes Mendoza, known to one and all as Peg, appeared in several of her mother's touring productions, and it was while working in one of them that she met her future husband, a gifted pianist called Will (later Bill) Sellers (originally Sel*lars*), in 1921. The couple married in 1923, and together toured the variety circuit, and although not part of their act, the young Sellers traveled with his parents, idling away his time behind the scenes in a series of shabby dressing rooms and damp lodgings, which can't have been much fun for the child, yet throughout his life he retained an affection for the music halls, which was reflected in several of his films. Even Clouseau's many disguises in the later Panthers have a musty whiff of the music hall about them.

Though Sellers didn't perform as a youngster, he did make his professional debut in an ad for Mazda Lamps while still a child, and began taking dance lessons long before his compulsory education commenced, at which point Peg finally gave up touring to look after him full time, though Sellers' father continued to work, making him absent for much of his childhood. By no means an academic, Sellers seemed merely to mark time during his school years, which ended in 1939 when he and Peg moved to the seaside town of Ilfracombe to escape Hitler's bombs, and it was here that his professional career began in earnest when he was engaged as a drummer by Waldini, a bandleader of minor celebrity for whom Sellers' father also played the piano, thus re-uniting the two within the profession.

Tours and summer seasons followed during the early forties, many of them for ENSA, the Entertainments National Service Association (or as it was more commonly known, Every Night Something Awful), while in 1943, when he turned eighteen, Sellers was conscripted into the RAF where, following basic training, he managed to get himself into the Entertainments Division, where he spent the duration as a member of Ralph Reader's Gang Show, playing the drums and appearing in routines and sketches (he also claimed to have impersonated several superior officers so as to gain access to their mess, which would have ended with a court-martial had he been found out). Being a part of the Entertainments Division saw Sellers travel to the Far East as well as throughout Europe, meeting along the way such lifelong friends as David Lodge, who would go on to appear with him in many of his films, including two of the Clouseau pictures.

After being demobbed in 1946, and with a Burma Star to show for his efforts, Sellers' career continued pretty much as it had done before, with gigs up and down the country. It was during this period that he began to develop a comedy act, no doubt spurred on by his success in the Gang Shows. Part of his routine involved an impersonation of the Northern singer and comedian George Formby, and it was this, along with various other impersonations, that helped earn the budding star a job at London's legendary Windmill Theatre, where he became a member of the *Revudeville* cast, which offered a mix of female tableaux and stand-up comedy performed by the likes of fellow aspirants Harry Secombe, Michael Bentine and Alfred Marks. It was during this period that he also broke into television, appearing in three episodes of *New to You* (1947–1950, TV), the first of which aired on 18 March 1948, while radio work followed soon after, with stints on such popular programs of the day as *Variety Band Box* (1945–1950), *Workers' Playtime* (1947–1964), *Show Time* (1948) and *Starlight Hour* (1950). In fact, so frequently did Sellers work on the airwaves during the following months, he very quickly established himself as a comic and mimic of note. At last, Sellers had arrived, and by way of confirmation, duly found himself appearing at the fabled London Palladium, opening for Gracie Fields on two successive Mondays in October 1949.

More radio work followed. Then in 1951 came the first step toward showbiz immortality with a new comedy program originally piloted as *The Junior Crazy Gang* but first broadcast as *Crazy People* (1951), which in turn mutated into *The Goon Show* (1952–1960), in which Sellers shared the microphone with Spike Milligan, Harry Secombe and Michael Bentine, who between them brought to life such improbably-named characters as Neddy Seagoon, Eccles, Major Bloodnok, Henry Crun, Bluebottle, Hercules Grytpype-Thynne and Minnie Bannister in a series of anarchic sketches scripted primarily by Milligan. The show's lunatic heights of surrealism changed the face of British comedy and would prove an influence on many performers and television programs that followed, and thanks to its popularity, its quartet of players became household names, enabling them to use their fame as a platform to launch their television careers with *Goonreel* (1952, TV), which also featured Graham Stark, another longtime friend and future Panther co-star, *The Idiot Weekly, Price 2d* (1956, TV), *A Show Called Fred* (1956, TV) and *Son of Fred* (1956, TV). The group also jumped to films during this period, albeit haltingly at first with such low budget obscurities as *Penny Points to Paradise* (1951), *Down Among the Z Men* (1952), *The Case of the Mukkinese Battle Horn* (1956) and *The Running Jumping & Standing Still Film* (1959), the latter of which earned an Oscar nomination for best live action short subject, though it was only Sellers whose career truly bloomed on celluloid as a consequence of these early efforts, resulting in eye-catching turns in the likes of *The Smallest Show on Earth* (1957), *The Naked Truth* (1957), *Up the Creek* (1958) and *Tom Thumb* (1958), which brings us pretty much back to where we set out.

Recalled Blake Edwards of the first time he laid eyes on his new Panther co-star, who by now looked more like a leading man, having slimmed down to better suit his aspirations: "I met Sellers for the first time at the airport. I'd only seen him in a couple of films back then, like *I'm Alright Jack*. Anyway, by the time we got from the airport in Rome back to the hotel we had discovered that we were soul mates when it came to all the great comedians, particularly Laurel and Hardy. It was at that point that Sellers said he wanted to come up with something original for the part of Inspector Clouseau—something that hadn't been planned for Ustinov. He suggested that we bend his character more towards the Laurel and Hardy vein. So I said that'd be fine, and after that it was like being in a room full of Cadbury's chocolate!"[11]

2. Send in the Clowns

Camera ready. Peter Sellers (left) and Blake Edwards between scenes during the making of *The Pink Panther* (1963) (Mirisch/G-E/United Artists/MGM).

Recalled Sellers of his concept for the role during the making of *The Return of the Pink Panther* (1975), one of the later films in the series, "When I first did *The Pink Panther* in Rome years ago he was just a straightforward French detective.... We just decided to make him very serious. The size of his moustache is to give him, in his own mind, masculinity. Very serious, but completely hopeless at his job.... He believes he's one of the greatest detectives in the world, and also, on top of it, the sad thing is that he knows deep down that he isn't, but he doesn't want anyone else to know."[12] Also among the ideas Sellers came up with was Clouseau's Franglais accent, which became more exaggerated as the films progressed, and his constant posturing, which he based on Captain Matthew Webb, the celebrated English cross–Channel swimmer whose image adorned matchboxes for many years. As for his legendary clumsiness, this was Edwards' contribution. "As far as I know, it's based on the fact that I really am Clouseau! I've broken every bone in my body in very funny ways."[13]

Filming eventually went ahead two weeks after originally planned on 19 November 1962, with Sellers now officially onboard for a not insubstantial $80,000 for his services (he was contracted for five weeks). For the actor, this was clearly an exciting time, as he recalled: "I arrived in Rome to work for Blake Edwards. Wow! Suddenly people at the airport to meet me. Wow! What am I walking into? Wow! Here we are. New life. Rome. Smells. Beautiful wonderful things. Anything could happen."[14] Shooting began with studio work at Cinecittà and in the streets of Rome itself. This went on until just before Christmas, after which the cast and crew moved to the sparkling slopes of Cortina in the New Year, where they made the most of the dazzling alpine scenery. A stop off in Paris followed for a brief sequence, after which Edwards and co. returned to LA for a handful of establishing shots, with principal photography finally in the can by mid–March, as noted in an article in *Daily Variety* on 15 March 1963.

Remembered Edwards of working in Italy, "This was the first time I had been to Rome. It was a wonderful experience, particularly in those days, in the sixties. Great city. I enjoyed myself immensely…. It was great to make a movie and, at the same time, between scenes, be able to walk across the street and examine where the lions used to feed on the Christians…. Who wouldn't want to be a director in the film business if you could go to all those great places and work and enjoy the food and wine?"[15] In addition to enjoying *la dolce vita* in the eternal city, he also recalled the holiday atmosphere while filming in the glorious Italian Alps: "What a good time we had. What a good time everybody had…. It wasn't the worst location in the world, and when we had time off, which was fairly frequently, we skied and sledded and all the other things that were available in Cortina…. It had great nightlife and beautiful scenery."[16]

Thanks to his contract, Edwards felt particularly secure while making the film. "I was under contract to the Mirisch Company, who had a deal with UA, so I didn't have to bother with UA. Part of my deal with Mirisch, one of the ways they enticed me to join their ranks, was to say, 'Look, you and I will decide what films are to be made, and then you leave the rest to us. If there's any problem with UA, we'll take care of it. You never have to answer to UA about anything.' 'We'll protect you,' was the idea, and it was a great relationship. Not that the people at UA didn't turn out to be nice guys. They most certainly did."[17] Said Walter Mirisch of the outlook he shared with his brothers, "Our philosophy was to create a family. We gravitated naturally to Blake Edwards, who we felt was a potential natural heir of Billy Wilder's,"[18] while of the company itself, editor Ralph E. Winters noted, "They had their own publicity department and production department, their own everything. They were like a miniature major."[19] However, as Edwards revealed, one of the Mirisch brothers did have reservations about the *Panther* script. "Harold Mirisch didn't particularly want me to do it. He didn't understand it, and he told me so. Not in so many words, but he said, 'Can't you come up with something else?' And I said, 'No, I feel good about this.' And I was really testing him to see whether or not his promise to me was genuine. And it was."[20]

2. Send in the Clowns

As amicable as the shoot was, it quickly became clear that as filming progressed, Sellers' expanded turn as Clouseau was gradually stealing David Niven's thunder. Recalled Walter Mirisch, "When the picture started out, David Niven had the leading role. When it finished, Peter Sellers did. And the script was barely changed."[21] Remembered Robert Wagner of the situation, "That first Panther really was supposed to be his [Niven's], but when they suddenly brought in Sellers instead of Ustinov, he could see it being taken away from him scene by scene, and he knew there was nothing he could do about it."[22] Ever the professional, Niven took the matter on the chin, though interestingly, he doesn't mention the film once in either of his best-selling memoirs, *The Moon's a Balloon* (1971) and *Bring on the Empty Horses* (1975). In the meantime, Edwards and Sellers hit it off and were clearly having a ball, coming up with all kinds of business for Clouseau. "So two bad little boys ventured off into this madness of humor,"[23] said Edwards of the situation.

As for making the character work, Edwards revealed, "We decided that the one thing about Clouseau that could make him succeed was that he embodied what I consider to be the eleventh commandment. He was the embodiment of that commandment. He lived by that commandment, which is 'Thou shalt not give up.' He just never considered he could lose. He never figured he'd fail. As a consequence, he never does fail. Somehow, he always comes through."[24] Meanwhile, of his working relationship with Edwards, Sellers said, "His sense of humor is very like mine. He finds the same sort of things funny that I do.... He's also a great giggler. It's great working with him."[25] However, the propensity to spend the day snickering did have its repercussions, as Edwards revealed: "That was half the fun and half the trouble. If you were Harold Mirisch and were sitting back in Hollywood and you heard that we'd lost half a day of shooting because we were laughing through the whole day, it would be pretty hard to understand. Harold, very nicely, said to me once, 'Can we do anything about this?' And I said, 'We either do it this way, or not at all. If this thing doesn't happen, this thing between us, then you're not going to have a funny movie.'"[26] As for his rapport with Sellers, Edwards simply observed, "We're both crazy!"[27]

The work of Edwards and Sellers can be seen at its most inventive in the various bedroom scenes between Clouseau and his wife Simone, in which the hapless Inspector, convinced of his virility, tries to seduce his clearly uninterested wife with endless sweet nothings and caresses. Unfortunately, each attempt to bed her results in disaster, with the Inspector further frustrated by a dressing gown that won't untie and doorknobs that come off in his hand. Even the playing (or rather the screeching) of his violin fails to do the trick and it ends up being crushed

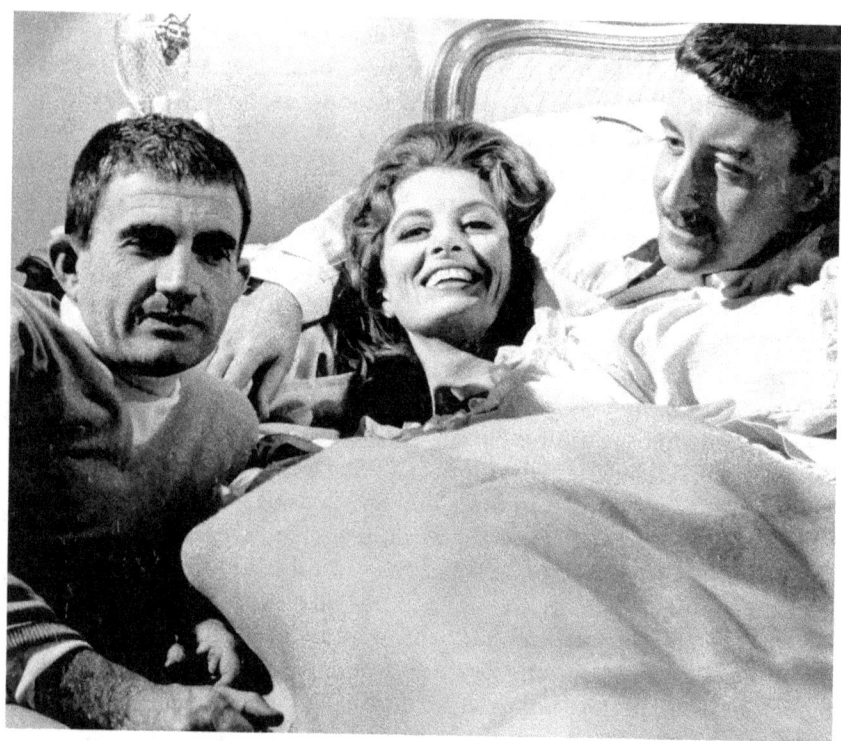

Taking cover. (From left) Blake Edwards, Capucine and Peter Sellers rest a moment while filming of one of the bedroom scenes in *The Pink Panther* (1963) (Mirisch/G-E/United Artists/MGM).

underfoot ("When you've seen one Stradivarius, you've seen them all," he sighs). He even acquiesces to her request for a glass of warm milk from the kitchens, most of which ends up on the corridor floor. Recalled Edwards of this elongated sequence, a good deal of which was ad-libbed, "It starts very simply and continues on for I don't know how many minutes. I choreograph leaving certain characters off camera. I find that's something I stole, or took, from Lubitsch. He was the master of that kind of stuff.... I let the actors move more than the camera, and I let a lot of stuff go on off-stage."[28] As for Sellers' penchant for improvising, Walter Mirisch recalled, "Blake was very smart and realised what was happening, and, instead of fighting it, he encouraged it.... Peter was a great improvisational actor. You're talking about comic invention that borders on genius."[29]

Of course, none of this would have worked without the cooperation of Capucine as Clouseau's wife, and in this regard she is a willing player in all the mayhem. Said Edwards of the model-turned-actress, with whom he shared his agent, Charles Feldman, and who he had previously directed in some uncredited re-shoots for *A Walk on the Wild Side* (1962), "She was just perfect for it. I adored her. She was a pain in the ass a lot of the time, but a sweet pain in the ass.... And look at that face!"[30] As for the staging of this sequence and others, editor Ralph E. Winters noted of Edwards' approach, which tended to observe the action with a sustained shot as through a proscenium, "Always in his movies, every scene, every shot, was mounted with class.... He always had his actors moving around. The important line took place in front of the camera, then the actor would move away ... then something else would happen.... You never had to cut."[31]

Aside from its Feydeau-like bedroom sequences, with their banging doors and people hiding under beds, the film is packed with comic incident pretty much from the get-go. Opening with the legend "Once upon a time," it first sets up the history of the Pink Panther, which sees the Maharajah of Lugash receive a priceless diamond necklace. "A gift to your father from his grateful people. Someday it will be yours," he tells his young daughter Dala, describing the pendant as "The most fabulous diamond in all the world." He then beckons her to him so that he can put it round her neck, at which we zoom into its heart and get our first glimpse of the Pink Panther himself, whose animated feline antics accompany the following credit sequence.

This is followed by a montage of scenes set in Rome, where we observe the Phantom carry out a jewel robbery, leaving behind his trademark white glove embroidered with a golden P; in Hollywood, where we see George Lytton posing for a fake graduation photo; in Paris, where a beautiful woman fences the jewels stolen by the Phantom before being chased by the police, who she dodges by slipping into a hotel and switching her clothes in an elevator, after which we cross fade to police headquarters to Inspector Clouseau, who we discover is on the trail of the Phantom and his female accomplice, who is revealed to be the Inspector's wife; and in Cortina d'Ampezzo, where the Princess Dala, now grown into a beautiful young woman, is enjoying a skiing vacation, all the while observed by the Phantom, who is planning his next heist.

The story proper then kicks in as we see the Princess taken under the wing of social climber Angela Dunning and her set; Dala's dog Amber kidnapped by the Phantom's accomplice Artoff, so that he can ingratiate himself with her by attempting to rescue it (pretending to have injured his leg while doing so); the arrival of Clouseau and his wife at the resort (the Inspector manages to fall onto Sir Charles as he is being carried through the hotel lobby on a stretcher); the disclosure that Mme. Clouseau's wardrobe contains all the latest fashions ("How you can manage on a police inspector's salary! I ask you, how many women could save enough out of the housekeeping to buy such a beautiful mink coat as this?"); and the revelation that Sir Charles is staying in the room next to the Clouseau's, thus allowing him to confer with Mme. Clouseau (and carry on their affair) via the connecting door. We then follow the continuation of Clouseau's investigations, in which he is joined by Tucker, a representative of Lloyd's of London who are insuring the gem, the theory being that the Phantom (who we discover has been operating without capture for some twenty years) is a member of Angela Dunning's inner circle, several of whom have been robbed. We also follow Sir Charles' attempt to woo the Princess, who has invited him to dinner to thank him for his efforts to save Amber (unfortunately, the fawning Dunning and her clique have also been invited), and witness the arrival of his nephew George at the resort, much to the surprise of Sir Charles and Mme. Clouseau.

The ladder of success. Peter Sellers and Capucine laugh it up between scenes during the making of *The Pink Panther* (1963) (Mirisch/G-E/United Artists/MGM).

The aforementioned bedroom sequence follows, in which Clouseau is constantly frustrated in his attempts to make love to his wife, along with a scene in which Sir Charles continues his courtship of the Princess in his room over a bottle of champagne. Having never drunk before, she proceeds to get plastered and passes out on his tiger rug, on which he drags her to his bed to sleep it off, only to discover his nephew in residence, who the following day starts his own campaign to win the heart of the Princess, while Mme. Clouseau attempts to woo *him* by keeping him out of the way of his uncle's activities. Unfortunately, Sir

2. Send in the Clowns

Charles learns that the Princess is planning to leave the resort later that afternoon, and so stages the return of her dog, to which end he chases down his accomplice in a horse-drawn sled, only to have his moment of glory ruined when his nephew, who has been having skiing lessons with Mme. Clouseau, manages to ski right over him (leaving ski marks on him) and deliver the dog to the Princess himself. At this point we repair to the local village inn, where one of Angela Dunning's group entertains everyone with a song, following which Sir Charles continues to romance Dala, who becomes defensive when Mme. Clouseau brings up the subject of a dispute over the Panther's ownership (a newspaper headline noticed by Sir Charles earlier had claimed "Rebels demand princess return fabulous gem"). "It belongs to me. It was a gift from my late father. I shall never surrender it," says Dala indignantly. She also reveals, "When the present government seized power, they claimed the diamond was the property of the people. There's even some talk of the international court deciding the issue."

George next rings Clouseau's room pretending to be the prefect of police, informing him that he has information regarding the Phantom that will require him to go to Brunico some thirty miles away, thus allowing him to continue his pursuit of Mme. Clouseau, not realizing that his uncle, who has also been visiting her room, is hiding under the bed. However, when Clouseau returns unexpectedly, George has to hide out in the bathroom (in a bubble bath being taken by Mme. Clouseau), while Sir Charles manages to escape through the window, landing in a snow drift below, from which he emerges much to the surprise Angela Dunning and her friends who are chatting unawares on the sidewalk. By this time, George has learnt that his uncle is the Phantom, having discovered his heist kit, along with a telltale monogrammed glove, in his closet, which he purloins in order to steal the Pink Panther himself from the Princess, who has now returned to Rome, where the diamond has been secreted all along in her safe. Thanks to intelligence provided by Tucker, Clouseau by now knows the true identity of the Phantom, prompting Sir Charles, disguised as Clouseau, to leave the hotel with haste ("My Sureté Scotland-Yard-type mackintosh has gone," exclaims the Inspector), at which the action switches to the Princess's villa in Rome.

Here, Clouseau, accompanied by Tucker, reveals to the Princess the identity of the Phantom ("He is a fraud, and I shall prove it," he says of Sir Charles), asking her permission to surround her villa that night, only to be told that she is throwing a lavish fancy dress party that evening. And so Clouseau (dressed as a knight) and Tucker (dressed as a court jester), along with various representatives of the law (among them two policemen disguised as a zebra) join in the frivolities in the hope of catching the Phantom red-handed, not realizing that the Princess hopes to prevent Sir Charles from incriminating himself. George is also at the party disguised as a gorilla, intending to rob the safe himself, while unbeknownst to him his uncle (disguised as a masked burglar) has a similar plan, managing to slip past the security guards on the front gate, who are distracted by his sidekick Artoff asking for directions. Unfortunately, Sir Charles is spotted by Tucker, who sees him dancing with another guest, the drunken Lord Cravenwood, who is also wearing a gorilla outfit. In the meantime, the lights have been turned out by Dala's manservant upon her nod, and Clouseau, intending to shed some light on the proceedings, mistakenly lights a Roman candle intended for the midnight firework display, which results in the rest of the fireworks going up and chaos ensuing in the ballroom. Meanwhile, Sir Charles purloins Lord Cravenwood's gorilla suit, and both he and George end up vying for the diamond, only to discover the safe to be empty, save for a glove bearing an embroidered letter P.

At this point Clouseau and Tucker, accompanied by several policemen, burst through the doors, and both Sir Charles and George dive out of the windows and make their escape, following which a major car chase ensues through the hills of Rome involving Clouseau, Tucker and various members of the constabulary (including the zebra), only for them all to end up in a massive pileup in a piazza. Sir Charles and George now find themselves banged up in the cells, given that the diamond is missing and that Clouseau is convinced they have colluded to take it, but it transpires that the Princess has stolen it herself, so as to prevent it being returned to her people by the international court, as she tells Mme. Clouseau, who has called by to ask for help in saving Sir Charles. In order to do so, they decide that the finger of blame must fall on someone else, and at the following trial, Clouseau finds himself implicated, given that he has been following the Phantom's footsteps during the same period he was carrying out his activities, with further damning evidence coming in the form of Mme. Clouseau's lavish wardrobe ("You're aware that your wife spent $7,000 at Yves Saint Laurent last month?" he is asked). At this point, Clouseau pulls out a handkerchief from his breast pocket to wipe his brow, only to discover it to be a monogrammed glove around which the Panther necklace is wrapped, leaving him no option but to accept his fate, which proves to be not so bad after all, given that he subsequently finds himself a national hero with an adoring female following. Leaving the courthouse with George and Mme. Clouseau, Sir Charles reasons that the Inspector will be free soon enough, once the Phantom resumes his criminal activities. As for

2. Send in the Clowns

A proper cup of coffee. Peter Sellers in full Clouseau garb takes a breather during the filming of *The Pink Panther* (1963) (Mirisch/G-E/United Artists/MGM).

Clouseau, when asked by one of the cops escorting him to jail how he carried out all the robberies, he replies with a nonchalant smile, "Well, you know ... it wasn't easy."

Following the fairy tale opening and the animated credits, Edwards and his editor Ralph E. Winters get the proceedings off to a flying start with the scene-setting montage sequence, which establishes the film's various characters and plot strands with both style and economy in just six brisk minutes, which is no mean feat given that it was filmed piecemeal over many weeks in several different locations (Rome, Hollywood, Paris, Cinecittà). From the get-go, the atmosphere is light and playful, and Edwards even manages to slip a few sly in-jokes into the proceedings. For example, the name on the door where George is getting his fake graduation picture taken is Pierre Luigi, the fabled Italian paparazzo who was actually working as the film's official set photographer, while in Paris, the hotel Mme. Clouseau slips into to evade the police is the Carrere, named after the film's art director Fernando Carrere (one of the gendarmes chasing her is played by cinematographer Philip Lathrop, while the film's other set photographer, Sherm Clark [another Edwards regular], can later be spotted as the hotel doorman in Cortina). As for Clouseau, he makes his screen debut accompanied by the strains of "The Marseillaise" following which comes one of the film's great sight gags as he idly spins the globe in his office while pondering the case with a colleague ("We *must* find that woman"), leans on it and falls flat on the floor ("What was that? What did you say?" he asks getting up quickly, trying to cover his blunder).

The location sequences in the azure-skied Italian alps are nothing short of breathtaking, and the ski runs and snow-capped mountains are captured in all their glory by Philip Lathrop's spectacular Technirama cinematography, whose professional, old-style Hollywood sheen also shows off the elegantly appointed Cinecittà interiors to their full Technicolor advantage, among them an eye-catching pink and white palace (all cushions and filigree) for the opening scene, along with the plush hotel rooms in Cortina and the Princess's villa in Rome, whose ballroom is vast enough to host one of the wild parties Edwards seemed to have a penchant for staging during this period. The film is then capped by the zany, Keystone Kops–like car chase, which enabled the director to fully indulge his love for the silent

Fall guy. Peter Sellers' Clouseau is caught red- (or possibly pink-) handed during the courtroom scene in *The Pink Panther* (1963) (Mirisch/G-E/United Artists/MGM).

comedians ("My entire early life was spent watching the great early comedians. They took my mind away from a life that I was not particularly happy in,"[32] he revealed). The proceedings then conclude with the trial, in which Clouseau finds himself framed for the Phantom's crimes. Comic highlights in these various sequences include Clouseau's inability to walk through a door without it either springing back on him or the handle coming off in his hand; George's yellow jumper getting increasingly longer after he has hidden out in Mme. Clouseau's bubble bath; a bottle of champagne exploding (prematurely ejaculating?) in the Clouseaus' bed as the Inspector is *finally* about to get to first base with his wife ("At last!" he exclaims as the love theme from Tchaikovsky's "Romeo and Juliet" swells on the soundtrack); and Sir Charles' fall into the snowdrift. The villa party is meanwhile a riotous affair involving dozens of elaborately costumed extras (Sellers' own costume allowed stuntman Dick Crockett to double for him on occasion), and climaxes with the explosive indoor fireworks display.

This scene also features the film's two best verbal gags: upon

2. Send in the Clowns

Court in the act. Peter Sellers (left) and Blake Edwards during the filming of the same scene in *The Pink Panther* (1963) (Mirisch/G-E/United Artists/MGM).

noticing the zebra with its head in the punchbowl, Clouseau admonishes, "Any more behavior like this and I'll have your stripes!" while later, during the chaos caused by the fireworks, Clouseau, crawling along the floor in search of Tucker, picks up a rubber snake, which is snatched from him by a woman dressed as Cleopatra who tells him to "Take your filthy hands off my asp," a joke that would have greatly amused audiences at the time, given the then-notoriety of *Cleopatra* (1963), a version of which Edwards' step-grandfather had directed all the way back in 1917. Incidentally, the two policemen inside the zebra skin reveal their names to be Sergeant Wilder and Sergeant Quine (though the DVD subtitles provided by Adrian Isaac mistakenly have them as Sergeants Walter and Coff, thus losing the in-joke). The sequence also contains a variation on the celebrated mirror routine between Groucho and Harpo in the Marx Brothers classic *Duck Soup* (1933), albeit this time featuring Sir Charles and George in their matching gorilla suits. The car chase meanwhile (shot in the small town of Rocca di Papa just outside Rome) contains another film reference: as the various vehicles zoom through the piazza ("I'll take the high road, you take the low road," suggests George to his uncle as they try and escape the authorities), an old man (played by J. Gordon Edwards' property master) tries to cross

Earning their stripes. (From left) Colin Gordon, Peter Sellers and friend during the party sequence in *The Pink Panther* **(1963) (Mirisch/G-E/United Artists/MGM).**

the square, only to return to his point of departure when things get too hairy. This was a direct reference by Edwards to a similar scene in Hitchcock's *Foreign Correspondent* (1940), in which an old man gives up trying to cross a road during a car chase through a Dutch village. "That's my homage, and nobody has ever gotten it,"[33] said the director (one also might argue that Niven's Phantom bears a striking resemblance to Cary Grant's John Robie, aka the Cat, in Hitchcock's *To Catch a Thief* [1955]). As for the pileup, which takes place off camera, Edwards observed, "I think it's funnier seeing the wreck after it has happened. And a hell of a lot less expensive."[34]

On the performance front, Sellers clearly steals the film as the bumbling Clouseau, and audiences familiar with the later films may well find themselves pining for more of him here. That said, there is ample compensation from the film's de facto leading man, the ever-dapper David Niven, who more than stands his ground as the raffish Sir Charles, while Capucine brings an air of patrician *froideur* to the role of the two-timing Mme. Clouseau. Elegance itself in her Yves St. Laurent wardrobe, she also makes for a surprisingly game foil to Sellers during their involved bedroom shenanigans in which she suffers a number of indignities with dead-pan resilience (one can't imagine Ava Gardner subjecting herself so keenly to such humiliations).

Elsewhere in the ensemble, Claudia Cardinale (likewise immaculately dressed by Laurent) makes for a charming Princess, who proves to have a little fire in her belly (the actress was faultlessly dubbed by an uncredited Gale Garnett), while Brenda de Banzie has some fun as the overbearing society hostess Angela Dunning, always on the lookout for the next celebrity to corral into her circle. Robert Wagner also appears to be having a good time as George Lytton, eager to take on his uncle's mantle in more ways than one, while Colin Gordon as Tucker proves to be a solid straight man to Clouseau during the investigation. Also leaving their mark are James Lanphier as Dala's devoted manservant Saloud (for which he is clearly sporting a tan make-up), John Le Mesurier as the defense barrister who brings down Clouseau (he and Sellers had already crossed paths in a handful of British films, among them *Mr. Topaze* [1961] which Sellers had directed), and Michael Trubshawe as the major-like Felix Townes, one of Angela Dunning's inner circle (Trubshawe was a close friend of David Niven's, and appeared in several of his films, while in *Those Magnificent Men in Their Flying Machines* [1965] he played a character called Niven).

Although the film's running time is a little on the generous side at one hour and fifty-five minutes, Edwards manages to keep things moving at a fair pace throughout, and only really comes a-cropper twice, first in the scene in which Sir Charles seduces the Princess on the tiger rug (which goes on far longer than is necessary, and in which inexplicably her cigarette moves from hand to hand before disappearing entirely when she passes out) and the sequence in which proceedings come to a complete halt for the après ski musical number "Meglio Stasera" which is performed direct to camera in the village inn by singer Fran Jeffries (whose third husband [of four] would prove to be Richard Quine). Sung entirely in Italian (which doesn't help matters), the number is presented in two lengthy shots and was choreographed by an uncredited Hermes Pan (known for his work with Fred Astaire), and while entertaining enough, it could quite easily have been trimmed from the proceedings (an English version of the song titled "It Had Better Be Tonight" with lyrics by Johnny Mercer can later be heard during the party in Dala's villa). Recalled Edwards of the sequence, "I don't really know why I decided to put her in the film.... It always puzzled me why I suddenly stopped the plot to do a number. I was, to say the least, somewhat surprised that it did work."[35]

As good as the film's various elements are, the icing on the cake is undoubtedly Henry Mancini's much admired soundtrack. As well as penning the catchy "Meglio Stasera" (whose Italian lyrics were care of Franco Migliacci, best known for the 1958 Eurovision hit "Volare"), Mancini scored the film with a breezy collection of light jazz-pop pieces, which give it an air of cocktail party sophistication, while he accompanies the car chase with a frantic comic piece carried by a silent movie-style piano (the cue is aptly titled "Shades of Sennett"). However, the score's most celebrated track is undoubtedly the instantly hummable title theme, initially created

What's new, pussycat? David Niven and Claudia Cardinale in the seemingly endless seduction scene from *The Pink Panther* (1963). No wonder the tiger's eyes look glassy (Mirisch/G-E/United Artists/MGM).

to accompany the Phantom's criminal nocturnal activities. Recalled the composer, "There were a number of scenes in which David [Niven] would be slinking around on tippy-toes. I started to write a theme for him—one of the few times I wrote a theme before seeing the actual picture. That music was designed as the Phantom-thief music, not to be the Pink Panther theme."[36] As for its origins, he admitted, "I don't know where that came from. That was just my interpretation of the mood that was needed."[37] However, he was certain of what instrument should carry the tune: a tenor sax. "I just heard it as the sound,"[38] he revealed, adding, "It wasn't *a* tenor sax, it was a particular *man*, Plas Johnson, who did the first one.... I heard Plas playing, and he had that wispy, kind of sassy way that he plays, and I really tailored it for him."[39]

Like Edwards, Mancini liked to work with familiar faces, and in addition to Johnson (who'd already worked on a handful of films and albums with him), the composer assembled such talents as pianist Jimmy Rowles, drummer Shelly Manne (who'd had a cue named after him on the LP *More Music from* Peter Gunn [1959] titled "My Manne Shelly"), guitarist Al Hendrickson, trombonist Dick Nash and flutist Gene Cipriano, each of whom would bring their unique style to the score, contributing to that unmistakable Mancini sound of the period, with its laid back vibes, lush strings, snazzy percussive riffs, big band blasts and easy Latin rhythms. He even manages to make the accordion (played by Carl Fortina) sound cool. Said the composer of his core ensemble, "I never had an orchestra really. I used a lot of the same men. They were all session players that happened to get together."[40] Among the cues they contributed to are "Royal Blue," "Champagne and Quail" (which Sir Charles actually plays on the record player secreted in his drinks cabinet when preparing to seduce Dala in his hotel room), "The Tiber Twist" and "Something for Sellers," all of which appeared on the resultant album, albeit in slightly different versions, given that Mancini always re-recorded his film scores for LP release at the time so as to ensure better sound quality, hence the occasional disparity in orchestrations. For example, in the film, when we first see the ski slopes of Cortina, it is scored with a playful version of "Meglio Stasera" accompanied by sleigh bells, whereas on the album, which was recorded on 16, 17 and 18 September at RCA's Music Center of the World in Hollywood, the cue has a more traditional percussion (the soundtrack itself [which wouldn't be released on CD until 2024] had been recorded earlier at the Goldwyn Scoring stage on 14, 17, 18 and 19 June and 24 July).

Strike a pose. Singer Fran Jeffries in a startling publicity shot by Rome's coliseum taken during the filming of *The Pink Panther* (1963) (Mirisch/G-E/United Artists/MGM).

Edwards described the impact of Mancini's music on the film as "Enormous,"[41] while of the theme's enduring popularity, the composer admitted, "Well, it feels very, very good of course. I'd love to do it again.... It is quite well known."[42] The album proved to be another triumph for Mancini, reaching a high of number eight during its incredible 41 week run in the Billboard pop album chart, all of which must have been pleasing for him given that his agent, MCA's Bobby Helfer, had secured him half the publishing rights (the other half being owned by UA). Peter Sellers was even persuaded to pen some comic liner notes for the LP's back cover ("I've never written record notes before and I'm sure I will never be asked again. The poor fools, they don't know what they are missing,"[43] he wrote). In addition to the album (which went gold), the title theme was also released as a single, and itself reached number 10 in the charts. The album was nominated for six Grammys and won three (for Instrumental Composition, Arrangement and Performance), while the score was nominated for the film's only Academy Award. In this instance Mancini lost out to the Sherman Brothers for *Mary Poppins* (1964), though the music has since been ranked at number 20 in the AFI's list of the 25 greatest film scores of all time (the number one spot being taken by *Star Wars* [1977] by Mancini's one-time pianist, John Williams).

If Mancini's contribution to the film was the icing on the cake, then the cherry on top is undoubtedly the animated opening credits. Recalled Blake Edwards of the title sequence, "I remember coming up with the idea of turning it into a cartoon, and all of the discussions that we had between the cartoonists, DePatie-Freleng, and myself.... We talked about this pink cat, what kind of character he should be."[44] For the animators David H. DePatie and Friz Freleng, the job offer couldn't have come at a better time. Having worked together at Warner Bros., the duo found themselves out of a job after the studio shut down its animation department in 1963, following which they had established their own company, DePatie-Freleng Enterprises, which initially survived on a diet of TV ads. Recalled DePatie, "Then my life changed. One day the telephone rang and it was Blake Edwards. I went over to his office and he handed me this script called *The Pink Panther*. He said, 'I want you to design for me a pink panther character.'"[45] The connection between Edwards and the cartoonists came via his uncle, Owen Crump, who had become close to the duo while making travelogues for Warner Bros. for many years (hence his usefulness as the film's second unit director). Consequently, hundreds of variations on the character were drawn up by the duo and their team of cartoonists. These were then submitted to Edwards, who selected one penned by another Warner Bros. veteran, Hawley Pratt.

Some three months later, once the film had gone through post-production, the animators were called in again to get Edwards' final ideas for the main titles, which would be directed by Pratt under

2. Send in the Clowns

LSP-2795 STEREO

the PINK PANTHER

RCA VICTOR
DYNAGROOVE
RECORDING

Music from the Film Score Composed and Conducted by

HENRY MANCINI

The cat's whiskers. The original "dynagroove" LP release of Henry Mancini's landmark score for *The Pink Panther* (1963) (Mirisch/G-E/United Artists/MGM/RCA/DePatie-Freleng).

the supervision of DePatie and Freleng, who would produce it. The sequence commences following the zoom into Dala's necklace, where we are greeted by the Panther himself, crouched smoking a cigarette in an elegant gold cigarette holder. He subsequently finds himself involved in a number of comic vignettes as the credits flick by. These see him interact playfully with the star names (he spins Wagner's name so it looks like propeller and flies away on it, snuggles up to Capucine's credit, and pants and whistles at Claudia Cardinale's, for which he receives a slap from an opera glove), after which he appears as a conductor in tails for Mancini's credit (for which he is quickly given the hook), while for Lathrop's nod he gets his photo taken with an old-style camera only to find himself blown up when the flash goes off. He also appears as a gondolier during the credit for "Meglio Stasera" and plays with the letters of Blake Edwards' name, mischievously putting them up as Elabk Sdrawed before being forced to correct them at gunpoint. All of this (which also includes appearances by Clouseau and the Phantom's monogrammed glove) is accompanied by Mancini's signature title music, about which DePatie observed, "It complemented so beautifully the action."[46] And from the get-go, the sequence proved to be a hit with audiences, as the animator remembered: "We take the picture out to preview. After the main title sequence is over with, they had to turn on the lights and shut off the projector. People were jumping up and down in the aisles and applauding ... screaming and yelling. I've never seen such a reaction."[47]

Following the film's sneak screening in LA (in August 1963) and a second in New York (in September), plus a special New Year's Eve showing in Boston, a trailer was released in March 1964, for which additional animated sequences featuring the Pink Panther were produced by DePatie-Freleng. These find him rifling through footage of the film and reacting to clips, which are accompanied by the title theme. "Oh, sir, what are you looking at now? Are those the bedroom scenes? Aha, they are, aren't they? Come on, don't be so selfish," cajoles the narrator, before going on to reveal, "I understand that the picture features the music of Henry Mancini and introduces Fran Jeffries?" at which point we get a blast of "Meglio Stasera" which is followed by a tantalizing glimpse of some of the film's comic highlights (Sir Charles being skied over by George, Sir Charles falling from the window and emerging from the snowdrift, the fireworks going off at the ball, etc.). A poster by illustrator Jack Rickard featuring caricatures of Niven, Sellers, Capucine, Wagner and Cardinale in a giant bed, over which hovers the Pink Panther himself, was also issued by UA, bearing the tagline, "You only live once ... so see *The Pink Panther* twice!!!" The studio also sent out a press book fronted by the poster, inside of which were portraits of the cast and a synopsis of the story. Newspaper ads meanwhile encouraged audiences to "Meet the zaniest characters ever gathered under one bed!" A novelization of the screenplay penned by crime writer Marvin Albert (best known for *Tony Rome*) was also published by Bantam on 1 January 1964 to further whet appetites during the run up to the release. "Now a sizzling United Artists picture," ran the cover blurb, which promised "a riotous romp through the bedrooms and boudoirs of international high society." And all for forty cents!

The movie was finally released in America on 20 March 1964 at the Hollywood Paramount and in New York shortly after at the legendary Radio City Music Hall on 23 April (this proved to be something of a coup fort United Artists, given that they hadn't had a film shown at

In the frame. Poster artwork for *The Pink Panther* (1963) (Mirisch/G-E/United Artists/MGM/Jack Rickard/DePatie-Freleng).

the venue since *The Men* [1950] some fourteen years earlier). It was an instant hit, and went on to earn $10.9m in the U.S. and Canada alone during its original theatrical run, eventually coming in at number ten in the year's box office rankings (the equivalent of 11,696,889 admissions at 1964 ticket prices), with the top spot being taken by *Mary Poppins* (1964), which was followed in second and third place by such favorites as *My Fair Lady* (1964), which also took the best picture Oscar, and *Goldfinger* (1964), the latter of which was also released by UA. In fact the company had four films in the top ten that year (by contrast, Ustinov's *Topkapi* [1964] came in at number 17 on the list).

Perhaps surprisingly, given its now classic status, the reviews were something of a mixed bag. On the plus side, *Variety* found the film to be "intensely funny" and singled out Sellers' "razor-sharp comedy timing," though *The New York Times* sympathized with the star for having "to work so persistently and hard at trying to be violently funny with weak material," finding the script to be a "basically unoriginal and largely witless piece of farce carpentry that has to be pushed and heaved at stoutly in order to keep on the move." *The Hollywood Reporter* was generally more positive, revealing that "the laughter begins early and sustains," adding that "the style is sharp and clipped, and studded with great sight gags that play on their own." It had minor reservations about the bedroom scenes, noting that "an exploding bottle of champagne has very obvious double meaning," but saved its most salient observation for Sellers, pointing out that, "in a picture about thievery, it is Peter Sellers who proves the most outrageous larcenist," adding that "the character is set in Sellers' first scene and the audience never relaxes thereafter waiting for the next doorknob to come off in his hand." The review also praised Philip Lathrop's photography, Mancini's score (which it found to be "perhaps his best to date"), Fernando Carrere's art direction and DePatie-Freleng's main titles, and also had kind words for Niven, saying that he "plays his own brand of comedy with immense success."

The film had actually been released in Europe a little earlier, having opened in Italy on 18 December 1963, followed by West Germany, Finland, Greece and Sweden over the next few days. It opened in London on 9 January 1964 with an A certificate, no doubt because of the bedroom shenanigans, and went on general release across the country on 14 February, proving to be another great success, particularly given Sellers' popularity in the UK, where *Dr. Strangelove* (1964), in which he also starred, opened soon after on 29 January 1964 (as it also did in the U.S.), thus proving to be something of a double whammy for the actor. The Kubrick film eventually came in at number 12 in the annual rankings and earned Sellers an Oscar nomination for best actor, while another of the star's vehicles, *The World of Henry Orient* (1964), opened in America on 19 March and in the UK on 18 June. Consequently, 1964 was something of a banner year for Sellers, who also found himself nominated for both a BAFTA and a Golden Globe as best actor for his performance as Clouseau, while Edwards and Richlin were nominated for best screenplay by the Writers Guild of America.

Revealed trade journal *Kine Weekly* of the film's boffo box office in London in its 30 January 1964 edition, "The David Niven-Peter Sellers farcical comedy, *The Pink Panther*, (UA) is firmly entrenched at the Odeon Leicester Square. In the second week it nearly reached five figures, and weekend business was very good, especially so on Sunday. It also opened very big at the Odeon Kensington, on Sunday, not far short of record figures." As for British press reaction, the *Monthly Film Bulletin*, like *The Hollywood Reporter*, had a few minor reservations, notably regarding "the confusions of the minuscule plot" and the inclusion of "yet another of those exhaustively cute drunk scenes," yet found time to praise the "happy combinations of ingenuity and genuine fun in the direction and style in the playing," singling out Capucine for her "masterly quick-change in a lift" and Sellers' "inability to walk across a room without sending the furniture flying," highlighting "his way, for instance, with a door handle." *Sight and Sound* also admired Capucine, claiming that "she is the most endearing accession to the comic world since the late Kay Kendall."

Commented Blake Edwards of the film's enormous success, "It did surprise me. I was delighted it was such a hit."[48] As for the loss of Ustinov as Clouseau, recalled Walter Mirisch, "When the picture came out and was a huge success, I remember our lawyer saying to me, 'Can you prove any damages?' We weren't damaged, we were helped."[49] Yet despite the movie's triumph, Edwards revealed, "I had no intention of going beyond the original."[50] Consequently, the cast and crew went their own ways, happy to pursue other projects. But as we know, history had other plans. However, in the meantime…

3

Getting Animated

Following the hugely positive reaction to the title sequence at the preview of *The Pink Panther* (1963) in August 1963, animator Dave DePatie was struck by an idea. "After that screening I started to think, 'You know, there may be life after the main title. This character may have a place in animation'"[1] Consequently, he spoke to his partner Friz Freleng about the matter. But to his disappointment, Freleng didn't see things quite the same way, believing the sequence to have been a one-shot. Convinced that his idea had legs, DePatie went to see producer Harold Mirisch in the hope that he might back the making of a theatrical cartoon of the type that he and Freleng had previously made during their years as animators at Warner Bros. Having consulted his brothers and United Artists, Mirisch got back to DePatie a week later with the astonishing news that UA wanted to give the animators a contract for 156 cartoon shorts, much to DePatie and Freleng's surprise.

However, as DePatie recalled, he wanted something more out of the deal. "I said, 'Friz, we have one problem that I want to discuss with you. You and I have always worked for somebody. We've never owned anything in our life. We didn't go into business to continue that. I'm gonna go back to Harold Mirisch and tell him that I want our company to own twenty-five per cent of the copyright.' He says, 'You'll never get it.'"[2] Nevertheless, a week or so after relaying his ultimatum, the Mirsich's lawyers called DePatie in and presented him with a contract for the 156 cartoons and twenty-five per cent of the copyright. A group was subsequently created that included the Mirisch company, Blake Edwards (via Geoffrey) and DePatie-Freleng, through which the first cartoon was made. This was titled *The Pink Phink* (1964), following which began a busy program of producing one six-minute Pink Panther cartoon per month, which United Artists then distributed as supports to their main features.

For *The Pink Phink*, the Panther was slightly modified, becoming less feline in appearance and more human in his physical reactions. He

The gang's all here. (From left) Friz Freleng, David DePatie, Harold Mirisch and Blake Edwards pose with the Pink Panther (Mirisch/G-E/United Artists/MGM/DePatie-Freleng).

is, however, just as mischievous as he was in the feature film's credit sequence. "Remember me? First I was a movie title.... Now I'm a movie star!!!" says the Panther in a speech bubble for the cartoon's poster, which is framed with little black paw prints. It also informs audiences that "he's back on screen in his new, hilarious, very own Cartoon Series!" In the short, we see the Panther enter a battle royal with a decorator who is painting everything blue. The Panther sees things differently, and begins re-painting everything pink, much to the decorator's increasing anger and frustration. Walls, doors, staircases and even the landscape come in for the treatment, until everything is pink, much to the Panther's delight, following which we see him move into his own pink house, but not before painting his defeated adversary pink too.

The short was directed by Friz Freleng and Hawley Pratt, and animated by Don Williams, Bob Matz, Norm McCabe and La Verne Harding, all of whom had worked on the title sequence for *The Pink Panther* (1963), as had background artist Tom O'Loughlin. Williams, Matz and McCabe had previously worked in the Warner Bros. animation department with DePatie and Freleng, as had the cartoon's writer John W. Dunn, editor Lee Gunther and its composer William Lava, each of whom would go on to work on many of the subsequent entries in the series. Lava scored the short with a heavy dose of "The Pink Panther Theme" for which Henry Mancini receives an upfront credit, as does Blake Edwards (the short is announced as "Blake Edwards' Pink Panther" prior to the appearance of the title *The Pink Phink*).

With its minimalist style and plenty of inventive visual gags (it contains no dialogue), the cartoon immediately set the pattern for what was to follow. Ready for release by the end of 1964, it was sent out by United Artists on 18 December 1964 as a support to their biggest movie of the year *Goldfinger* (1964), which would be seen by 54,946,236 patrons in the U.S. and Canada alone (as would the cartoon presumably, assuming half the audience weren't at the concession stand stocking up with Milk Duds and Raisinets for the main feature while it was playing). "Seven minutes of absolute madness!" ran the newspaper ads for the cartoon, while another (for the Country Club Plaza in Kansas City) announced, "*Goldfinger* and *Pink Phink*.... Just about the most colorful show we've ever had!" Audiences loved the cartoon, and so did the Academy of Motion Picture Artists and Sciences, which nominated it for an award in the best animated short film category, for which a new poster was sent out featuring a rattled Panther taking nerve pills, accompanied by the amended strap line, "First I was a movie title. Then I became a movie star. Now I'm a nervous Academy Award nominee." The poster also encouraged theater owners to "Book the entire series now thru United artists." The cartoon subsequently went on to win the Oscar, much to the delight of all concerned. Recalled Blake Edwards, "I had no idea that character would take off. I thought it was fine for the film, but I had no idea that it would take off like that. That it would have that kind of a life of its own."[3]

The second cartoon, *Pink Pajamas* (1964), was ready for release on Christmas Day 1964, with credits the same as the first short. This time the Panther tries to grab a little shut eye in an empty house, only for its drunken owner to return unexpectedly, resulting in much chaos. The following year saw the series really take a hold, with a further twelve cartoons released (some of which featured canned laughter), among them *We Give Pink Stamps* (1965), *Sink Pink* (1965), the latter the first of two shorts in which the Panther actually spoke care of impressionist Rich Little, *Pinkfinger* (1965), which sent up the secret agent phenomenon, *Pink Ice* (1965), in which the Panther was again voiced by Rich Little, *The Pink Tail Fly* (1965) and *Pink Panzer* (1965).

A further ten cartoons followed in 1966, among them *The Pink Blueprint* (1966), which brought the series its second Academy Award nomination (though in this case it lost out to *Herb Alpert & the Tijuana*

Brass Double Feature [1966]) and *Pink, Plunk, Plink* (1966), in which the Panther sabotages a concert, replacing the classical repertoire with "The Pink Panther Theme" much to the delight of an applauding Henry Mancini, seen at the climax in a live action insert. The cartoons

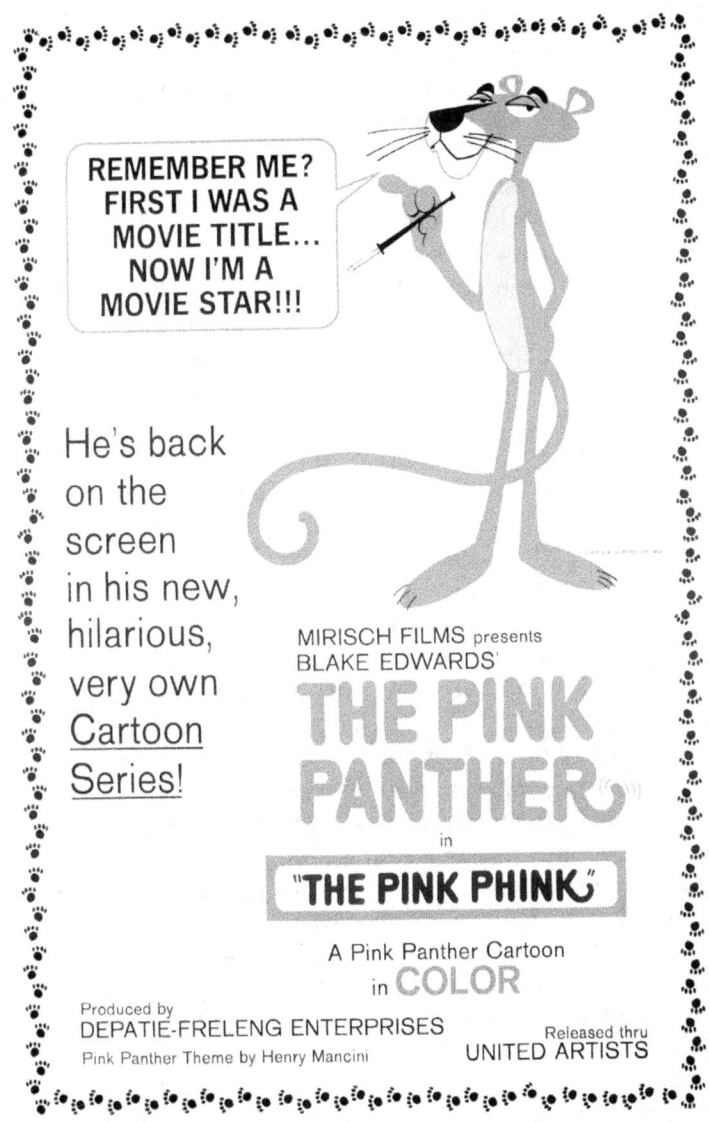

Poster child. The Pink Panther proves he has star value all of his own in this poster for *The Pink Phink* (1964) (Mirisch/G-E/United Artists/MGM/DePatie-Freleng).

continued on throughout the sixties and seventies, producing such titles as *In the Pink* (1967), *Prehistoric Pink* (1968), *Think Before You Pink* (1969), *The Pink Flea* (1971), *Pink 8 Ball* (1972), *Pink Aye* (1974), *Pink Elephant* (1975), *Sherlock Pink* (1976) and *Therapeutic Pink* (1977). Following this, the shorts went on to be made for television, though they were all subsequently released theatrically, among them *Pink Pictures* (1978), *Star Pink* (1978), *String Along Pink* (1978) and *Supermarket Pink* (1978), which was the last to be released theatrically in 1980, bringing the original run to a close at 124 episodes, the majority of them directed either by Hawley Pratt or Gerry Chiniquy.

Running parallel with the Panther shorts, DePatie-Freleng launched a second series of cartoons in association with Mirisch and Blake Edwards (again via his company Geoffrey), this time involving the exploits of a bumbling French detective working for the Sureté. Known as The Inspector, he is clearly based on Sellers' Clouseau, and is assisted by a young Spanish sergeant named Deux-Deux (pronounced Doo-Doo), both of whom were voiced by Pat Harrington, Jr., while their short-tempered Commissioner was voiced by the likes of Larry Storch, Paul Frees, Mark Skor and Marvin Miller. Thirty-four of the cartoons were released theatrically between 1965 and 1969, thus bringing the total number of Panther-related shorts made for UA by DePatie-Freleng to 158. The first of the Inspector cartoons, *The Great De Gaulle Stone Operation* (1965), was released by UA on 29 December 1965 as a support to the James Bond film *Thunderball* (1965), the year's third most popular film, which meant it was seen by 62,970,297 ticket holders during its run in the U.S. and Canada. Written by John W. Dunn and directed by Friz Freleng and Gerry Chiniquy, it sees the Inspector tasked by the Commissioner to guard a diamond worth ten billion francs, only to lose it pretty much immediately to a three-headed jewel thief known as Weft, Wight and Wong, whom he now sets out to catch (a similar-looking villain had already appeared in DePatie-Freleng's credits for the Panther sequel *A Shot in the Dark* [1964], more on which anon, and from which Mancini's new title theme is also featured, as it had already been in the Panther short *Dial "P" for Pink* [1965]). Styled in the by now established DePatie-Freleng manner, albeit with verbal as well as visual jokes, the cartoon proved to be a perfect set-up for the installments that followed, among them *Reaux, Reaux, Reaux Your Boat* (1966), *Ape Suzette* (1966), *Bomb Voyage* (1967), *London Derriere* (1968 [surely one of *the* great puns]), *La Feet's Defeat* (1968) and, finally, *Carte Blanched* (1969).

This was by no means the end of the Panther and the Inspector, however. Sixty-two of the Panther cartoons were subsequently featured in the Saturday morning TV series *The Pink Panther Show* (1969–1970,

3. Getting Animated

TV), whose initial two-season run of thirty-two episodes began airing on NBC on 6 September 1969. Most of the shows featured two Panthers either side of an Inspector short. For instance, episode one consisted of *The Pink Blueprint* (1966), *Bomb Voyage* (1967) and *The Pink Tail Fly* (1965). The series was an instant hit with kids, and proved particularly memorable for its opening credits sequence in which we see a young boy drive his Panthermobile to see the show at Grauman's Chinese Theatre, where the Panther and the Inspector emerge from its side door (the one-off vehicle, the envy of every schoolboy, was designed by Ron Reisner and fabricated at his California Show Cars garage by custom car builder Ed Newton). Accompanied by a catchy theme tune "Panther Pink Panther from Head to Toes" composed by Doug Goodwin, the sequence also featured cartoon clips along with live action images of animals mentioned in the song's clever lyrics (rhinoceroses, tigers, cats and mink), while the closing credits see the car drive off minus the Panther, who is forced to give chase.

The program proved to be such a success it was followed by several more incarnations, among them *The New Pink Panther Show*

Car share. The Pink Panther and Inspector Clouseau make their entrance in the titles for *The Pink Panther Show* (1971–1972, TV) (Mirisch/G-E/United Artists/MGM/DePatie-Freleng/NBC).

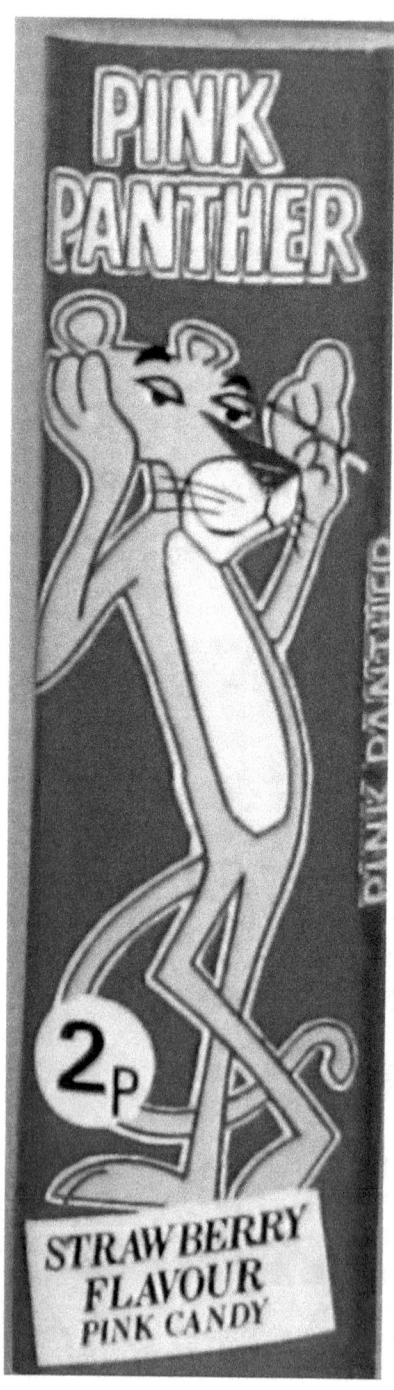

(1971–1972, TV), which had a new theme tune "Pantherly Pride" again provided by Doug Goodwin, and which replaced the Inspector segment with installments from DePatie-Freleng's *The Ant and the Aardvark* shorts (shown theatrically between 1969 and 1971 care of UA), *The Pink Panther and Friends* (1974–1976, TV), *The Pink Panther Laugh-and-a-Half Hour-and-a-Half Show* (1976–1977, TV), *Think Pink Panther* (1977–1978, TV), *The All New Pink Panther Show* (1978, TV) and *The Pink Panther Show* (1980, TV).

If that weren't enough, there was also a matter of the merchandising which, over the years has seen the licensing of a wide variety of Panther products, including tee-shirts, coffee mugs, cuddly toys, key fobs, model cars, onesies, pez dispensers, socks, ties, baseball caps, pins, computer games, comic strips, annuals and candy bars. There was even a set of commemorative stamps issued in the UK in 1985 featuring Peter Sellers and David Niven, while in 2001 the U.S. post office issued a stamp featuring Henry Mancini and the Panther. Said a thankful Blake Edwards of the additional benefits of creating the Panther character, "Needless to

Sweets for my sweet. British Pink Panther candy bar, and all for just two pence of your pocket money (Mirisch/G-E/United Artists/MGM/DePatie-Freleng/NBC/Nestlé).

3. Getting Animated

Top and bottom: Stamp of approval. The franchise is given official recognition by the UK (top) and U.S. post offices (Mirisch/G-E/United Artists/MGM/DePatie-Freleng/NBC/Benham/British Post Office [UK], Mirisch/G-E/United Artists/MGM/DePatie-Freleng/NBC/U.S. Post Office [U.S.]).

say, he's been very good to me, considering the merchandising empire that he sponsored."[4] However, as he revealed, the run of movies might well have ended before it began: "I didn't envision a whole series of Panthers. I was surprised to even find myself going back for a second one."[5] Luckily, a fortuitous development saw him change his mind, which prompts us to head all the way back to the sixties again...

4

A Second Shot

Just as *The Pink Panther* (1963) had gone through some last minute cast changes, with Peter Ustinov being replaced by Peter Sellers, so too did its immediate follow-up, *A Shot in the Dark* (1964), which had begun life as a different kettle of fish entirely (Blake Edwards described the film as "an unintentional Clouseau"[1]). The film was based upon the 1960 French play *L'Idiote* by Marcel Achard, which had enjoyed a lengthy run at the Theatre Antoine in Paris between 1960 and 1962. This was subsequently adapted for the American stage under the title *A Shot in the Dark* by the prolific screenwriter Harry Kurnitz (*Land of the Pharaohs* [1955], *Witness for the Prosecution* [1957], etc.) and likewise enjoyed a lengthy stay on Broadway at the Booth Theatre, where it opened on 18 October 1961 and went on to run for 389 performances prior to being sent out on tour.

In the play (which was produced by Broadway veteran Leland Hayward and directed by Harold Clurman), a pretty young French maid, Josefa Lantenay (played by Julie Harris), finds herself accused of murdering her lover Miguel. Yet despite being found naked in the room with a gun and the body, the Examining Magistrate, Paul Sevigne (William Shatner), is convinced that Josefa is innocent, much to the incredulity of his superior, Lablache (Hugh Franklin), his clerk Morestan (Gene Saks) and Josefa's employer, the wealthy banker Benjamin Beaurevers (Walter Matthau), who has also been having an affair with her, and who, it transpires, is the guilty party, despite her attempts to shield his identity (Matthau would go on to win a Tony as best featured actor in a play for his performance).

Like many successful Broadway productions, the three act play (which is set primarily in the Examiner's chambers) was seen as a viable film property, and was subsequently acquired by the Mirisch Corporation as a vehicle for Sophia Loren, with Anatole Litvak, who had just worked with her on *Five Miles to Midnight* (1962), set to direct from a script to be written by Alec Coppel (best known for co-writing the

4. A Second Shot

The play's the thing. Julie Harris is featured on this *Playbill* cover for the stage version of *A Shot in the Dark* (Playbill/Total Theatre).

screenplay for *Vertigo* [1958]). Peter Sellers was subsequently cast in the part of the Examining Magistrate while Matthau retained his role as the duplicitous Beaurevers (Sellers, who had an infatuation for Loren, had already worked with the actress on *The Millionairess* [1960] during the making of which they had recorded the hit novelty song "Goodness Gracious Me"). Sellers, whose casting was announced in *Daily Variety* on 9 May 1963 (just over a month after the completion of filming on *The Pink Panther* [1963]), was less than satisfied with how the project was panning out, however, and eventually decided to take matters into his own hands and approached Blake Edwards to take over.

As Edwards recalled, "Peter came to me and said he was going to be doing a film with the Mirisch Company. It was a stage play called *A Shot in the Dark* and he was not happy with the director, which means that the director was probably great and that Sellers was up to his usual tricks. Anyway, Peter asked if I would direct it and I said I'd have to read the script. Well, it didn't appeal to me, so I rang him up that afternoon and said I'd only do it if the lead could be Clouseau, and Peter just screamed on the other end of the line! So off I went to London to make *A Shot in the Dark*, and I wrote the damn thing on the Queen Mary, and by the time I got to London—which was five days, working day and night—I had half a script."[2]

Litvak left the picture in October 1963, by which time Edwards had been hired as writer, director and producer (the latter via his company Geoffrey again). Said Edwards of the situation, "The Mirisches had no alternative but to either cancel, and cough up a lot of money, or to put me on as director and let me re-write it to suit the Clouseau character."[3] Time was now of the essence, given that soundstages had been booked at the MGM-British Studios in Borehamwood (where Sellers had filmed *The Millionairess* [1960] with Loren), to which end work had already started on building the sets designed by Michael Stringer, who had recently worked for Mirisch on *633 Squadron* (1964). Also onboard by this point were Walter Mirisch as executive producer and Cecil Ford as associate producer. Like Michael Stringer, Ford had just come off *633 Squadron* (1964), and several of that film's crew now joined him on the Clouseau picture, among them editor Bert Bates (who worked in conjunction with Ralph E. Winters), sound recordists John Bramall and J.B. Smith, sound editor Teddy Mason and continuity supervisor Connie Willis. The film's other British crew included cinematographer Christopher Challis (shooting in Panavision and DeLuxe color), his camera operator Austin Dempster, costume designer Margaret Furse (who would go on to earn a BAFTA nomination for her work on the movie), assistant director Derek Cracknell and production manager Denis Johnson. By using so many local crew, the film qualified to be termed British, and was therefore liable for a tax break via the Eady Levy, the terms of which required that 85 percent of the film be shot in the UK and that only three non–British salaries could be excluded from the film's production costs, thus securing maximum British employment for artists and technicians (this was one of several films Mirisch went on to make in Britain under the scheme in the sixties).

In the meantime, Edwards continued to beaver away at the

screenplay, in which task he was helped by William Peter Blatty, who had travelled with him to London on the *Queen Mary* (conveniently, Sellers had also been onboard). Although hailed today for penning the classic 1971 horror novel *The Exorcist*, and for writing and producing the 1973 film version (which won him an Oscar for best screenplay and a nomination for best picture), Blatty at the time was known primarily as a writer of comic novels (*John Goldfarb, Please Come Home!* [1963]) and screenplays (*The Man from the Diners' Club* [1963]), all of which was enough to recommend him to Edwards, who must have been pleased with his work, as he went on to write a further three films with him, making him the latest addition to his coterie.

However, the radical changes to the script saw Walter Matthau leave the production, by which time Loren had already bailed, in this case owing to her slow recovery from an operation on her throat. Matthau was subsequently replaced by the suave Hollywood actor George Sanders, whose character was renamed Benjamin Ballon, while Shirley MacLaine (who had already made a handful of films for Mirisch, among them the recent *Irma la Douce* [1963]) was considered as a replacement for Loren before her role, now named Maria Gambrelli, was assigned to the Austrian actress Romy Schneider. However, when her schedule overran on *Good Neighbor Sam* (1964), she in turn was replaced by the German actress Elke Sommer, whose English-speaking career was just taking off thanks to her appearances in such large-scale films as *The Victors* (1963), in which Schneider had also appeared, and *The Prize* (1963), in which she starred opposite Paul Newman (Schneider would go on to work with Sellers in *What's New Pussycat* [1965]).

Other casting choices for the film included character star Herbert Lom as Clouseau's superior, Commissioner Charles Dreyfus (Lablache in the play), Graham Stark as his sidekick Hercule LaJoy (a variation on the play's Morestan character) and Burt Kwouk as his houseboy Kato (later Cato). All three would go on to become staples of the later sequels, with Lom and Kwouk reviving their roles multiple times, while Stark would play a variety of characters. Stark was good friends with Sellers, as he had appeared in a number of films and TV shows with him, such as *Down Among the Z Men* (1952), *A Show Called Fred* (1956, TV) and the recently released *The Wrong Arm of the Law* (1963), not to mention *The Millionairess* (1960), and though he would go on to become a valued member of Edwards' company of players, he was at the time unknown to the director.

As the actor recalled, "Blake and Peter were coming back from America by ship so they could work on the script a bit, and halfway across Blake suddenly said, out of the blue, 'Who's going to play

Hercule?' And Peter, without a pause, bless him, said, 'Graham Stark—I want Graham Stark to play him.' Naturally, Blake looked a bit blank. He didn't know who I was then—and why should he? So Blake said to get a copy of *Spotlight* which they had with them for casting purposes, to see what I looked like. Well, by an extraordinary coincidence I'd made a small film in France called *San Ferry Ann*. It was a little comedy in which I played a gendarme, and there was a good still of me wearing a kepi, looking like General DeGaulle, which I'd decided to use in *Spotlight*. So when Blake opened it up and saw my picture he said, 'Oh, for Christ's sake, he's perfect!' So for years, I've never taken that picture out of *Spotlight* as a compliment to them. So that's how it all began."[4]

For Herbert Lom, the film proved to be something of a gear change for the Czech actor (real name Herbert Charles Angelo Kuchacevich ze Schluderpacheru). Known primarily as a dramatic performer with a penchant for villainous types, he'd played key supporting roles in *North West Frontier* (1959) and *Spartacus* (1960), as well as Captain Nemo in *Mysterious Island* (1961). He'd also appeared with Sellers in *The Ladykillers* (1955) and *Mr. Topaze* (1961), the latter of which Sellers had

Getting the point. Herbert Lom (left) and Peter Sellers have a heated exchange in *A Shot in the Dark* (1964) (United Artists/Mirisch/Geoffrey).

directed. Recalled Lom of his experience working with Sellers on the Ealing classic, "After *The Ladykillers*, Peter came to my dressing room and asked me whether I could do him a favor. I told him of course and asked him what the favor was, and he asked me if I could help him find another good part! So I said to him, 'My dear chap, you won't need *me* to find you a good part! You'll be offered so many you won't know which one to take first!' And that certainly proved to be the case!"[5] Lom also remembered being offered the role of Dreyfus by Edwards. "Blake rang me and asked me to have lunch with him at The Dorchester, and he said to me, 'You've been playing all these heavies, and I think you're very funny!' And I said, 'How am I supposed to take that?' Anyway, he offered me the part and I was delighted. I've always been interested in the funny side of things, and I've always looked for the funny streaks in the heavies I'd been asked to play."[6]

Also joining the cast, and set to become a series regular, was Burt Kwouk, a jobbing Anglo-Chinese actor (born in Warrington, near Manchester) who had been playing minor supporting roles in the likes of *The Inn of the Sixth Happiness* (1958), *Visa to Canton* (1960) and *The Terror of the Tongs* (1961). His performance as Clouseau's karate-chopping houseboy Kato, who challenges the Inspector to a series of surprise fights in his apartment by way of practicing the finer aspects of martial arts with each other, proved to be one of the highlights in *A Shot in the Dark*, and these sequences became increasingly elaborate when repeated in the subsequent films. Recalled Kwouk, "The whole point is that Clouseau and Kato think they are these great martial arts masters when actually they're total rubbish! All they succeed in doing is smashing up the house in which they live!"[7] The bumps and bruises Kwouk received during the filming of these scenes proved to be worth it, however, as the part helped to raise the actor's profile, even if he did become known primarily for this one role. "I'm delighted to be known for *something* rather than nothing at all!"[8] said the actor. "It's had a huge effect on me, of course. What Kato did was take me from one level of being a working actor onto a higher level. What I'm trying to say is, it made me more expensive!"[9]

The remainder of the cast was rounded out with the French actor André Maranne as Dreyfus's hapless assistant François Chevalier (who would likewise go on to be a series regular) and, as members of the extended Ballon household, Tracy Reed as Ballon's wife Dominique, Douglas Wilmer as the head butler Henri LaFarge, Vanda Godsell as the cook (and LaFarge's wife), Maurice Kaufmann as the second chauffeur Pierre (the first being the murdered Miguel Ostos), Ann Lynn as the head maid Dudu (and Pierre's wife), David Lodge as the gardener

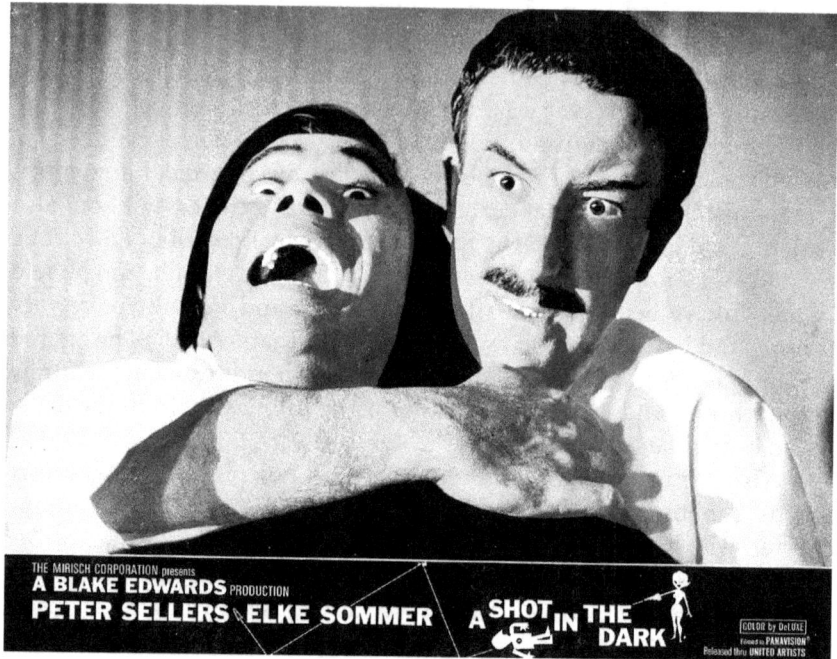

Surprise attack. Burt Kwouk (left) and Peter Sellers in one of the fight scenes from *A Shot in the Dark* (1964) (United Artists/Mirisch/Geoffrey).

Georges (Lodge was another of Sellers' chums who had already appeared with him in the likes of *The Naked Truth* [1957], *Up the Creek* [1958] and *Two Way Stretch* [1960]), Moira Redmond as Simone the second maid (and Georges' wife) and Martin Benson as the second butler Maurice, all of whom it seems have something to hide when Maria (the third maid) is accused of murder.

Indeed, the film, which finally began its twelve week shoot on 18 November 1963, opens with an elaborate sequence in which the Ballons and their servants are seen creeping about the house (the Chateau de la Pierre Blanche) in pursuit of their nightly romantic liaisons with each other, all of which climax with the firing of four shots in rapid succession. Following the credits, we cut to the office of Commissioner Dreyfus, who is informed by his assistant Duval of the shooting, and that he has mistakenly assigned Clouseau to the case, much to shocked chagrin of his superior, who fears the worst, given Monsieur Ballon's status and the potential for sensationalism in the press. Having arrived at the chateau (and immediately fallen into the ornamental fountain in the courtyard after getting out of the wrong side of his car), Clouseau, assisted by Hercule, begins his investigations, and discovers that Miguel the

4. A Second Shot

head chauffeur has been killed, and that the prime suspect appears to be the maid Maria Gambrelli, with whom the Inspector is clearly smitten, and who he believes to be innocent, despite indications to the contrary, given that she had been discovered with a smoking gun in her hand by Maurice, who had to break open the door to her room, which was locked from the inside. But Maria protests her innocence as to how the gun got in her hand ("I don't know how it got there, I really don't"), and Clouseau clearly believes this isn't the whole story ("I believe everything. And I believe nothing. I suspect everyone. And I suspect no one. I gather the facts, examine the clues, and before you know it, the case is solved"). However, before he can cause any real trouble, Dreyfus arrives on the scene to take over, much to the Inspector's disappointment.

Waking the next day, Clouseau is set upon in his bedroom by what appears to be an Oriental assassin, but who turns out to be his houseboy Kato, but their "workout" is interrupted by a call from Dreyfus, who informs the Inspector that he is now back on the Gambrelli case, at which we cut to Clouseau's office as he goes over the evidence with Hercule with the aid of a giant blackboard ("Facts, Hercule, facts"). Yet despite all the evidence against her, Clouseau believes the maid to be innocent and shielding somebody, and determines to wheedle their identity from her. In the meantime, we learn that Dreyfus had to reinstate Clouseau to the case upon the insistence of "extremely influential parties" as he terms it. Determined to catch the perpetrator, Clouseau thus arranges for Maria to be released from prison and follows her from there in the guise of a balloon seller, only to be arrested for not having a license.

Back at the chateau, Georges the gardener informs Monsieur Ballon that he saw him climbing down from Maria's room on the night of the murder, and that he will require 100,000 francs to ensure his silence. Clouseau is also on the scene watching Maria, and follows her into the greenhouse where he discovers her holding a bloodied pair of garden shears and a body at her feet—this time that of Georges the gardener, with all evidence again pointing to her having committed the crime. Yet Clouseau still maintains her to be innocent ("Only a fresh-faced novice would come up with a conclusion like that," he informs Hercule, who has surmised that she must be guilty). Determined to find out who Maria is covering for, Clouseau has her released from prison again, much to Dreyfus's now twitching anger, and disguises himself as a street artist outside the prison so as to follow her, only to be arrested again for not having a license.

At the chateau, Ballon and his wife, who is about to leave for a recital, are discussing Maria, who Dominique wants to sack, much to her husband's reticence ("We can't just fire her. She has given us no cause," he says, to which comes the response, "Cause? We are up to our necks in dead bodies. What are you waiting for? The last act of *Hamlet*?"). Clouseau soon after turns up, and seeing Mme. Ballon depart in her car with speed sends Hercule to follow her while he interrogates Monsieur Ballon over a game of billiards, during which he accuses him of murdering Miguel. However, despite admitting to not liking Miguel, and that he too has been having an affair with Maria, Ballon insists that he did not kill the chauffeur in "a rit of fealous jage" as Clouseau has it. The Inspector is subsequently called away following a call from Hercule, who has tracked Dominique to an apartment block where, mistaking the high note of an opera singer for a scream, Clouseau barges in on the soiree, only to fly straight through the room and out of the window into the river below.

Determined to get to the bottom of things, Clouseau next disguises himself as a gamekeeper so as to spy on the comings and goings at the chateau, only to mistakenly shoot a crow, which sees him confronted by the real game warden and arrested for not having a hunting license. Dreyfus is now apoplectic ("Give me ten men like Clouseau and I could destroy the world") and manages to cut off his thumb with his desktop cigar guillotine. Following a phone call from Hercule, Clouseau next tracks Maria to Camp Sunshine, where she is joined by Dudu. Not realizing that it is a nudist colony, Clouseau is forced to strip naked in order to enter and, covering his embarrassment with a guitar acquired from the locker attendant (played by Sellers' pal Brian Forbes, who would go on to direct him in *The Wrong Box* [1966]), he attempts to track her down, only to find her hiding behind a bush near the body of Dudu, who has been murdered, by which time Dreyfus and his men have arrived on the scene, prompting Clouseau and Maria to escape in his car without their clothes. Back at the chateau, where Dreyfus and François have gone to search for the girl, Henri the butler is found dead in a closet, while out on the streets of Paris, Clouseau and Maria find themselves stuck in a traffic jam to the delight of a gathering crowd, and are arrested for public indecency.

Dreyfus again throws the Inspector off the Gambrelli case and puts plans in motion to send him to the department of records in Martinique. He also surmises that it was Ballon who had wanted Clouseau on the case in the first place, given his incompetence. Indeed, Clouseau is back on the job again almost immediately, and determines on setting a trap to catch the killer, which he does by arranging to meet Maria at the Café Olé that evening in the hope of making her mysterious lover jealous and forcing him into the open. Indeed, during the noise of the

4. A Second Shot

flamenco floor show, an attempt is made on Clouseau's life, only for the assassin to miss and shoot another patron, while outside, as they are getting into a taxi, a thrown knife instead sees off the doorman. The bodies now start to pile up: a blow dart kills another patron at a Polynesian night spot, while at another a Cossack dancer (played by Tutte Lemkow) is poisoned after imbibing vodka intended for Clouseau. The assassin then follows Clouseau to his apartment, where the Inspector has taken Maria for a nightcap, and leaves a bomb in the guise of an antique clock at his door ("That's very strange"), only for it to go off as he is attempting to make love to Maria (this after another badly timed attack from Kato).

"Phantom killer murders four. Trail of death follows Inspector Clouseau," exclaims the front page headline in *Le Figaro* the next day, which brings the killings (including the Ballon murders) to eight, according to the calculations of the twitching Dreyfus, who by now has had to resort to analysis. But Clouseau has devised a plan to finally expose the killer that night, to which end he assembles everybody in the drawing room at the chateau, not realizing that the assassin, who is revealed to be Dreyfus, is in the grounds, where he places explosives under the hood of the Inspector's car. During the subsequent interrogation an argument breaks out between those assembled, in which all the affairs are laid bare, and it is revealed that it was Dominique who shot Miguel by mistake, expecting to find her husband with Maria, and that it was Monsieur Ballon, who'd been hiding in Maria's closet, who put the gun in her hand. But it seems that *everyone* is guilty of either infidelity, murder or blackmail, and when the lights go out, as per Clouseau's instructions to Hercule, they all make a run for it, piling into Clouseau's car, only for it to blow up (off camera) as it drives off, adding six more to the body count. "They were all murderers except Maurice who was a blackmailer," says Clouseau, by which time Dreyfus has truly lost the plot, and falls to the floor, biting the Inspector's leg like a dog. With the case now solved, Clouseau and Maria kiss, at which Kato attacks, and all three end up in the ornamental fountain...

For a lighthearted detective comedy, the plot is at times somewhat complicated (one can just about follow what is being done by who and to whom), and the final revelation in the drawing room has all the hallmarks of a Poirot denouement. Otherwise, the film provides ample opportunity for Clouseau to do what he does best: make a perfect fool of himself while trying (and failing) to retain a modicum of dignity amid the self inflicted pratfalls and catastrophes. Clearly enjoying the fact that he is now the undoubted center of attention, Sellers is fully confident in his performance as the clodhopping detective, determinedly

Laughing stock. The cast crack up while filming the denouement of *A Shot in the Dark* (1964). From left: Vanda Godsell, Maurice Kaufmann, Peter Sellers and Tracy Reed (United Artists/Mirisch/Geoffrey).

sticking to his theory that Maria is innocent, despite the insurmountable evidence against her. It is here, second time round, that the character (now minus Madame Clouseau, who is never mentioned) is more fully formed, especially regarding his accent and its various exaggerations. Recalled Blake Edwards, "It wasn't until we were well into the film that the mispronunciation came out.... He went to France for the weekend, and when he came back he said he'd run into a concierge who talked like this, so it developed itself."[10]

The character (who is again introduced to the strains of "The Marseillaise") is at his comic best while interviewing the various suspects in the case, during which he frequently falls foul of his own clumsiness. For instance, during his initial investigation, he manages to splatter Maurice's shirt with his pen, get a splodge of face cream on his nose after sniffing the contents of a pot of face cream on Maria's dressing table, suck the ink from his pen ("Ugh") and set his mackintosh on fire after lighting cigarettes for himself and Maria (this despite the fact that it still supposedly wet from his soaking in the fountain, which has already prompted Maria to worry that he might catch his death of pneumonia, to which he stoically replies, "Yes, I probably will, but it's all part of life's rich pageant, you know"). Later, while interviewing Monsieur Ballon over a game of billiards, he causes mayhem with a bent cue, with which he rips the gauze ("I'm dreadfully sorry, Monsieur Ballon. I appear to have grazed your billiard table"), gets caught up in the cue rack, and makes his exit via the wrong side of an open door, straight into the wall ("I suggest you have your architect investigated as well").

Other highlights include Clouseau instructing his driver "Back to town" as he and Hercule leave the chateau, only for him to immediately drive off leaving the two of them behind, the running joke about Clouseau being constantly arrested for his lack of a license, at which we instantly cut to a shot of a police van taking him away (note the way Sellers bounces as he walks with the balloons), the scenes in the nudist colony, which climax with Clouseau and Maria being carted off to the police station (this time with four policemen clinging to the back of the van and gawping through the window), Clouseau's exit from Dreyfus's office during which he manages to shatter the glass of the closing door ("And another thing!" he says, pointing), his inability to synchronize his watch with Hercule so that the lights at the chateau can go out at the appropriate moment (much of this scene was apparently improvised by Sellers and Stark) and the climactic denouement during which he manages to stumble over every outstretched leg and piece of furniture available (amid the argument between those gathered, he even breaks the fourth wall by looking into the camera in typical Oliver Hardy style).

Cue the mayhem. Peter Sellers causes havoc on the billiards table in *A Shot in the Dark* (1964) (United Artists/Mirisch/Geoffrey).

Elsewhere, the spinning globe gag from the previous film is revived to hilarious effect, though this time Clouseau manages to get his hand caught in it ("Look, I've got Africa all over my hand now," he says, which Sellers apparently adlibbed on the spot), while the fights with Kato add further chaos to the proceedings. Said Edwards of these scenes, which were inspired by his own training with grand master Ed Parker, "At that time I was just beginning martial arts, which I'd been interested in most of my adult life. I can't remember the genesis really, except that it just came to me that he [Clouseau] had someone training him who was just as fucked up as he was, who would jump out of refrigerators and attack him all the time. I thought that would be a pretty bizarre situation. I told Peter the idea and he just collapsed."[11]

Despite the monumental presence of Sellers as Clouseau, the film mercifully isn't a one-man show. Elke Sommer, perfectly coiffured in various sixties hairdos, makes for a charming suspect as Maria Gambrelli, while George Sanders is all gentlemanly deadpan restraint as Monsieur Ballon, particularly during the billiards scene where he just about manages to maintain a straight face. "He was rehearsing not to laugh,"[12] revealed Graham Stark, who himself brilliantly exudes stony contempt as Clouseau's sidekick Hercule. Although Stark was pals with Sellers, and had already appeared in several of his films, he wasn't cast as Hercule simply because they were buddies, as the actor revealed. "It was more professional than that.... It was very much geared to if you were right for the part, and Christ help you if you weren't, because he [Sellers] could be quite ruthless.... He liked people he knew, but if you weren't right he could be quite terrifying, there was no question."[13] Things were clearly right on this occasion, and the two developed something of a double act during their appearances. Said Stark of the situation, "It was divine. Blake liked what I was doing and we got on very well. It was very easy that film—not complicated. It was a strong, funny story, all shot on one stage at MGM with nothing outside. We just got on with it and it was a very big success."[14] As for breaking up with laughter on set with Sellers, Stark recalled, "Every time we did a scene together, people would come down to watch because they knew what was going to happen!"[15]

The other actor on the film previously unknown to Edwards was Burt Kwouk, who certainly leaves his mark as Kato, and all with very little dialogue. Recalled Kwouk, "No actor ever knows why a director has noticed him. Blake had perhaps heard of me, or seen my work or whatever, and the phone call came for me to go to The Dorchester to meet him. So I went along."[16] Like several of the other actors on the film, he subsequently became a mainstay of the series, despite the limitations of

4. A Second Shot

Time, gentlemen, please. Peter Sellers (left) and Graham Stark attempt to synchronize their watches in *A Shot in the Dark* (1964) (United Artists/Mirisch/Geoffrey).

the role, which he managed to tailor to his own talents. "An actor always develops a personality within the structure of the script, and *A Shot in the Dark* was structured in such a way that everything Kato did was physical other than verbal. It made it possible for the actor, who happened to be me at the time, to, as it were, expand the personality physically rather than verbally. In other words, as an actor, I was not locked into the words."[17] As for the fight scenes, Kwouk revealed that they were choreographed "sometimes very carefully, sometimes very carelessly. It was how we felt at the time. As with everything, some things are difficult and you have to solve problems, which take a long time, other things you just go *bang* and they're done."[18]

As for Herbert Lom's turn as the increasingly unstable Dreyfus, whose tics and twitches became something of a trademark, the actor revealed, "The twitching was not in the script, it happed on the set. In one of the scenes, Clouseau leaves my office and says, 'Don't worry, the case will be solved," and he gives me a stupid wink. That makes me so mad I wink back, and once I start winking I can't stop! So that's how the twitch developed. And as the films went on, it got worse and worse! When the scriptwriters ran out of ideas, they'd always say to me, "Herbert, can you do some winking?" And I'd say, "No, I won't. You write me some decent scenes then I won't *have* to wink!"[19]

Lom certainly got his fair share of decent scenes in *A Shot in the Dark*, among them his opener, in which we find him answering the phone in his office. "Ah. Yes, my darling. I was just about to call you. I'm on my way. I've got the cheese and beaujolais. What? My love. Kiss the children for me." At which the buzzer goes, and he is informed, "Your wife is on the other line." "Tell her I'm out of town," he responds. Priceless. Of his casting in the role, however, he revealed that it didn't always work in his favor in the long run. "In a way, it's been a double-edged sword. On the one hand I was offered lots of funny parts with twitching eyes and so on, whilst on the other hand, whenever I was after a big dramatic part, producers would say, 'Oh, yes, a very good actor Herbert Lom, but too much associated with crazy comedy.'"[20] Of working with Sellers he meanwhile noted, "I'll tell you my attitude to Peter in a nutshell. He is known to have been difficult on the set and difficult at home. I didn't find him difficult. I found him charming, very co-operative and great fun to work with. I think it must have been due to the fact that we really liked eachother."[21]

As Graham Stark has noted, save for some long shots of the chateau (actually the Luton Hoo estate in Bedfordshire), some second unit shots in Paris (photographed by Skeets Kelly) and a brief back lot scene as Clouseau arrives at the apartment at which Madame Ballon is attending the soiree, the movie was filmed entirely in the studios, including the pillared exterior of the Ballon chateau, its grounds and greenhouse, and the nudist camp, complete with swimming hole, all of which proved to be a challenge for the film's cinematographer, Christopher Challis, who'd already worked with Sellers on the crime drama *Never Let Go* (1960) and with Sommer on *The Victors* (1963). Admitted Challis, "You needed a lot of light because they were very big sets. But I think it was because Blake wanted to keep tight control of the picture.... I think it was largely to avoid problems with the weather."[22]

The biggest challenge proved to be the opening sequence, in which the camera pans and cranes about the exterior of the chateau as its inhabitants move from room to room and corridor to corridor, up and down the stairs for their nightly liaisons, all of which were shot in a series of lengthy, unbroken takes. "It was Blake's idea and was worked out between us," said Challis of the complicated sequence. "My camera operator, Austin Dempster, of course had the toughest job on that. It wasn't easy to light, either, but he had a terrific job timing all the crane movements, because cranes in those days were pretty primitive. They were pushed by anyone they could find who was around! So it was an enormous job of timing and cueing."[23] As for his experience of working with Edwards he said, "He was great to work with.... Blake is very good at keeping discipline and is a very good director. He knows exactly what he's doing and he doesn't over shoot or anything like that. He knows when he's got what he wants. He keeps very tight control on his pictures, and though the films are hilariously funny, they're done in a very calculated way."[24] Indeed, one impressive high angle shot, taken from outside the billiards room from the hall staircase, sees Maria and three other members of the household staff eavesdropping on the conversation between Clouseau and Monsieur Ballon from various vantage points, only for them to be sent scattering by the ringing of a phone. Brilliantly staged and photographed by Edwards and Challis, it wouldn't look out of place in a Hitchcock film. As for Sellers' penchant for breaking up, Challis admits he didn't see much of it himself. "He didn't do much of that on that picture. He was miserable most of the film, behind the scenes. I don't quite know why. There were no difficulties like that. He was pretty good. He didn't break up on that one at all. I think that came later."[25]

Sommer madness. Elke Sommer and Peter Sellers in the nudist camp scene from *A Shot in the Dark* (1964) (United Artists/Mirisch/Geoffrey).

Edwards certainly seemed to enjoy working in England with the local cast, and returned several times to make films there during his career. As he recalled, "The original Panther was set up to do in Italy.... Anytime that Peter could use England as his base, he preferred that. And I got to know all his friends, and learned much about the people he'd been on the radio with, such as The Goons. I have always admired English films, as well as American. I certainly admired the English actors—they're so damned professional and very good. I really enjoyed that stock company."[26] He also appeared to be happy with the work of the British crew, as he revealed in an interview during shooting. "I was warned of certain difficulties, but I have had a very good experience here. We are on schedule; I've had one hundred per cent efficiency from the entire crew. There is a lot of enthusiasm and I'm as satisfied as I would be at home."[27] However, when asked about his experience making the previous film in Italy, he described it as "Quite terrible. Outmoded equipment, confusion and bad management. I even had a strike on the set with fights. Maybe I had too many Americans on the crew and they [the Italians] resented it. There's absolutely no comparison here. And I don't think the efficiency of Hollywood is all that it's cracked up to be—at least not now with the economic worries. I'm averaging about three pages of script per day here against 2½ in America."[28]

Once the film was in the can (by which time Sellers had also married his second wife, the actress Britt Ekland, on 19 February 1964, just ten days after meeting her at The Dorchester), it was handed over to the editing department for post-production, after which Henry Mancini added his score, which was recorded at the C.T.S. (Cine-Tele Sound) Studios in Bayswater, London (home of the early Bond soundtracks), where Mancini had recorded *Charade* (1963) the previous year. However, this time there was no Panther theme "Because there was no Pink Panther!"[29] as the composer pointed out. Instead, he provided a killer new theme with a vamping *Peter Gunn*–style rhythm, this time carried by bass guitar rather than a piano, over which plays a four-note "mystery" motif performed on an Indian pump organ the composer had acquired from a shop in London (this theme would go on to feature in the DePatie-Freleng Clouseau cartoons). With its keyboard riffs and big band breaks, it's another Mancini classic.

In fact the sixties were proving to be something of a golden period for the composer. "It just happened that it was my decade, and the kind of pictures that were popular then suited what I did. That was when I started coming to London to work on pictures.... In fact *Charade* was written in a suite in the Mayfair Hotel. But when you're on a roll it's great!"[30] Mancini's "roll" actually carried on well into the eighties, and eventually took in such classic soundtracks as *Arabesque* (1966), *Wait Until Dark* (1967, with its disconcerting "wonky piano" motif), *Silver Streak* (1976), *Who Is Killing the Great Chefs of Europe?* (1978, aka *Too Many Chefs*) and *Santa Claus: The Movie* (1985) among many others, with the only real blip occurring when he worked for Alfred Hitchcock on *Frenzy* (1972), which saw his score replaced by another by Ron Goodwin. Recalled the composer of the incident, "The replacement of the music wasn't the problem—it was the *rejection*! I had no inkling.... Hitchcock was there the whole time [during the recording], nodding yes, yes, yes. Then when I got back home it was all of a sudden no, no, no! I think he thought it was too macabre. That was the word he used. Maybe he wanted more of a Pink Panther feel to it. I could go down a list a mile long of composers who've had their scores replaced—very *prominent* composers. But it happens. You feel a great depression about it, but it happens."[31]

The title theme for *Shot* aside (which is also featured during the nudist colony sequence in a swing version played by a "live" orchestra of naked musicians), Mancini's other major contribution to the film is the song "Shadows of Paris" which plays over the opening sequence at the chateau. A yearning romantic ballad sung by an uncredited Gina Carroll (then under contract to Decca), its purple lyrics by Robert Wells (who'd co-written *Knockout* [1953, TV] with Edwards) provide an ironic counterpoint to the onscreen activities of the Ballon household as they furtively creep about the house in pursuit of their amorous assignations. Elsewhere, a comedic effect in the form of a single descending guitar note accompanies Clouseau's various arrests for not having the correct license, while during the assassination montage, an ominous, low register orchestral rumble builds in power to the point when the killer (Dreyfus) makes his deadly move.

Of his working methods with Edwards, Mancini recalled, "Usually, I don't see anything unless there's a special scene that he wants me to see. We then talk a bit about what he sees; if he has any special needs. Then I go ahead and kind of figure it out. I usually spot alone, then I give him the notes and he takes them home and sees if there's anything I've missed."[32] Of the time it takes to score a film, he admitted that he could be "Pretty fast, if I have to. I can move quickly. Something like the Panthers would take four weeks.... Pictures which are loaded with more music than usual can take anything up to eight or even ten weeks."[33] Unfortunately, a full LP of the music failed to appear this time round, though the title music and "Shadows of Paris" were issued on a 45 single by RCA.

Work on the animated title sequence also took place during

For the record. The rare single release of Henry Mancini's music from *A Shot in the Dark* (1964) (United Artists/Mirisch/Geoffrey/RCA/Twin Chris Music Corp./ASCAP).

post-production (note that Sellers and Sommer share equal billing, appearing on the same card together, albeit with Sellers listed first on the left; the credits also feature the line "and introducing Turk Thrust" which was the pseudonym under which Bryan Forbes appeared, and which was a running joke between Sellers and Forbes at the time). This time the action focuses on the exploits of Clouseau himself, who finds himself shot at numerous times during the sequence, which also features a three-headed villain, a chorus of legs dancing the can-can, flashing cameras for Christopher Challis's credit, a giant gorilla which causes the Inspector to turn white and shatter into pieces, and a giant chicken whose egg explodes over the Inspector. Edwards' credits for producing and directing float down on six parachutes. As on the previous film, the

4. A Second Shot

sequence was created by DePatie-Freleng, with animation production provided by George Dunning & Associates (Dunning would go on to direct *Yellow Submarine* [1968]), while returning animators included Bob Matz, Norm McCabe and Don Williams. DePatie-Freleng was also involved in the production of the trailer again, which features an animated bullet which introduces scenes from the film ("Elke Sommer is the number one sexpot.... I mean suspect," he informs us, while at the conclusion he reveals, "Confidentially, the murderer is..." before being shot himself). As for the accompanying poster, it contains three panels featuring Sommer in various alluring outfits with Sellers in the background. "Meet the inspector who was always on the job. In the bedroom.... In the nightclub.... In the nudist colony!" runs the accompanying text, while the strapline announces the film to be "The picture that gets away with murder!"

The film was originally slated for a Christmas 1964 release, but following the success of *The Pink Panther* (1963), this was brought forward by United Artists, who opened it at both the Trans-Lux East and Astor cinemas in New York on 23 June 1964, where it raked in a combined opening day gross of $68,000, despite industry fears that two films featuring Clouseau might cancel each other out. Commented *Variety*, "Wisdom remains to be seen of projecting a second appearance of the hilariously inept detective so soon after the still-current first run of *Panther*." Audiences thought otherwise, and the film ultimately went on to earn $12,368,234 in the U.S. and Canada alone (the equivalent of 13,299,176 tickets), outstripping its predecessor by some one-and-a-half million dollars and coming in at number seven on the year's list of top grossing movies (*The Pink Panther* came in at number ten), making Sellers the king of comedy. In fact such was his status by now, he had been accorded the honor of placing his hand and foot prints outside Grauman's Chinese Theatre just before the film opened on the West Coast at LA's Vogue and Fine Arts theaters on 15 July. The film premiered in London on 28 January 1965 at the Odeon Leicester Square, where it played for three weeks before transferring to the London Pavilion in Piccadilly Circus for a further twelve. It carried an A certificate, no doubt because of the implied nudity and the discussion of a possible sexual assault ("He did not rape me," says Maria of Miguel at one point when questioned by Clouseau in his office).

As before, the reviews were on the mixed side, though most agreed that the film was worth seeing for Sellers. Commented *The New York Times*, "The wonderful dexterity and the air of perpetually buttressed dignity with which Mr. Sellers plays his role make what could quickly be monotonous enjoyable to the end," to which *The New Yorker* added, "A

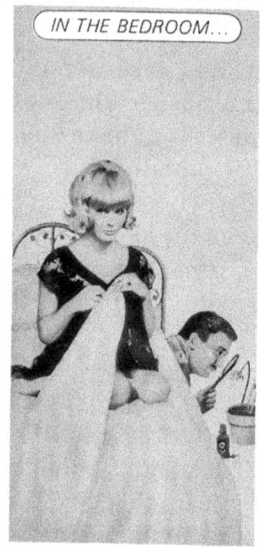

On the job. Saucy poster artwork for *A Shot in the Dark* (1964) (United Artists/Mirisch/Geoffrey).

Biting humor. Elke Sommer and Peter Sellers in *A Shot in the Dark* (1964) (United Artists/Mirisch/Geoffrey).

Shot in the Dark as done on Broadway was a mediocre comedy, but Blake Edwards, who directed the film and collaborated on the script with William Peter Blatty, had the good sense to toss the foundation stock out the window and let Mr. Sellers run amok." *The Washington Post* found that "the real fun comes from sight gags, an old if neglected ingredient," though Britain's *Monthly Film Bulletin* described it as "slapstick of the crudest kind." It also felt that "as the bumbling inspector, Sellers is this time absolutely out of hand," though it did admit that "no expense has been spared in sets or decoration." The *LA Times* averred that the film was "all variations of falling down and going boom," and pleaded that "enough is enough already." *Variety*, however, found that "the laughs are still there abundantly through imaginative bits of business and a few strike belly proportions."

Inevitably, given the success of both films, Mirisch and United Artists were keen to repeat the formula, but things had begun to fracture between Sellers and Edwards during the making of the second film. Commented Walter Mirisch of the situation, "You know, both he and Blake reacted very fiercely to their relationship after *A Shot in the Dark*. Both said they didn't wanna work together again. Peter actively disliked the picture. I remember him talking to me once and telling me he didn't think it should be released. I think it is as good, if not a better picture, than *The Pink Panther*."[34] As for Edwards, he revealed, "At one time I did say, 'I'll never make another film with him again,' and that was [after] *A Shot in the Dark*."[35]

But if Sellers and Edwards weren't keen to continue what was now shaping up to be a potentially lucrative series of films, then who would?

5

The Interloper

Following the success of *A Shot in the Dark* (1964), Blake Edwards and Peter Sellers went their separate ways. Recalled producer Walter Mirisch, "Despite the fact that we were very anxious to make a third Pink Panther with the combination at that time, they simply did not want to work with one another."[1] Mirisch tried to cajole the two, but the answer was still no: "I told Blake I'd like to prepare another script, which we called *Inspector Clouseau*. Peter again said he didn't want to have anything to do with the character."[2] Remembered Henry Mancini of the situation, "It was one of those things. They wanted to continue the series, and neither Blake nor Sellers at that time were up to it."[3] Admitted Edwards, "I decided at that point it just wasn't worth the pain and the discomfort that one had to go through in order to have fun. It's great to be able to laugh while you're working ... but it's not going to last for long if you end up so stressed."[4]

Instead, Sellers went on to make *Kiss Me, Stupid* (1964), again for Mirisch, and in which he was directed by the great Billy Wilder, while Edwards made *The Great Race* (1965) for Warner. Bros., which helped to continue his love for old-style slapstick (the elaborately produced comedy included such ingredients as a saloon brawl and the greatest pie fight ever staged). Despite its huge production costs ($12m), the film was a big success, raking in some $25m at the box office, making it the sixth most popular film of 1965. Unfortunately, Sellers fared less well and clashed with Wilder on set. He then famously suffered a series of almost fatal heart attacks on 5 April 1964, which forced his withdrawal from the film (he was replaced by Ray Walston). After a period of recovery, he was nevertheless back in front of the cameras later in the year, appearing in the television movie *Carol for Another Christmas* (1964, TVM), which he followed with the comedy *What's New Pussycat* (1965), which reunited him with Capucine, and which proved to be another major success, coming in at number eight in the year's box office rankings with a take of $18,820,000.

Sellers continued to be prolific during this period, and went on to appear in such films as *The Wrong Box* (1966), *After the Fox* (1966), *The Bobo* (1967) and (taking top billing over David Niven, with whom he didn't share any scenes) the Bond spoof *Casino Royale* (1967), albeit to rather more variable commercial impact, while Edwards went on to make *What Did You Do in the War, Daddy?* (1966) and *Gunn* (1967), neither of which set the world alight either, after which the duo decided they *did* want to work together again after all, although *not* on a new Clouseau film. Instead, they made *The Party* (1968) for Mirisch, a silent movie-style comedy of disasters with little dialogue concerning a perpetually clumsy Indian actor, Hrundi V. Bakshi, who is mistakenly invited to a swank Hollywood party, only to wreck both it and the deluxe home in which it is taking place. Like his character in *The Millionairess* (1960), Sellers played the role in brown-face make-up and assumed an exaggerated sing-song accent, and while the film is no longer PC in this regard, its heart is undeniably in the right place. With much of the action improvised (the script was just 63 pages long), the film includes sequences of genuine hilarity, among them a scene in which Bakshi attempts to feed a parrot with the encouraging cries of "Birdie num num" and a toilet roll gag that's a real doozy, and though it occasionally falters, it nevertheless contains some of Edwards' and Sellers' most inventive work, as well as a great set care of Fernando Carrere (complete with indoor pools and moving floors), plenty of tuneful muzak from Henry Mancini (including a cheeky rendition of "Meglio Stasera" from *The Pink Panther* [1963]), a scene-stealing turn by Steve Franken as a drunken waiter (the actor would go on to appear in Sellers' final film, *The Fiendish Plot of Dr. Fu Manchu* [1980], as well as one of the later Panthers), and a climax that involves an elephant and a giant bubble bath. Made on a budget of $1.5m, the film went on to earn $2.9m following its release by United Artists on 4 April 1968, and though it has gone on to be recognized as a cult classic, it was by no means regarded as a hit at the time. But then again, neither was the film that Edwards and Sellers *should* have made, *Inspector Clouseau* (1968).

Interestingly, both *The Party* (1968) and *Inspector Clouseau* (1968) were in production via Mirisch at pretty much the same time. The two films also had something else in common: their writers, brothers Frank and Tom Waldman, a couple of TV veterans whose credits included everything from sit-com episodes to specials. As well as *The Party* (1968), the duo had also worked with Edwards before on the Bing Crosby comedy *High Time* (1960) and a failed pilot, *Boston Terrier* (1963, TV), which was spun from a 1962 episode of *The Dick Powell Show* (1961–1963, TV) which Edwards had directed from a story by himself and

5. The Interloper

The elephant in the room. Peter Sellers, Claudine Longet and friend make a splash in *The Party* (1968) (Mirisch/Geoffrey/United Artists).

Tom, who'd also worked on an episode of *Peter Gunn* (1958–1961, TV) titled *Jacoby's Vacation* (1961, TV), again from a story by Edwards, while Frank had worked on an episode titled *Voodoo* (1961, TV), likewise from a story by Blake. The brothers would therefore clearly have been trusted by Edwards to take the Clouseau character forward into his next adventure. However, as we shall see, without the vital ingredients of Sellers and Edwards (and Mancini), they were on a hiding to nothing.

Like *A Shot in the Dark* (1964), the new Clouseau adventure was to be filmed in London at the MGM-British Studios in Borehamwood so as to take advantage of the tax breaks provided by the Eady Levy, as a consequence of which the majority of the cast and crew were again local, and who this time worked under the aegis of the American producer Lewis J. Rachmil, whose credits for Mirisch already included *Kings of the Sun* (1963), *Rage to Live* (1965) and *Hawaii* (1966), along with two British-based productions, *633 Squadron* (1964) and *Return from the Ashes* (1965), both of which had also been made at MGM-British. Returning from *A Shot in the Dark* (1964) to work on the film was production designer Michael Stringer, who'd also worked on *633 Squadron*

(1964) and *Return from the Ashes* (1965), as well as Sellers' *Casino Royale* (1967), and second unit photographer Skeets Kelly. They were joined by the likes of cinematographer Arthur Ibbetson (shooting in Panavision and DeLuxe), editor John Victor Smith, sound recordist Gerry Turner, production supervisor Charles Orme and assistant director Kip Gowans (who'd worked on *Return from the Ashes* [1965] as well as three films with Sellers, including *Mr. Topaze* [1961]). Another American, Bud Yorkin, was now in the director's chair, and although he'd helmed TV specials for Fred Astaire, Jack Benny, Danny Kaye and Carol Channing, he'd made only three films: *Come Blow Your Horn* (1963), *Never Too Late* (1965) and *Divorce American Style* (1967). The cast meanwhile included such familiar British faces as Frank Finlay, Barry Foster, Patrick Cargill and Beryl Reid, all of whom supported the new Clouseau in town, the respected American comedy character actor Alan Arkin, who'd just made a big splash in the Mirisch comedy *The Russians Are Coming, The Russians Are Coming* (1967), for which he'd earned an Oscar nomination for best actor.

When interviewed on set about it at the time of filming, Arkin admitted that his chief concern on taking over the role of Clouseau was actually the accent. "French came very hard to me. The Russian for *The Russians Are Coming* was easy, but the French was difficult. I worked on it for about a month before I got the part."[5] And when asked if he felt any pressure in taking over from Sellers, he replied, "Not really, because I'm not doing the same scripts he did. If I was doing the exact same thing over again I probably would feel it, but I'm playing the character, I'm not playing him.... I don't really feel like I'm competing with him. I'm a great fan of his."[6] As for the screenplay, he admitted, "I read the script and fell down laughing. I thought it was one of the funniest things I'd read. And when I'm moved by something it means I want to do it.... Then I had a couple of misgivings and went back and saw his films again and just felt that I could do something different with him than what he did. Not better not worse, I just think different. It's up to people who watch it to decide. I don't even think anybody has to decide which they like better. One is one thing, and this is something else."[7]

This time the plot sees Clouseau sent to London at the insistence of the British Prime Minister to assist a flummoxed Scotland Yard in the recovery of the loot stolen from the infamous great train robbery (said to be £2.5m), which it is feared will be used as capital to fund another, even greater crime (which proves to be the case). However, while many of those involved in the robbery have been apprehended, the identities of their evasive leaders remain a mystery, with one of them thought to be a mole at the heart of the establishment, while of the organization's three

5. The Interloper

Doppelganger. Alan Arkin takes on the mantle (and hat and moustache) of the world's most incompetent detective in *Inspector Clouseau* (1968) (Mirisch/United Artists).

top men, two have already escaped jail. Says Sir Charles Braithwaite, the Commissioner in charge of the case, to Clouseau, "The thought was, since you couldn't possibly be the traitor, we can trust you. But you must trust no one. The viper in our bosom could be anyone." To which Clouseau responds, "Anyone? I suspect everyone."

Clouseau thus makes his way to Blackpool Prison to interview the remaining gang member still in custody, Addison Steele, who is working in the prison barber shop, where the Inspector finds him cutting the hair of the warden's wayward son, Clyde Hargreaves. During their meeting, Clouseau learns from Steele that he and the other members of the gang never met their ringleader, known to them as Johnny Rainbow. Steele also offers to give Clouseau a shave, but instead drugs him and then makes his escape down a laundry chute. We then cut to Clouseau as he is being kitted out by Superintendent Weaver, his liaison on the case, with a variety of Bond-style gadgets that he has requested, among them smoke-signal matches, a high-intensity laser beam disguised as a cigarette lighter, a high-frequency transmitter and recorder, a belt whose buckle contains three miniature missiles, and inflatable underwear, all of which prove handy given that two of the escaped men, Steven Frey and Frenchy Lebec, accompanied by their driver Bull Parker, are on the trail of the Inspector, whom they plan to assassinate.

Having been invited to Weaver's home for dinner, Clouseau meets the family's au pair, Lisa Morell, with whom he becomes smitten, and Weaver's Scottish wife, who turns out to have designs on him, though not until after they have all visited the Edinburgh International Festival, where Frenchy attempts to assassinate Clouseau, only to be inadvertently shot dead by his exploding belt when he expresses joy at having won the Grand Door Prize of a giant plum pudding. Reporting to Sir Charles at his club, outside of which he again meets the warden's son, Clouseau comes to suspect that there is a bomb in the pudding, and wrecks the club in trying to disarm it with the assistance of the bomb squad, only to discover that it instead contains a cyanide capsule, which at least proves that the bad guys are indeed out to get him after all.

Clouseau next follows up a clue found in Frenchy's pocket, a book of matches, which leads him to the Tudor Arms, where he is seduced by two female members of the gang. Again he is drugged and a cast is made of his face, so as to enable the members of the gang to disguise themselves as the Inspector in order to carry out their grand plan, which is to rob thirteen banks in Switzerland. Having travelled to France for the funeral of Frenchy Lebec, so as to gather more clues, Clouseau now teams up with Lisa, who turns out to be a member of Interpol, so as to eavesdrop on the gang's plans, but in firing a microphone into their den with a crossbow, he overshoots and latches onto a TV in the house opposite and ends up eavesdropping on a western in which the bad guys are planning a robbery. By now it has been revealed that the warden's son is actually Johnny Rainbow, while Clouseau's seemingly friendly liaison, Superintendent Weaver, is the mole in the establishment, who throws the Inspector off a moving train so as to be rid of him, allowing Johnny Rainbow to take Clouseau's place at a meeting with the Minister of Finance, during which he informs him that a gang plans to rob one of thirteen banks, and that when he discovers which one, he will turn up and remove all the funds and transfer them for safekeeping. However, the plan is to carry out this ruse at all thirteen banks, and then get the money out of the country by having it wrapped up as Lindt chocolate bars.

Clouseau eventually turns up on the scene to reveal Weaver's part in the plot and ends up in a fight with him wearing one of the disguises ("My face. You've stolen my face"). Weaver is killed in the melee, after which Clouseau tracks down the stolen money, which is being sent

5. The Interloper

down the Rhine, and which he follows by giving chase to Addison Steele, whose car also proves to be a boat (when Clouseau follows him into the water in his own car, his inflatable underwear helps to save his skin). Brought onboard the gang's vessel, he is finally face to face with Johnny Rainbow ("You'll soon be laughing on the other side of my face!") and is locked up in the hold with Lisa, who has also been picked up by the gang. Following a rare moment of self reflection ("I ruin everything I touch") Clouseau finally defeats the gang by using his laser lighter to make a hole in the side of the boat, which then begins to sink, and though the gang escape in Steele's car-boat, Clouseau and Lisa are picked up by Sir Charles, who has been tracking him, so that all ends well, with Clouseau returning to France in triumph, with the prospect of a romantic relationship with Lisa to boot. However, onboard the plane, he finds himself sitting next to Weaver's wife in her widow's weeds, and the film ends with him escaping her advances by parachuting to safety.

If any of this sounds even remotely funny, then sad to report, it isn't (when Clouseau bumps into the warden's son outside Sir Charles' club, they have an exchange of views during which Clouseau comments, "There is a time for laughing and a time for not laughing, and this is not one of them," which just about sums things up). Indeed, the animated titles, again designed by DePatie-Freleng and executed by TVC London under the supervision of Gerry Chiniquy from storyboards by John W. Dunn, in which we see Clouseau attempt to catch a frog-like criminal, during which he is shot at and blown up on numerous occasions, is about as good as things get, save for some mildly amusing business between Clouseau and Sir Charles as they work their way around the latter's office, moving photos and lamps so that they can see each other, with Clouseau ending up in Sir Charles' chair. Otherwise, there is barely a smile, never mind a laugh, to be had in the whole film, and a sequence at Frenchy Lebec's funeral in which Clouseau falls into an open grave and pulls in a young boy after him with whom he then struggles to get out is about as bad as things get (keep an eye out for a cross in the graveyard bearing the legend "Repose in paix Norman Lear 1903–1962" which is an in-joke, as Lear had produced Bud Yorkin's previous film, *Divorce American Style* [1968]).

The central notion for the robbery is pretty good, particularly the idea of wrapping up the money as chocolate bars, though it should be noted that the great train robbery had already been dealt with in two British films by this point: the slapstick comedy *The Great St. Trinian's Train Robbery* (1966) and the rather more serious *Robbery* (1967), the latter of which also features Frank Finlay and Barry Foster. Otherwise, the situations here are labored in the extreme, particularly

Clouseau's introduction, in which he exits his plane without his shoes and gets soaked in the rain while trying to re-board to retrieve them, and the sequence at the Edinburgh International Festival, which is just plain embarrassing, as Clouseau finds himself embroiled in trying to toss a caber before inadvertently seeing off Frenchy Lebec (played by Tutte Lemkow, who had appeared as the Cossack in *A Shot in the Dark* [1964]). It would seem that Clouseau might well have been involved in even more shenanigans at the festival given what Sir Charles says to him later at his club: "I gather you behaved disgracefully. Drinking on duty, flirting with woman after woman. Even reciting vulgar limericks." However, save for him having a drink, we witness none of this, making one wonder what ended up on the cutting room floor, given that for such a brief sequence (just over a minute-and-a-half in length) the setting is a somewhat elaborate affair, complete with a highland marching band, painted castle backdrops and dozens of extras. Indeed, a still exists of Clouseau with an apple in his mouth which does not appear in the film, which was trimmed from an original length of 105 minutes down to a release print of 96 minutes.

Admittedly, a couple of members of the cast leave their mark, notably Patrick Cargill as the flustered Sir Charles and Beryl Reid as the creepily flirtatious Mrs. Weaver, whose full-on Scottish accent makes Mike Myers' Fat Bastard character sound refined, while Delia Boccardo adds a little glamor to the proceedings as Lisa Morell (the film purports to introduce her, despite her having appeared in a couple of European productions). Otherwise, the actors struggle with the threadbare material, and the script sees such established players as Frank Finlay (as Weaver) and Barry Foster (as Steele) left dangling. Other members of the cast with not enough to do include Clive Francis (as Clyde Hargreaves/Johnny Rainbow), Michael Ripper, Geoffrey Bayldon, Eric Pohlmann, Richard Pearson and real life gangster John Bindon (as Bull Parker), while the film's designer, Michael Stringer, pops up briefly as Prime Minister Harold Wilson (he'd go on to appear as Wilson again in the TV series *Paradise Postponed* [1986, TV], which he also designed). Meanwhile Arkin himself (undoubtedly a fine comic actor) comes across as a particularly cold fish as Clouseau. Sellers managed to make the character a loveable bumbler, but in Arkin's hands, he is merely irritating and self-aggrandizing (note that when the various gang members don their Clouseau masks, Arkin plays these characters, albeit dubbed with the other actors' voices).

The film's swinging London backdrop also dates the proceedings, coming as it does at the end of a cycle which saw such indulgent affairs as *Salt and Pepper* (1968); *Don't Raise the Bridge, Lower*

5. The Interloper

Radio shack. Alan Arkin in action in *Inspector Clouseau* (1968) (Mirisch/United Artists).

the River (1968); and *One More Time* (1970) foisted on audiences (the first and last care of United Artists). In terms of handling, Bud Yorkin's direction lacks the visual panache that Blake Edwards would undoubtedly have brought to the production, though even he and Sellers would surely have been undone by the Waldman brothers' dire screenplay (note that Edwards and Maurice Richlin are listed in the opening credits for having created the character of Clouseau, an acknowledgment Richlin failed to receive for the previous film). Flatly photographed by Arthur Ibbetson and rather casually edited by John Victor Smith, the film seems much longer than its running time, and is only enlivened on occasion by the breezy score by Ken Thorne (best known for his work for director Richard Lester), though even this is diminished by some rather poor sound editing (the LP, released by UA, at least makes amends for this, among its cues being such charming Mancini-esque pieces as "Bossa Nova Restaurant"). The location work handled by second unit director Michael Frewin is adequate enough, though trying to pass off Billingsgate Fish Market and its environs as Paris simply by putting up freshly painted French signs on all of the

In the groove. The LP cover for Ken Thorne's soundtrack for *Inspector Clouseau* (1968), one of the film's few saving graces (Mirisch/United Artists).

shops just doesn't cut it, and would have been particularly noticeable to British audiences.

Given the absence of Edwards and Sellers, it seems natural that others from the previous films weren't involved on this occasion either. So were they even approached? "Not at all, I'm glad to say,"[8] revealed Herbert Lom, while Burt Kwouk admitted, "The first thing I knew about the Arkin movie was when it came out."[9] Henry Mancini put his own absence down to the rules of the Eady Levy. "Although I did a lot of films here [in the UK], there were some I couldn't do because of the quota system. This meant you had to use a certain amount of British talent. The bulk of it. And in this case I think they were allowed to bring the director and Arkin, so that filled out the quota of people allowed to come in. When

5. *The Interloper*

In the picture. Poster artwork by *Mad* cartoonist Jack Davis for *Inspector Clouseau* (1968) (Mirisch/United Artists).

we did the Panthers after, the system had eased up. Blake and I were the Americans."[10] As for the reaction to Sellers' replacement, commented Graham Stark, who likewise hadn't been asked to return at this point, "Arkin is a fascinating actor but his approach was much more realistic. The public had got besotted with Peter's Clouseau, so it was like doing a Chaplin film without Chaplin."[11] Walter Mirisch agreed: "Audiences didn't want anyone but Peter, and, consequently, the film suffered."[12]

In fact it performed particularly poorly when released by UA in America on 19 July 1968 (following a preview in Los Angeles on 28 May), taking in just $1.9m at the U.S. box office. It also fared badly in Britain, where it had been released with a U certificate slightly earlier on 14 February, again by UA, and where it was sometimes double billed with the adventure thriller *Twist of Sand* (1968). "After *The Pink Panther* and *A Shot in the Dark*.... How could they put Clouseau on another case?" queried the poster. How indeed, wondered most of the critics. Observed the *Chicago Sun-Times*, "The camera lingers on Arkin, waiting for moments of inspiration that never come," while *Time* described the film as "a parody of a parody." *The Washington Post* called it "a mirthless failure" and

The New York Times "relentlessly awful," though the *Los Angeles Times* at least didn't blame Arkin, reasoning that "he tries and tries (and occasionally succeeds) but the uninspired script is hopeless from the start." *The New Yorker* actually found that "Alan Arkin is sometimes very funny in it, especially when he doesn't try to be," while the *Monthly Film Bulletin* declared it to be "more inventively directed that *A Shot in the Dark*," which is just astonishing, though it did admit that "this third film in the Clouseau series finally demonstrates that the joke has run out of steam."

Things certainly weren't looking good for the Inspector, and as we shall see, it would take a downturn in the careers of both Edwards and Sellers before he eventually made his return to the big screen again.

6

The Panther Returns

Following the making of *The Party* (1968), Blake Edwards and Peter Sellers decided to go their separate ways a second time. During this period, Edwards directed the World War I musical *Darling Lili* (1970), which starred his second wife, Julie Andrews, whom he'd married on 12 November 1969. The film, made for Paramount, eventually had a whopping $17m budget, yet despite its spectacular aerial sequences and a tuneful soundtrack care of Henry Mancini, who was Oscar nominated for best song ("Whistling Away the Dark") and score, the film bombed at the box office and did considerable harm to both Andrews' and Edwards' status at the time. As a consequence, Edwards stepped away from a few of his long-standing collaborators for a period, among them Mancini. Recalled the composer, "There was a slight, what you might call, falling out, because Blake was so devastated by what had happened on *Darling Lili*. Paramount Studios, and everything connected with it, was kind of distasteful to him. And it was dramatic."[1]

As a consequence, Edwards' next three pictures were scored by other talents: Jerry Goldsmith did *Wild Rovers* (1971), an elegiac western which was much re-cut by the studio (MGM), much to Edwards' distress; Roy Budd did the medical thriller *The Carey Treatment* (1972); and John Barry did the romantic thriller *The Tamarind Seed* (1974). None of these fared particularly well at the box office, despite each being more than competent of their kind, particularly the last, which saw the director teamed with his wife for the second time. The film was made as part of a two-picture deal Edwards had signed with ITC, which was run by TV mogul Lew Grade, who was branching out into films, and who was hoping to lure Andrews into making a TV special for him (ITC had previously been involved in the star's Emmy Award–winning series *The Julie Andrews Hour* [1972–1973, TV]). The program eventually went ahead as *Julie: My Favorite Things* (1975, TV), which Edwards directed from a script by himself, Robert Wells (who also produced) and Frank Waldman, and featured extravagant Busby Berkeley–style musical numbers, guest spots by Peter Sellers (who appeared in three sketches) and a routine in which Andrews performed with four dancers dressed as the Pink Panther, as Henry Mancini's celebrated theme tune played. The program aired on ABC on 18 April 1975, and was a canny marketing tool for Edwards' second film for ITC, the recently completed *The Return of the Pink Panther* (1975), the *real* reason for the reunion between Edwards and Sellers, which was released on 21 May, hence the star's involvement in the special (Sellers and Andrews also appeared, separately, in a tribute program to Lew Grade titled *Salute to Sir Lew– The Master Showman*, which aired in the UK on 18 April 1975 and in America two months later on ABC on 13 June).

Sellers' own career had taken an even more spectacular nose-dive than Edwards' in recent years with such films as *Hoffman* (1970); *Where Does It Hurt?* (1972); *Soft Beds, Hard Battles* (1974); and *Ghost in the Noonday Sun* (1974), among others. The actor had again clashed with his director, Peter Medak, on the latter, yet despite their differences, they managed to make a commercial together for Benson & Hedges cigarettes during the shoot in Cyprus. The ad was written by Sellers' fellow Goon and *Noonday* co-star Spike Milligan, who also appeared in the commercial, along with another *Noonday* cohort, James Villiers. Shot in just five hours on their day off from the feature, the ad sees Sellers as a time and motion man supervising a bullion robbery at a small harbor-side customs authority post office, only for Milligan, who is carrying six purloined bars of gold in his mackintosh pockets, to scupper the enterprise when he jumps into the gang's escape boat and goes through the bottom, prompting it to sink. A miniature masterpiece running just one minute and fifteen seconds, the ad, which is full of quirky gags and detail, went on to win several awards. Recalled Peter Medak, "Peter decided to play it as Clouseau, and we had more fun with this commercial than on the whole movie. This is when Peter had the idea to revive Clouseau—originally for television, backed by Lew Grade. Within six months he was making *The Return of the Pink Panther*."[2]

It would seem that great minds do think alike, as it turned out that Blake Edwards was also having similar thoughts, though who actually had them first is a moot point, given that Walter Mirisch had already tried to encourage Edwards back to the series following the Arkin debacle. Said the producer, "Talking to Blake, later in the sixties, I said, 'It's just a crime not to make another Clouseau picture with Peter.' And he said he'd been thinking that too."[3] When Edwards eventually submitted an outline for a new film to Mirisch in the early seventies, the producer was delighted. Astonishingly, United Artists nixed the movie, given that Edwards' and Sellers' careers were in decline at this point.

6. The Panther Returns

Ciggy break. Peter Sellers as the Clouseau-like time and motion man in the Benson & Hedges ad that inspired *The Return of the Pink Panther* (1975) (B&H/Altria/Peter Medak).

Consequently, Edwards eventually turned to Lew Grade with the idea, Grade having turned down his plans for their second film together, a remake of *Rachel and the Stranger* (previously filmed in 1948), which Blake had hoped to shoot in Canada. In fact, Grade had even suggested buying Edwards out of the second commitment when the director suggested the Panther project as an alternative (interestingly, Sellers had once been a client of the booking agency run by Grade and his brother Leslie many years earlier).

Recalled Edwards, "I had made a deal with Lew Grade, who said he could get the rights to it. And I said great. And then I thought, 'Oh what a bloody shame,' because it had done well, and I thought we were only just scraping the surface."[4] So, rather than the proposed TV series, which would have run to 24 episodes like such Grade productions of the period as *The Persuaders!* (1971–1972, TV) and *The Julie Andrews Hour* (1972, TV), and which Sellers, who could barely get through a film, would inevitably have tired of making almost immediately, Edwards suggested they instead make a film, which would also honor their remaining commitment together. Recalled the director, "So I begged Lew. I said 'Let's do a movie,' and Lew said, 'I'm a television man.' And so I'm a considerable huckster, getting people to do something I think is great and they don't. I took advantage of the fact that he didn't know much about the film business. I on the other hand did, being a third generation. You learn a lot, particularly of that side. In this case I said,

'Look, Lew. Peter and I have talked and we'll do the movie for nothing!' And he said, 'What?!' Then I said, 'Not *exactly* nothing. This is the deal we'll make with you. We'll work for expenses, and those will be minimal. We won't be excessive about it. We just want to be comfortable. And we want a percentage of the gross. We won't take any money now, but if the picture's a success we'd like to have a piece of the success.' And he leapt at it. And I don't think he's ever forgiven me, because he doesn't think about all the money *he* made, he thinks about all the money *I* made!"[5]

As a consequence of this deal, Edwards was able to make the film for just $5m, provided by Grade's Pimlico Films, Ltd. This included location work in Switzerland, France and Morocco, as well as at Britain's Shepperton and Twickenham studios, with principal photography expected to last a total of ten weeks. Keeping to his side of the bargain, Grade persuaded United Artists to give him the rights allowing him to make a film featuring the Clouseau character in exchange for a share of the profits and the right for UA to distribute the film worldwide as a negative pickup, following which the global rights to the film would revert to him. Still believing that the movie would be a flop, UA's then–President and CEO Erik Pleskow (who had been with the company in various capacities since joining it 1951) agreed to the terms.

The film, which again sees Clouseau called in to investigate when the fabled Pink Panther diamond is stolen, was a return in more ways than one, with several of the cast and crew from the previous installments back onboard, among them Herbert Lom as Chief Inspector Charles Dreyfus (with all references to his previous murderous habits seemingly forgotten or erased), André Maranne as his assistant Sergeant François Chevalier, and Burt Kwouk as Cato Fong (previously Kato), along with Sellers' pals David Lodge and Graham Stark, albeit in different roles from those they had played in *A Shot in the Dark* (1964). Although Sir Charles Litton (previously Lytton in *The Pink Panther* [1963]) is part of the plot, and again under suspicion for the theft, given that a white glove monogrammed with the letter P has been left at the scene of the crime, it was Christopher Plummer who was this time cast in the role, which was first offered to Douglas Fairbanks, Jr., who proved to be unavailable. Said Edwards of David Niven's failure to return to the part, "It may have been that he simply wasn't available."[6] Of course, Niven, who instead went on to make *Paper Tiger* (1975), had previously had his thunder stolen by Sellers in the first Panther (and here, in a reverse to the first film, would also have had to submit to the indignity of either equal or second billing), though this didn't prevent Niven from later appearing with Sellers in the all-star crime spoof *Murder by Death*

6. The Panther Returns

(1976), which also reunited Sellers with Alec Guinness, the star of *The Ladykillers* (1955), in which he had been a supporting player along with Herbert Lom.

Familiar faces behind the scenes included Frank Waldman, who co-wrote the screenplay with Edwards; Connie Willis, who supervised the continuity; Dick Crockett and Joe Dunne, who were in charge of the stunts; and, of course, Henry Mancini, who was back on the music stand where he belonged. Said the composer, who had been kept busy in the interim with work on such movies as *The Thief Who Came to Dinner* (1973) and *The Great Waldo Pepper* (1975), as well as his own 26-part TV series *The Mancini Generation* (1972–1973, TV), "It was a re-union, you know. Everyone came back together again…. Everybody was back together after ten years, and in the meantime Sellers became a cult hero as Clouseau via all the TV showings, and it was almost as if people were waiting for this to happen."[7] In fact, so familiar had Clouseau become, he was even referenced in other films (for example, in *Pulp* [1972], Michael Caine refers to an overweight cleaning woman as "Inspector Clouseau in drag").

Someone who hadn't been involved in any of the previous films, yet who would go on to play a major part in all the subsequent Panthers, as well as many of Edwards' other projects, was Tony Adams, who at this point joined the production team as an associate producer, and would become one of the director's most important and trusted collaborators. So how did his long-standing association with Edwards begin, and at such a comparatively young age (he was just 21 when shooting began)? Remembered Adams, "I went to the United States for a summer with John Boorman when he was shooting *Deliverance*, and basically I was looking after his kids, which I'd done a previous summer back in Ireland where I'd grown up. I got along well with everyone so well that Burt Reynolds sponsored me to work on his ranch and go to college in the States. He introduced me to Blake and Julie, and then I went to work for them as an assistant. They moved to London soon after I joined them, so it was fortuitous timing. I also helped out on some musical specials that Julie was doing at the time. Very soon after that *Return of the Pink Panther* came about and I was associate producer on that, and that began everything. It was something I hadn't set out to do, then suddenly there I was in the midst of it, and I haven't stopped since."[8]

Of his experiences on the film, Adams recalled, "I was really thrown in the deep end. I remember we had something like ten weeks to get the whole thing together because of Peter Sellers' availability. So it came about very fast."[9] In fact Edwards was still busy writing the script when Adams was called upon to help with the various pre-production chores required to help set up the film, which the director advised him on. As Adams revealed, "Blake hadn't even finished writing it, and he said to me, 'You go and do it.' I said, 'I dunno,' and he said, 'I'll teach you.' But he was locked away. It was trial by fire, which was the greatest experience. So by fortuitous circumstances, I had a lot more to do on that one than would have happened in any other kind of situation. That kind of increased as they went along. I'd be with Blake from the first time he put pen to paper, right through to the end of post-production."[10]

This time the story sees the Pink Panther stolen from a supposedly impenetrable museum in Lugash, where it sits on a trigger device in a special glass case surrounded by all manner of gadgets to help protect it, including sensor beams which, if crossed, set off the alarms and bring down a series of steel shutters over the windows and entrances, all backed up by a team of armed guards. As a consequence of the daring theft, the country's General Wadafi decides to call in "The famous French detective who recovered the Pink Panther the last time it was stolen." Unfortunately, Clouseau has been demoted, and is working as a beat cop, all of which requires him to be reinstated by the Commissioner to his former position, much to the chagrin of the increasingly twitchy Chief Inspector Dreyfus. As a consequence of being put on the case, the Inspector finds his life in danger from the hands of an assassin, whose first attempt sees him blow up Clouseau's apartment with a bomb following one of Cato's impromptu attacks ("Cato is in hospital. They nearly blew his little yellow skin off," he tells Dreyfus [this was one of several now dubious references to the houseboy's skin color in the series]).

However, once he arrives in Lugash, Clouseau is quick to identify the culprit of the theft, thanks to the tell-tale glove ("So we meet again"). But the Phantom, who is now living in splendid retirement in a villa in the South of France with his wife Claudine, is adamant that he is not the thief, and is prompted to set out to prove his innocence before he is arrested by the police for a crime he did not commit (no mention is made of his previous relationship with Clouseau's former wife Simone). Consequently, Sir Charles flies to Lugash to make his own investigations, and with the help of a former associate, a low life called Pepi, he arranges a meeting with a local bigwig known as the Fat Man, who he suspects is behind the job, only to find his life in danger when the Fat Man assumes that Sir Charles is in possession of the diamond himself. Meanwhile, Clouseau has made his way to the South of France where, disguised as a telephone repair man, he infiltrates Sir Charles' villa to look for clues, only to be sent on a false trail to Gstaad in Switzerland by Claudine (keen-eyed viewers will note that the registration of Sir Charles' car in the villa's driveway is LIT 1).

6. The Panther Returns

Following his near fatal encounter with the Fat Man, Sir Charles subsequently allies himself with the police in Lugash, led by the corrupt Colonel Sharki, to help find the real culprit (and the diamond), while Clouseau, this time disguised as a wealthy playboy called Guy Gadbois (named after Julie Andrews' business manager) attempts to get closer to Claudine, herself now in Switzerland to further trick him along. Things finally come to a head when it is revealed that it is Dreyfus who is attempting to kill Clouseau (again), and that Claudine is the perpetrator of the theft, her motivation being to give her husband a purpose in life again after becoming overwhelmed by boredom during his forced retirement ("You nearly had me killed, you know," he says, to which she responds, "I'm sorry darling. It's just that I never realized how tedious life could be for a retired jewel thief"). The film then ends with the diamond restored to its rightful place in the museum and Dreyfus incarcerated in the lunatic asylum. As for Clouseau, he is promoted to Chief Inspector, only to fall foul of another of Cato's attacks, this time in a Japanese restaurant, which is trashed in the ensuing mêlée ("Take those little yellow hands off of me," he admonishes).

With its freewheeling atmosphere, jet-setting background and variety of eye-catching locations, the film sees a return to the glamor of the first film in the series, with the various characters travelling hither and yon in luxury across Europe and Morocco as per the demands of the plot, which is a surprisingly involved affair for such a piece of froth. However, the film's more serious aspects actually work in its favor (the initial robbery, the plight of Sir Charles, who finds himself in genuine peril), so that when they come, the comedy scenes have an even greater impact.

The film opens with the museum's guide providing a group of tourists (and therefore us) with a detailed description of the various security devices at hand to protect "our nation's religious symbol, the Pink Panther, largest and most famous diamond in the world." Then, following the titles, we see the thief fire a line with a crossbow from a nearby building, glide across the abyss and enter the museum via the roof and, avoiding the detection of the guards, slowly and methodically deal with each and every one of the obstacles in order to steal the Panther (note that the glass case covering the diamond later appeared in Peter Sellers' final film, *The Fiendish Plot of Dr. Fu Manchu* [1980]). Impeccably presented by Edwards from a variety of shadowy angles, this is a genuinely thrilling sequence to watch, with the thief cleverly using aerosol spray to detect the whereabouts of the sensor beams and liquid wax to pull themselves across the floor before using two specially made metal arms to hold the trigger device in place and carefully lift the diamond from its stand, replacing it with the monogrammed glove of the Phantom. Equally serious is Sir Charles' attempt to clear his name by discovering the genuine culprit of the theft himself, which leads to encounters with the Fat Man (a parody of the Kasper Gutman character played by Sydney Greenstreet in *The Maltese Falcon* [1941]), who sends several of his goons to kill him following their meeting ("I'm awfully sorry, old boy"), and the corrupt Colonel Sharki, whose motives are not only self serving but potentially deadly ("I will be forced to shoot you," he says to Lady Litton at one point, to which comes her retort, "Who's forcing you?").

As for Clouseau, we first encounter him on the beat, unable even to salute the passing of a pretty girl without hitting himself in the eye with his baton. Then comes one of the classic scenes in the series, as he berates a blind busker and his monkey for playing on a street corner, not realizing that a robbery is taking place in the bank behind them, to which we, but not Clouseau, are privy through the window. He even returns a dropped bag of money to one of the departing masked robbers and waves their car on as they make their escape, capping off his misfortune by knocking out the bank manager when he runs out into the street to fire his gun after them. Naturally, Dreyfus is less than impressed when he hears Clouseau's version of events, informing him that "the beggar was the lookout man for the gang."

Having been suspended by Dreyfus, Clouseau heads home, where we are treated to another of his and Cato's impromptu fights, with Cato surprising his master when he goes to put his groceries in the refrigerator, only to be greeted by his manservant, who jumps out of the ice box and attacks him. A hilarious sequence of posturing and calamity ensues, climaxing with Clouseau flying through the air in slow motion (accompanied by a suitable slo-mo growl on the soundtrack) as he attempts to get one up on Cato. This is then capped with the delivery of the bomb, the explosion of which we see from the vantage point of Clouseau's neighbor, an elderly woman who attacks him with her knitting bag when he comes flying through her living room wall after she and all her furniture (including her TV set and the pictures on the walls) have momentarily been levitated by the blast (Edwards seems to have been inspired here by a similar moment in Laurel and Hardy's *Blockheads* [1938]).

Having been informed that he is on the Panther case, Clouseau heads for Lugash, where his examination of the crime scene not only sees him accidentally active the metal shutters, but also slip on the wax, cover the place with finger print powder, almost castrate himself with one of the metal grabbers and pull at a fishing line the thief has used, which brings a shield crashing down onto a statue and a glass case of

6. The Panther Returns

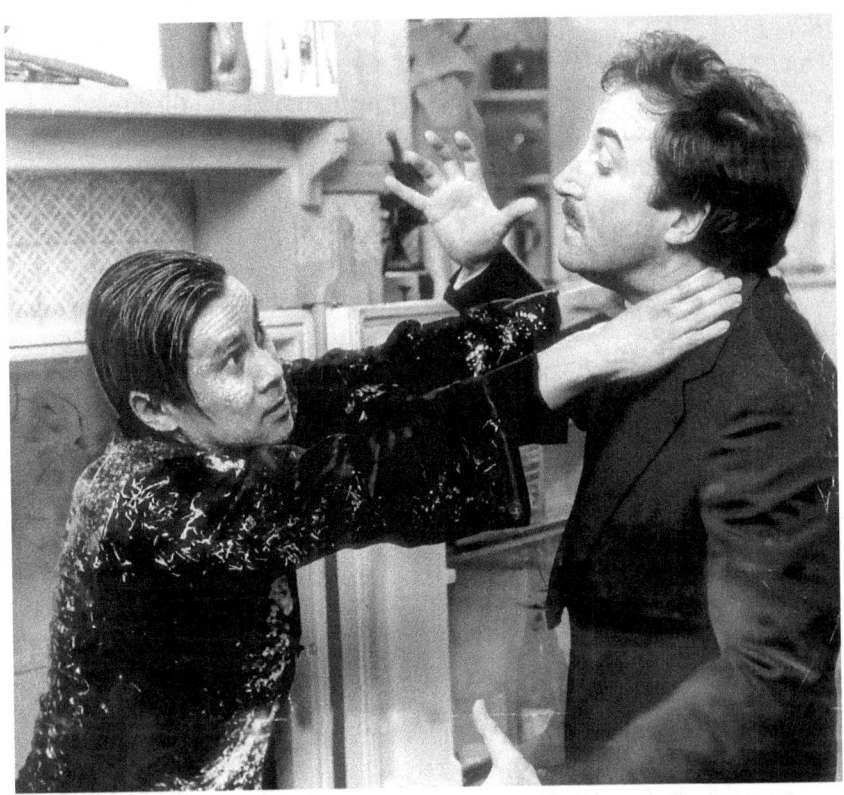

The ice man cometh. Burt Kwouk's Cato (left) emerges from the refrigerator to attack Peter Sellers' Clouseau in *The Return of the Pink Panther* (1975) (ITC/Pimlico/Jewel/Mirisch/UA/Geoffrey).

artifacts. Clouseau's attempts to infiltrate Sir Charles' Riviera home, first as a pool man and then as a telephone repair man, provide further comic highlights, especially when he gets stuck between the drawers of Sir Charles' pedestal desk and has to perform a somersault to escape. That he loses control and ends up ditching the vans of *both* characters into the same swimming pool, given that their brakes have been tampered with, is the topper to end all toppers, especially as the second van plunges into the water just as the first is being lifted out by a crane.

Once in Gstaad, the mayhem continues ("Today a paradise in the Swiss Alps, tomorrow a wasteland," predicts Dreyfus). Here, we get a variation on the gag at the end of *A Shot in the Dark* (1964), when Clouseau orders a taxi driver to follow Lady Litton's car, only to see the driver get out and run after it. This is followed by a shot of Clouseau pursuing on foot with his luggage and asking a passerby, "Excuse me, do you know the way to the Palace Hotel?" to which comes the flat reply, "Yes," after which the man carries on his way. Elaborate sequences involving Clouseau getting stuck in a revolving door at the hotel and disguised as its ancient cleaner follow, the latter seeing him use a very powerful vacuum which not only sucks a painting out of its frame and a parrot from its cage, but also gets itself attached to the bosom of the buxom lady who arrives to give Lady Litton a massage, after which it is switched to blow and the whole room is filled with debris. This scene also features a brilliantly timed gag with a faulty light bulb which keeps popping out of a lamp, and which Clouseau miraculously manages to catch each time it does so, and a sequence in which he and the hotel's bellboy, who has been assisting him, end up ducking into Lady Litton's bathroom when she unexpectedly returns to her room, the floor of which becomes extremely slippery when she turns on the sauna in which they are forced to hide (and through the steamed up glass panel in the door Clouseau wipes a peephole so that he can observe her).

As well as the "Follow that car" joke, other gags revived from the previous films see Clouseau attempt to enter Sir Charles' study via the wrong side of the open door and crashing into the wall beside it, plus a variation on the spinning globe routine, though this time it's a drinks trolley Clouseau leans on, only for it to roll away and send him crashing to the floor. New comic business sees him sitting fully clothed on the edge of a swimming pool, only to fall in when he leans back too far when watching a pretty girl dive in, and a running gag involving Dreyfus and a cigarette lighter that looks like a revolver, which he inevitably gets mixed up with the real thing, managing to shoot both himself and Chevalier at various points ("Call a doctor ... and then help me to find my nose," he implores his assistant after one such accident).

Another running gag involves the crushing of Pepi's fingers, which sees them bandaged with increasingly elaborate splints, while slapstick rears its head as Clouseau attempts to take a bath in his tiny Swiss hotel room during which all the taps fail and he ends up flooding the place and producing a giant wall of bubbles (echoes of *The Party* [1968] here). He can't even cross a dance floor without being punched in the face by an energetic dancer. As for the best verbal joke, that comes as Clouseau, disguised as Guy Gabdois, is attempting to impress Lady Litton by boasting of his prowess skiing "Up the mountains, down the slopes, on the piste," though his attempt to dry off Dreyfus after soaking him with a carafe of water with "Allow me to blot you" comes pretty close (in addition to the near the knuckle "piste" joke, the film contains the series' only expletive, which occurs when Sir Charles, trying to evade the Fat Man's goons, jumps out of a window and, landing badly, mouths the word "shit" which is bleeped out by car horns; just prior to this, sharp eyed viewers will note that as Sir Charles is running along an interior balcony he passes behind a pillar, from which a stuntman emerges in his stead, who then uses a rope to jump down to the ground floor). The final scene, in which Cato, disguised as a waitress, attacks Clouseau as he is enjoying a meal at a Japanese restaurant, brings things to a satisfactorily elaborate comic climax, given that it concludes with a repeat of the Inspector's slo-mo karate kick through the air (again with slo-mo sound effects), this time landing in the kitchen.

Knowing that they were potentially onto a winner from the start, both Edwards and his cast are fully confident with their handling of the material throughout the film, with Sellers in particularly fine form as Clouseau, his character, with all his exaggerated verbal ticks and mispronunciations, now in full bloom. Also making the most of their return appearances are Herbert Lom as the increasingly crazed Dreyfus, Burt Kwouk as Cato and André Maranne as Chevalier, with David Lodge this time onboard as Sir Charles' chauffeur Mac (for which he sports a rather odd Scottish accent) and Graham Stark as the disheveled Pepi. Recalled Stark of his casting following the disappearance of the Hercule character he'd played in *A Shot in the Dark* (1964), "When they reorganized the Panthers in the seventies, Hercule did not exist. I don't know why. So the part they offered me was Pepi, which was very successful too. I was quite glad in a way. I've always been a law unto myself. I hate doing series. I turned down the Carry Ons and *The Army Game* on TV. I hated playing the same part again and again. So I was delighted that it turned out the way it did, because I got some very nice parts to play."[11] However, playing Pepi did have its downside, given the increasingly elaborate splints the character finds himself wearing. "That was charming when I wanted to go to the lavatory! It was out in Africa, so the crew, the wicked buggers, kept giving me cold drinks all day. Then waited. I couldn't take the bandages off. Peter grinned, 'Well, now you know who your best friends are!'"[12]

Sadly, Stark didn't have any scenes directly with friend this time out, but still enjoyed himself, given that Edwards gave him free reign with his character. "Blake said, 'Do what you want with Pepi,' which was very nice of him. He always asked me first. So I said he was a walking disaster area. Things always happen to him. So he said, 'Right, do it. Anything you want to do, do it!' So I went off to Berman's in London and got the worst tropical suit you've ever seen. I stained it with tomato juice, tea, and scruffed it all up. I then got some dreadful shoes in Casablanca, which I destroyed in about twenty minutes. It was wonderful. Peter said, 'Pepi's sensational. He's a wonderful character.'"[13] Unfortunately, Stark's

All fingers and thumbs. Graham Stark as the accident-prone Pepi in a staged promotional still for *The Return of the Pink Panther* (1975), which must have delighted the camera company (ITC/Pimlico/Jewel/Mirisch/UA/Geoffrey).

appearance did have a downside, as he recalled. "Christopher Plummer invited me up to the balcony of a restaurant for a drink, but a vigilant policeman quickly barred me from going up the stairs, as vagrants were barred."[14] At least the location and the hotel made up for Stark's discomfort in the role. "That was Morocco and it was heaven. We stayed in one of the great hotels of the world there, the Mamounia.... You needed a road map just to get across the bedroom! It was a wonderful place with a great view. In fact it's where Churchill used to go to paint."[15]

Others joining the regulars on the film this time included Christopher Plummer (who'd starred with Edwards' wife in *The Sound of Music* [1965]), who brings a natural suavity to the role of Sir Charles (despite a slightly unconvincing hairpiece), Catherine Schell as his glamorous wife Claudine (that's her caught on camera disguised as a man while casing the museum, hence Sir Charles' comment, "There's something about a wife, even with a beard"), Peter Arne (who would go on to be an Edwards regular) as the sinister Colonel Sharki, Peter Jeffrey as Colonel Wadafi, Gregoire Aslan as the Chief of Police in Lugash, John Bluthal as the blind beggar, Mike Grady as the bell boy ("Keep up the good work, and I shall see to it that you become a bell *man*" Clouseau informs him), Eric Pohlmann as the Fat Man, Peter Jones as Dreyfus's psychiatrist (who the Chief Inspector inadvertently strangles during a session), Claire Davenport as Claudine's buxom masseuse, Nadim Sawalha as the museum guide, and Serge Tanney as the Chief of Police in Nice.

Of these, Eric Pohlmann had already appeared in *Inspector Clouseau* (1968) as the Minister of Finance (he'd also played a character similarly known as the Fat Man in *Carry on Spying* [1964] and, as a point of interest, had provided the voice of the unseen Blofeld in both *From Russia with Love* [1963] and *Thunderball* [1966]), while Serge Tanney, who is dubbed by David de Keyser and had already played small roles in Edwards' *Darling Lili* (1970) and *Wild Rovers* (1971), was actually the director's long-standing therapist Herb Tanney, and would go on to appear in several more of his films under a variety of pseudonyms (it should also be noted that Sir Charles travels to Morocco under the guise of Dr. Marvin Tanney; as for Schell's barely suppressed laughter during her scenes with Sellers, erroneously attributed by some to the fact that the actress just couldn't keep her face straight during filming, this is clearly part of the plot, or at least was made to appear so, given that her character can't hide her amusement at the absurdity of Clouseau's disguises, particularly the improbably named telephone repair man Emil Flournoy).

The film almost featured Edwards' wife, Julie Andrews, as well, but her scene ended up on the cutting room floor. As the actress recalled, "I did make a cameo appearance in *Return of the Pink Panther* as a maid. It was done more as a surprise for Peter Sellers, since he had no idea who was going to play the maid. I don't believe Blake had any serious intention of using it in the film, but in any case it ended up on the cutting room floor, much to my relief, as the joke didn't really come off."[16] Confirmed Edwards, "We shot some film, and it exists somewhere, of her [Julie] as a Swiss Fraulein. When Peter goes to see his tiny room, she enters all padded up and looks like she should be yodeling. And this was without him knowing who it was! I wrote a scene out and everything. Well, she came flying into the room, and you can see Sellers thinking, 'What the hell is this? Why on earth is this crazy woman running around the room cleaning up.' Then he suddenly realized, 'Oh my God, is that who I think it is?' Then he broke up, and it got to be too much of a joke, so we had to cut it."[17]

In fact far more material than could be used in the film had to be cut, including additional scenes of Clouseau trying to get through the revolving doors at the Palace Hotel with some skiing equipment, and a scene in which he manages to get a woman's dress caught in his flies in a restaurant. Some last-minute changes even saw some actors listed in the credits missing from the final print, among them Milton Reid, who is credited as the owner of the Japanese restaurant seen in the finale. Scenes involving Victor Spinetti as the concierge at the Palace Hotel, with whom Clouseau has an argument over his "reum" were also trimmed. Others who *did* make it into the film, and who are worth keeping an eye out for, include Monty Python star Carol Cleveland as the girl who dives into the pool, associate producer Tony Adams as a waiter in the disco scene (he's the one wearing a striped jacket who delivers a drink to Claudine from Clouseau [he even gets a line: "From the gentleman at the bar, madam"]) and the "swine bird" which gets sucked into the vacuum cleaner by Clouseau in Lady Litton's bedroom.

As before, giggling was prevalent during filming, with Sellers constantly breaking up, though according to Herbert Lom, "The biggest giggler was the director, Blake Edwards, who spoiled many-a take by laughing in the middle of it."[18] Said Burt Kwouk of these incidents, "It's like being on stage when something goes wrong. It's very funny for the audience, actors, stagehands. It's just funny. And if you're doing comedy, that kind of thing helps, I think."[19] In fact there were so many ruined shots and bloopers, several of them were put together for one of the film's trailers. "While filming his new movie, *The Return of the Pink Panther*, Peter Sellers had a serious problem. He couldn't keep a straight face. In fact neither could anyone else," the narrator informs us, as we are then treated to a series of outtakes, among them the scene in which Clouseau asks for directions to the Palace Hotel (which is already up to take seven according to the clapper boy), his arrival as the telephone repair man, and scenes in Claudine's hotel bedroom. Concludes the voice over, "If you think making *The Return of the Pink Panther* was fun, wait till you see it." In addition to the film's regular trailer, a promotional featurette titled *He's Also a Great Giggler* (1975) was made to help promote the film. This was written and directed by Ed Anderson, Bill Gunther and Edwards' son Geoffrey, who was also making his behind-the-scenes debut on *Return* as an assistant editor after appearing briefly in *Wild Rovers* (1971) for his father (he would go on to work with him on several more films in a variety of capacities, including writer and second unit director).

As before, Sellers could be awkward when the mood arose, which didn't always help matters. Remembered Burt Kwouk of the actor's behavior, "We can all be difficult on set when we choose to be. Sometimes we choose to be and sometimes we don't. Peter, being the head honcho as it were, was more noticeable when he threw a moody. When I threw a moody everyone just ignored me, so it was a bit pointless."[20] Associate producer Tony Adams had slightly less agreeable memories of the situation: "At the time, in my naiveté, I thought that's how stars behaved. So it was the greatest baptism by fire. Since then, I've worked with people that were perceived to be difficult, but I'd think, 'Hey, they're not that difficult. I've dealt with a lunatic.' He was most

On the beat. Blake Edwards (left) and Peter Sellers during the filming of the blind beggar scene for *The Return of the Pink Panther* (1975) (ITC/Pimlico/Jewel/Mirisch/UA/Geoffrey).

mercurial and unpredictable, and when you're making a movie that's the hardest thing to deal with. You literally don't know what person is going to walk in that day, or where he's coming from. There's just no way you can get a handle on it. You just had to wait and see. Things could be going fantastically well all week, then he'd come in the next morning and like nothing. Nothing is right and he doesn't want to do it. These are very hard things to deal with, especially with the studio. They'd look at the reports, and basically nothing had been shot for two days. People would be screaming, and you have to say, 'Well, you don't understand the actor. He won't do it.' Then they'd say, 'Well, you have to *make* him do it!' We always ended up catching up with ourselves because we always built in a few days for that kind of event."[21] In fact the greatest delay to filming occurred when Blake Edwards had to undergo an appendectomy during the shoot, which saw the schedule, expected to wrap on 14 August 1974, overshoot by one week.

Thanks to the fine work of cinematographer Geoffrey Unsworth (shooting in Panavision and DeLuxe), the film certainly looks glossy, and makes the most of its many glamorous locations, along with the sets by provided by production designer by Peter Mullins (who'd go on to work on all the subsequent Panthers helmed by Edwards). The film is also smoothly edited by Tom Priestley (the son of the writer J.B. Priestley) who, given the number of ruined shots and curtailed scenes, keeps the globe-trotting action moving from A to B to C in a surprisingly brisk and engaging manner. As before, the film's main titles are one of its great assets, though this time, given that DePatie-Freleng were busy with the Panther shorts and TV series, they were handled by the great Richard Williams, whose work in this field already included eye-catching sequences for such movies as *What's New Pussycat* (1966) and *Casino Royale* (1967), both of which had starred Sellers.

Williams, who had won an Oscar for his short *A Christmas Carol* (1971), and would win a further one (as well as a special achievement award) for *Who Framed Roger Rabbit* (1988), created what many regard as the best title sequence for the series here. Assisted by veteran animators Art Babbitt and Ken Harris, he uses a variety of superbly realized techniques, including dimensional animation, strobe and ripple effects and deco design to often dazzling impact. The sequence, which runs almost four minutes, pits the Panther (given a slick overhaul in design) in comic combat with the cartoon version of Clouseau in a series of situations involving the premiere of *The Return of the Pink Panther*, which allows for the cast to have their names literally spelled out in lights, to which our hero points with his cane, having opened the sequence performing a soft shoes shuffle. Arriving at the movie theater to cheering crowds and flashing camera bulbs in an incredibly extended pink limousine (followed by Clouseau on a scooter), we then follow our feline friend through a series of brisk movie skits, which see him appear as Carmen Miranda, a coin-tossing gangster, a bow-legged cowboy, Groucho Marx, Charlie Chaplin, Mickey Mouse (did they clear the rights?), a ballerina and Frankenstein's monster. After we've also seen him tap dance up a flight of stairs and swim backstroke, things reach a climax as several Panthers saunter in unison along Blake Edwards' name which is mirrored in a reflecting pool. It really is brilliant stuff, and prompted Benny Green writing in *Punch* to describe *Return* as "The first film in history to be upstaged by its own credit titles." The Panther also makes a return for the end credit roll, which is played out in Dreyfus's padded cell, in which we observe him writing Kill Clouseau on the walls with his feet. He then scribes The End and we iris in on the Panther's cigarette holder, which leaves a pink smoke ring as the screen zeroes down to blackness.

Naturally, the titles are accompanied by Henry Mancini's famous Pink Panther theme, also given a slick, finger-snapping make-over, with the sashaying tenor sax solos now performed by the British jazz musician Tony Coe. The Panther theme is also featured to more dramatic effect during the audacious robbery sequence, which is divided into three sections, with Mancini augmenting the shadowy proceedings with tablas and a low register alto flute as Claudine first enters the museum, while for her daring escape, blaring brass, slashing strings and a relentless electric guitar baseline are added to the mix, which help to ratchet up the tension to an almost unbearable level, all of which makes for one of the composer's most dynamic action cues. Wisely, he lets the central robbery itself play silent. Elsewhere, he accompanies Clouseau's arrival in Switzerland with the jaunty, accordion-led "Summer in Gstaad," while the many source cues include such catchy pieces as "So Smooth," "The Orange Float," "Dreamy" (which features a piano solo by Mancini himself) and "The Wet Look." There are also a couple of percussive "local color" pieces for the Marrakesh scenes—"Naval Maneuver" and "Belly Belly Bum Bum"—and a charming new love song, "The Greatest Gift," performed by a vocal group, which features touching lyrics care of Hal David, best known for his long-standing collaboration with Burt Bacharach.

Recorded at the Music Center in London, the music was subsequently released on LP by RCA and went on to earn Mancini a Grammy nomination for best original score written for a motion picture or television special. Said the composer, "All the Panthers had a lot of source music, and the albums were great sellers."[22] As for being reunited with Edwards after his recent forced absence following the upset with *Darling*

Cue the music. The Panther's tail becomes a treble clef in the cover artwork for Henry Mancini's tuneful soundtrack for *The Return of the Pink Panther* (1975) (RCA/ITC/Pimlico/Jewel/Mirisch/UA/Geoffrey).

Lili (1970), he commented, "When the Panther came back, we were kind of forced back into each other's arms! By that time he had made peace with himself and what had happened, or had either felt better about it, or tried to forget it."[23] Arguably the composer's best work for the series, the soundtrack also includes a sly nod to Hollywood's golden age, as Graham Stark revealed. "We met in London while he [Mancini] was scoring the film and, like a schoolboy, he told me he had lifted a few bars of music. I gathered this was quite legal so long as it wasn't more than five bars. He said, 'Seeing you make your entrance in that hotel in Casablanca, sweaty and disheveled, your tropical suit stained and dirty, I put in a few bars of 'As Time Goes By.' Of all the compliments I may have received in my lifetime, I think that is the one I shall remember most."[24]

6. The Panther Returns

It was during this post-production period that Julie Andrews managed to see an early version of her husband's new film, on which so much now rested. "I accompanied him to London for a few days to see a rough cut of *The Return of the Pink Panther*. Even in its unfinished form, the film was hilarious, and I dared to hope that it could be very successful."[25] However, as Tony Adams later learned, "There wasn't a great appetite for the movie at the time because it had been financed by Lew Grade. One memo that floated around said it wasn't even worth the price of the prints to release it! Of course, within a few months after its release we were already planning the sequel."[26] Adams' work even extended to helping with the film's promotion. "I was getting involved in areas that producers don't normally get involved in, such as the campaign,"[27] he revealed. This time the poster, designed by Richard Williams, featured a tiptoeing Pink Panther being pursued by the large shadow of Clouseau carrying a magnifying glass, accompanied by copy that listed a number of history's other great returns, among them the swallows of Capistrano, General MacArthur and the fifties, climaxing with "And now Inspector Clouseau returns in the greatest return of them all." There was also an exhibitor's campaign book and a novelization by Frank Waldman published by Futura on 13 January 1977 to help push things along. The film was also promoted on such TV programs as *The World of Peter Sellers* (1975, TV, aka *Peter Sellers og hans verden*), a Danish profile in which the star was interviewed on location during the shoot, and *Film '76* (1976, TV), which featured interviews with Sellers, Edwards and Catherine Schell.

Before the film was released to the public, it received its world premiere during a grand gala weekend in Gstaad, at which guests included Elizabeth Taylor and Richard Burton. Recalled Julie Andrews of the event, "The Gstaad tourist board and United Artists went all out for the gala weekend, which took place at the Palace Hotel. There was pink swag everywhere, and huge pink paw prints led up the road to the Palace and spilled over the side of the hill. It poured with rain for most of the weekend, but everyone was in a festive mood. The screening of the film was preceded by entertainment from the local brass band and an alpenhorn demonstration. Attendees gathered for dinner under a tent on the hotel grounds, where Henry Mancini conducted an orchestra. I sang 'Moon River' directly to Blake, and was surprised to see him tear up."[28] A second event subsequently took place at the La Costa Resort in California, during which Sellers did multiple television interviews and Henry Mancini again performed for the crowds.

A co-production between ITC, Pimlico and Jewel copyrighted to Mirisch and Geoffrey (Jewel had also been behind *The Tamarind*

Me and my shadow. Artwork for *The Return of the Pink Panther* (1975) (ITC/Pimlico/Jewel/Mirisch/UA/Geoffrey/Richard Williams).

Seed [1974]), the movie was finally released by United Artists in America with a G rating on 21 May 1975, and went on to do astonishing business, eventually coming in at number five in the year's list of top grossing movies, with a take of $41,833, 347 in the U.S. and Canada alone, which was the equivalent of 20,406,510 tickets sold, while the eventual worldwide take was a hefty $75m. Said Julie Andrews of its success, *"The Return of the Pink Panther* was a smash hit, breaking box office records in America."[29] Graham Stark concurred: *"The Return of the Pink Panther*, made in Marrakech, set box office records worldwide, and gave Peter's career a revival. Clouseau-speak became fashionable again, with a million bad impressions of the extraordinary voice

Page turner. Frank Waldman's paperback tie-in for *The Return of the Pink Panther* (1975) (Futura/ITC/Pimlico/Jewel/Mirisch/UA/Geoffrey).

Peter had invented circulating at parties. It became certain another Panther film would be made. And it was."[30] Said Tony Adams of the finished film, "I think it's probably my favorite of the group. There are pieces in the others I'm crazy about, but I think *Return of* is the classiest looking of them all. There are some great running gags in it."[31]

Also pleasantly surprised by the film's success was Burt Kwouk who hadn't expected to be invited back as Cato because *"Shot* wasn't really a Pink Panther movie."[32] As he recalled, "At the time we made *Return*, I thought, 'We'll have some fun and whoever's backing it will get some of their money back. The audience will laugh, then we'll go away and that will be that.' I had no idea it was going to explode into this *thing*. There are people who have worked on them who say, 'Oh, we always knew that we'd score with these films.' I was the only one who had no idea, and to this day I'm pleasantly surprised by the success of the Pink Panther series of films. And I'm even more surprised by the success of Cato. We get on quite well together!"[33] Meanwhile, of Edwards' and Sellers' collaboration on the movie, Henry Mancini observed, "They both started to reach their comic peak with that picture, and it just continued until Sellers died."[34]

The film's British release, again by UA, and for which it was awarded a U certificate, followed on 1 January 1976. Supported by the short subject *Where the Americas Meet* (1975), it was again an instant success, and although not all of the reviews were positive, it didn't really matter as audiences loved the film. *The New York Times* was among those who praised it, describing Clouseau as "the very special slapstick triumph of Mr. Sellers and Mr. Edwards." *The New Yorker* also found Sellers to be "working here at his best," while *The Washington Post* described his performance as "a frequently hilarious and generally satisfying return to comic form." Among those who found fault was the *Chicago Tribune*, which pointed out that "we not only know when each and every joke is coming; we know exactly what that joke will be," while the *Monthly Film Bulletin* described it as "a series of self-contained, self-destructing little set pieces." Elsewhere, the *LA Times* found it "not up to what went before," though it did admit that it was "a cheerful escape from all the things that ail us."

In addition to triumphing at the box office, the film went on to earn Golden Globe nominations for Sellers (as best actor in a comedy or musical), Mancini (for best score) and the film itself (in the comedy or musical category), while in London it won two prestigious *Evening Standard* awards, for best comedy (Edwards) and best actor (Sellers). The Writers Guild of America also nominated Edwards and Waldman for best screenplay (written directly for the screen).

Having proved the naysayers wrong (and become somewhat wealthy in the process), the question now was, how were Edwards and Sellers going to top it? More importantly, how willing were they going to be involved?

7

Lightning Strikes Twice

Having had to prove their worth again by making *The Return of the Pink Panther* (1975), Blake Edwards and Peter Sellers now had the film world at their feet, and suddenly, instead of shunning the duo, United Artists (not surprisingly) were keen to be involved with the franchise again, and pushed for an immediate follow-up. However, after some of the frictions encountered during the making of *Return*, it wasn't an immediate given that the director and star would be willing to reunite again so soon. Said Blake Edwards of the situation, "I think he [Sellers] secretly hated me for making him successful financially and critically a lot, too, when he felt—and justifiably so—that *Strangelove* and things like that were greater artistic achievements. And they were."[1] The director was also quite frank as to why he kept returning to the franchise: "I guess greed as much as anything else kept bringing us together. We'd do one, it would turn out to be successful, and everybody would want us to do another, and offer us more money, better deals. It got so it was hard to refuse."[2]

Consequently, the clarion call went out, and the team reassembled for *The Pink Panther Strikes Again* (1976), though according to announcements made by both *The Hollywood Reporter* and *Daily Variety*, which reported Edwards' deal with UA, the original title was to have been *Inspector Clouseau Strikes Again*, given that the Panther diamond doesn't actually appear in the plot this time. In addition to Sellers, the returning cast included Herbert Lom as Dreyfus, André Maranne as Chevalier and Burt Kwouk as Cato, all of whose roles were now deemed integral to the series, as was Graham Stark, who was also back for another of his classic cameos. Behind the scenes the script was again in the hands of Edwards and Frank Waldman, who were re-joined by production designer Peter Mullins, stuntmen Dick Crockett and Joe Dunne, sound supervisor Gerry Humphreys, production supervisor Derek Kavanagh and associate producer Tony Adams, while Alan Jones, who'd worked as the first assistant editor on *Return*, was promoted to editor, with Edwards' son Geoffrey joining him as assistant editor. As ever, the music was in the hands of Henry Mancini.

Observed Tony Adams of this core team of familiar faces both in front of and behind the camera, "In terms of using the same people over and over again, the comfort factor is very important because of how he [Blake] works, which is very organic."[3] Said Edwards of what was quickly becoming his favored group of supporting actors, "Whenever we got anyone from the original kind of stock company together there was always improv. And the actors contributed as much as I did."[4] Of course, Edwards' way of improvising also appealed to his leading man, as Tony Adams remembered. "Some of the best gags that are in those movies are ones he [Edwards] came up with on the spot. He'd act it out, then Sellers would do it and add to it, and things would build and build and build. The hardest part was to keep the crew from laughing. Finally, by the time the take took place, Sellers was floating off the ground."[5] In fact, this proved to be the case quite literally this time, as we shall see.

As they worked on the screenplay for *Strikes Again*, Edwards and Waldman found themselves devising ever more elaborate set pieces for Clouseau to become involved in during the solving of his latest case, taking things to a new level of lunacy. The plot line for *Return* had been based on one of the outlines the duo had prepared for the proposed

Back in action. Blake Edwards directs Peter Sellers in a moment from *The Pink Panther Strikes Again* (1976) (UA/Amjo/Geoffrey 1964).

Panther TV series, and *Strikes Again* came from another, and carries on from the previous film, with Dreyfus, having spent some three years in a psychiatric hospital following his attempts to assassinate Clouseau, now ready for discharge pending an appearance before the sanity board. However, a visit by Clouseau on the day of the hearing ("I thought a few words from me on your behalf...") sees Dreyfus quickly revert to his old ways, thus scuppering his chances of release. Consequently, he takes matters into his own hands, escapes from the hospital and, having broken into the apartment below Clouseau's, spies on him through a number of holes he drills through the ceiling before planting explosives to blow the place up, though things don't quite go according to plan, given that the Inspector, who has been trying out his new Quasimodo disguise, complete with helium inflated hump, manages to escape the blast by accidentally over inflating the costume and floating out of the window and past Notre Dame before finally deflating and falling into the Seine.

Completely mad by now, Dreyfus next recruits the notorious bank robber Jean Tournier, and with his help builds "an organisation so sinister, so powerful, that by comparison the Cosa Nostra will seem like the Vienna Boys' Choir," as he puts it. Funded by a bank heist, and peopled with criminals broken from jail, Dreyfus arranges for the kidnapping of Professor Hugo Fassbender and his daughter, his plan being to coerce the scientist into building a Doomsday Machine whose ray is powerful

Getting the heump. Clouseau tries out his Quasimodo disguise in *The Pink Panther Strikes Again* (1976) (UA/Amjo/Geoffrey 1964).

enough to hold the world to ransom, his sole demand being the life of Clouseau. And to prove his intent, he wipes the United Nations building from the face of the earth by way of a demonstration of the power he now bears. In the meantime, Clouseau is sent to investigate the disappearance of the Professor, whose country house staff he interviews, among them the butler Jarvis, who moonlights by performing in a Soho drag club called Queen of Hearts. Following the murder of Jarvis by one of the kidnappers, Clouseau discovers a pamphlet for the Oktoberfest in Munich, and follows the trail to Germany, where the underworld's greatest assassins have been sent by various governments to kill him, but whose attempts on his life he manages to evade by a series of lucky blunders and accidents.

He finally tracks down Dreyfus to the gothic Mondschein Castle, and after having failed to gain entry via the drawbridge, eventually does so in the guise of the local dentist, who has been summoned to tend Dreyfus, who at this point has been led to believe that Clouseau has finally been assassinated, though it was actually Tournier who, disguised as Clouseau in order to gain access to his hotel room and wait for his return, who was killed in his stead by an Egyptian agent who then, in the shadows, makes love to a beautiful Russian named Olga who has also been sent to kill him, and who subsequently falls in love with the Inspector, believing it was *he* who made love to her (following all this?). Having rumbled Clouseau after he pulled the wrong tooth, Dreyfus aims the ray gun to destroy England, only for the Inspector, by now disguised in a suit of armor, to land on top of it following an incident with a medieval catapult (don't ask), resulting in it firing at Dreyfus, who gradually disappears as he plays "Tiptoe Through the Tulips" on the organ, the last we see of him being his twitching eye before it goes up in a puff of smoke. Returning home, Clouseau discovers Olga waiting for him in his bedroom, which has now been modified to include a giant bed which tips down from the wall. However, just as he and Olga are about to make love, Cato attacks, prompting the bed to flip up and the whole lot to crash through the wall and into the Seine below.

Clearly, this is all a very long way from the sophisticated antics of the first Panther back in 1963. However, though the humor is undeniably broader, the film nevertheless contains some sequences that rank among the best in the series, among them Clouseau's encounter with Dreyfus in the grounds of the hospital, which sees Dreyfus end up in the lake not once but three times, with Clouseau's attempts to revive him ("Out with the bad air, in with the good") misconstrued for a sexual act by two passing old dears ("Pervert!" says one of them, hitting the Inspector with her purse). Other memorable moments include Clouseau

7. Lightning Strikes Twice

floating past Notre Dame as Quasimodo as the bells ring, much to the surprise of two on looking nuns; Clouseau having a go on the equipment in the Professor's gym, claiming that he was known as "The Pavlova of the parallels" at the Sureté, only to swing off the bars the wrong side and end up crashing down a flight of stairs; Clouseau's interrogation of the Professor's household staff which climaxes with the wrecking of a piano ("But that's a priceless Steinway," exclaims the housekeeper, "Not anymore," comes the response); the various attempts on Clouseau's life at the Oktoberfest, which end with the elimination of many of the killers (an assassination attempt in a toilet cubicle is particularly well worked out); a cleverly choreographed sequence in which the lights in his hotel bedroom are, unbeknownst to each other, turned on and off by Clouseau and Olga (Edwards would later finesse the routine for *Victor/Victoria* [1982]); Clouseau's various failed attempts to gain access to the castle, which involve a grappling hook, a canoe and a pole vault, all of which end with him in the moat; and Cato's final catastrophic bedroom attack.

Also among the film's highlights is Clouseau's encounter with Dreyfus in the castle. Covering for the local dentist Dr. Schirtz, who has gone fishing, Clouseau examines a cavity that Dreyfus is suffering from, during which the two end up getting high on nitrous oxide, with the nose of Clouseau's disguise (provided by make-up expert Harry Frampton) gradually melting in the heat. Recalled Herbert Lom of the sequence, "That's one of the best scenes I ever shot with Peter. It was

Visiting hours. Herbert Lom (left) and Peter Sellers in an early scene from *The Pink Panther Strikes Again* **(1976) (UA/Amjo/Geoffrey 1964).**

particularly difficult because we both had to laugh a lot, and as you know, one has to shoot many angles to cover such a scene, and in a nutshell we had to laugh all day, and that was quite difficult for our diaphragms. But the scene is one of the best scenes we ever shot."[6] As for Sellers' approach to Clouseau, Lom revealed, "He used to think of Clouseau as *him* not *I*. And he used to tell me, sometimes when I met him in the morning, he used to say, 'You know, I thought up some wonderful stuff for him last night.' And the *him* was Clouseau, and he'd thought up some new ideas to put into the script, because half the scripts were improvised by Peter, sometimes for much too long. But that's how he thought of him, as *him*. He lived life with a double."[7]

The film also contains another of Graham Stark's eye-catching supporting roles as an ancient hotel clerk at the Bavarian hotel Clouseau is staying at. However, this wasn't the role Edwards originally had the actor shoot. Recalled Stark, "I was originally going to play the hotel manager in Munich, and Blake wanted me to do it as Hitler, and I didn't like the idea. I was a bit dubious. I said, 'I'm sorry, I was in the RAF in the war and I don't think he's funny.' And Blake went, 'I'll tell you what we'll do. We'll film it, and if you don't like it we'll cut it. Well, we needn't have worried, because we filmed it in Munich at the hotel where Hitler actually stayed, and it got hysterical. It got very difficult. Peter got the giggles and I wasn't very happy. Then I went back to England. Then I got a call from Blake saying he'd got a better idea. Play the old man. And I did. They cut the Hitler thing completely."[8]

As a consequence, Stark instead played the ancient hotel clerk who is asked by Clouseau of a cute dog lying on the floor in reception, "Does your dog bite?" to which the old man replies "No." However, when Clouseau goes to pet the "nice doggy" it savages him. "I thought you said your dog did not bite," admonishes the Inspector, to which comes the response, "That is not my dog," at which a cuckoo clock strikes. "It's reckoned to be one of the funniest moments in films,"[9] recalled Stark. "The funny thing is, when I first saw the script, I remember thinking I'd love to do that bit. It's an old joke, but it's a belter.... It was my idea, like a fool, to play the scene with a big pipe. I didn't smoke at the time. I'd given up. So they filled the pipe with herbal tobacco. We started filming the scene at eleven in the morning, with me puffing away. Well, Peter kept getting the giggles and by lunchtime people were hanging onto the camera, they were laughing so much. By four in the afternoon Blake was going a bit potty, because we still hadn't got the scene. Peter somehow pulled himself together and we eventually got through it. After that I flew back to London to start *The Prince and the Pauper*, and I had this terrible headache on the plane. Well, much to my surprise, one day Blake

Edwards suddenly walked onto the set, screamed with laughter, and said to the director, Richard Fleischer, 'What are you using this well known drug addict for?' Nobody laughed. I said, 'That's not funny, Blake!' It was then that he told me they'd stuffed the pipe with marijuana! I'd no idea, but everybody else did, which is why they were all so hysterical! It's an amazingly good scene, considering!"[10]

Interestingly, Stark is listed for *both* the receptionist roles in the film's end credits ("Munich and Alpenros hotel clerks"), which means the Hitler scene must have been cut quite late in the day, though he *can* be seen briefly from the back as Hitler in the Munich hotel as he hands over keys to Tournier and Olga. In fact quite a few names appear in the end credits who do not appear in the completed film given some last-minute cuts, among them Jackie Cooper as a repair man, Priceless McCarthy as a flight attendant, Joanna Dickens as a "Fat Lady" on Clouseau's flight to London, newscaster Howard K. Smith as himself, Murray Kash as Dr. Zelmo Flek and Harold Berens as a hotel clerk. Other trimmed scenes involved Clouseau's car catching fire at the psychiatric hospital, an extended version of the scene in which he attempts to gain entry to his apartment, an entire sequence involving fancy dress proprietor Dr. Auguste Balls, as played by comedy actor Harvey Korman, from whom Clouseau acquires his Quasimodo disguise (Liz Smith also appeared in this scene as Martha Balls), and a scene in Clouseau's London hotel, in which he is accidentally pushed out of his window by the hulking maid who has come to turn down his bed (this role was played by Claire Davenport, who had appeared as the masseuse in *The Return of the Pink Panther* [1975]). Edwards would eventually make use of this cut material (and much more) elsewhere, as we shall later see.

One person who *did* make the cut this time, albeit on the soundtrack rather than in person, was Edwards' wife Julie Andrews, who provided the singing voice for Jarvis when he performs in the drag club. Recalled Andrews, "The character's name was Ainsley Jarvis and since he was in drag (if memory serves) Blake needed an androgynous voice if possible. He suggested that I sing the song—to keep it in the family, so to speak—and I did."[11] Said Mancini of Andrews' involvement, "It was just an inside joke. It was a comedic put-on, though where they got the name from I have no idea. Blake asked her to do it and she did it, that's all. It was a good effect."[12]

Recalled legendary stunt man Vic Armstrong, who appeared in the nightclub scene, "You've never seen anything so funny in all your life as dozens of butch stunt men dressed up as transvestites dancing. It was actually quite surprising the number of stunt men that wanted to wear dresses. 'Is my lipstick smudged?' they would say, and 'Are my seams

Life's a drag. Peter Sellers (left) and Michael Robbins in *The Pink Panther Strikes Again* (1976) (UA/Amjo/Geoffrey 1964).

straight?' It was absolutely hysterical, like a pantomime. Opened my eyes a bit, I can tell you. As for me, I spent the whole time trying to keep my face away from the camera so no one recognized me."[13] Added Armstrong, "That was the first time I saw Blake Edwards and Peter Sellers. There was always an aura that came on the set when Sellers arrived, a negative aura for me.... With Sellers, if he got bad vibes off somebody or if they were looking at him and he didn't like it, he'd whisper to his minion, 'Get rid of that guy. I don't like him.' He was totally paranoid. With some stars people let them get away with this kind of behavior and pander to them, and it gets worse and worse until they don't know which way is up any more. Very odd."[14]

The filming experience itself, despite all the gaffes and giggles, was an enjoyable one for Graham Stark, as he recalled. "The pleasure of working for Blake was that, when it came to going on location, there was nobody with more style. He knew that not only the wonderful character of Clouseau entranced the public, but also the exotic scenery surrounding him. Now it was Bavaria and *The Pink Panther Strikes Again*."[15] However, as it had been with the two previous entries, the film's actual base was England, in this case Shepperton Studios (as per *Return*), where even the exterior of the castle was shot.

Also joining Sellers, Lom, Kwouk, Maranne and Stark this time round were Leonard Rossiter, Colin Blakely and Dudley Sutton as the London cops offering assistance to Clouseau (Rossiter's character ends up being shot in the backside during the country house sequence), Richard Vernon as the kidnapped Professor Fassbender (which had been the name of Sellers' character in *What's New Pussycat* [1965], a variation on which he also played in a sketch in *Julie: My Favorite Things* [1975, TV]),

Lesley-Anne Down as the glamorous Olga (Maud Adams had originally been cast, but refused to perform nude, while Down's fellow *Upstairs, Downstairs* [1971–1975, TV] co-star Nicola Pagett had also been considered for the role), Omar Sharif as the Egyptian assassin (Edwards had just worked with him on *The Tamarind Seed* [1974]), stunt man Dick Crockett as the bumbling U.S. President and Byron Kane as his Secretary of State (clearly based on Gerald Ford and Henry Kissinger, respectively, and the only aspect of the film that dates it), Michael Robbins as the cross-dressing Jarvis (Robbins would eventually go on to appear with his "voice" Julie Andrews in *Victor/Victoria* [1982]), Geoffrey Bayldon as Dreyfus's psychiatrist Dr. Duval (Bayldon had appeared briefly in *Inspector Clouseau* [1968]), John Clive as Chuck, the maître d' of the drag club, actor/stunt man John Sullivan as Tournier (Sullivan had just appeared as a KGB agent in *The Tamarind Seed* [1974]), and Joan Rhodes and the wonderful Damaris Hayman as the two old biddies by the lake. The film also features Vanda Godsell, Norman Mitchell, Patsy Smart, Tony Sympson (who'd appeared with Sellers in *Soft Beds, Hard Battles* [1974]) and George Leech as the various members of Professor Fassbender's improbably named household staff, with Leech as the beekeeper Mr. Stutterstutt (which Clouseau mangles to Stuckerstuff, Stuffsucker and Stiffsticker) and Godsell (who'd played the cook in *A Shot in the Dark* [1964]) as the housekeeper Mrs. Leverlilly (which Clouseau pronounces Loveliver), while the assassins are played by the likes of Anthony Chinn, Eddie Stacey, Terry Maidment, Herb Tanney (billed as Sado Tanney) and the diminutive Deep Roy (billed as Roy Deep).

Of the regular cast, Sellers, despite the rampant giggles and behind the scenes tantrums, makes the most of the various comic situations he finds himself in as Clouseau, though he looks a little odd during the opening lakeside sequence thanks to a curious chestnut rise his thinning hair has been given, while Lom has a ball as the increasingly crazed Dreyfus, who not only flies the helicopter to help Tournier escape his guards while being transported by train, but also ends up in full Phantom of the Opera mode in his Bavarian schloss, playing an organ and swooping about in a cape (Lom had already played the role for real in *The Phantom of the Opera* [1962]). He even gets to star in the trailer, pronouncing direct to camera of the various assassins, "I brought them together to destroy the most dangerous man in the world." Elsewhere, Burt Kwouk gamely takes his usual beating as Cato, and gets to play a nice faux reaction to Clouseau's Quasimodo disguise ("Who are you? What have you done with Inspector Clouseau?"), while André Maranne is as deadpan as ever as Chevalier, never more so than when Clouseau, leaning back too far in his chair, rights himself by pulling himself back up on Chevalier's tie, resulting in him bashing his head on the desk.

Admittedly, the film gets off to a slightly hesitant start, with a rather lengthy sequence between Dreyfus and his psychiatrist ("Every day and in every way you're feeling better and better," encourages the doctor), but once Clouseau arrives on the scene, disorder is quickly restored, and while it doesn't quite have the same pace as *Return*, it moves from set piece to set piece with reasonable alacrity, with Clouseau's attempts to gain entry into the castle a particular highlight, though of all the entries in the series, it is undeniably the drabbest looking at times, with the work of cinematographer Harry Waxman (shooting in Panavision and DeLuxe) failing to compare to the glossy work of Philip Lathrop, Christopher Challis and Geoffrey Unsworth, while some of the sets (such as Clouseau's Munich hotel room) lack the Hollywood look.

Still, there are compensations aplenty, prime among them Henry Mancini's excellent score. Recorded at the Music Center in London and released on LP by UA, it generally eschews the usual easy listening source cues for a series of descriptive pieces which big up the action, among them "The Evil Theme" which accompanies Dreyfus's antics as he spies on Clouseau by drilling holes through the ceiling of the apartment below, and the surprisingly melancholy "Inspector Clouseau

The master of all he surveys. Herbert Lom's Dreyfus in full Phantom mode in *The Pink Panther Strikes Again* (1976) (UA/Amjo/Geoffrey 1964).

Theme" which accompanies the Inspector's failed attempts to get into the castle (other composers might have gone the comedy route here, but Mancini instead plays up the pathos, which makes the scene all the funnier). There is also "local color" in the form of the jaunty "Bier Fest Polka" for the Oktoberfest sequence, and a piece tailored for Sharif's brief appearance titled "Along Came Omar," as well as two songs: the plaintive "Until You Love Me," which Jarvis (Andrews) sings at the drag club, and the epic "Come to Me," which plays over the final bedroom scene. Both have lyrics by the prolific Don Black, best known for penning several James Bond title songs, among them those for *Thunderball* (1965) and *Diamonds Are Forever* (1971), with Tom Jones, who'd sung the former, here belting out the unreservedly florid lines. Recalled Black of his association with Mancini, "Writing with Henry, or Hank as we call him, was a dream. Not only did he write wonderful melodies, but he also knew all the best restaurants in London and Los Angeles."[16] Said Mancini of how Jones came to perform of the song, "I had known Tom a bit before, and we wanted someone who would have that big voice, and the song was tailored for that kind of singer. And he was perfect for it. It was played over the bedroom scene. That was a really good stroke, and I liked that. We did our track and Tom came in and put his voice over."[17]

As always, Mancini's celebrated theme tune, again featuring Tony Coe on the tenor sax, adds immeasurably to the film's opening titles, which were again in the hands of animator Richard Williams. As before they see the Panther and Clouseau confront each other in a deco movie theater, where the Inspector has arrived to watch a film, only for the screen to be bombarded with spoofs, this time featuring Alfred Hitchcock, Batman, King Kong, Julie Andrews (in *The Sound of Music* [1965]), Count Dracula, Gene Kelly (in *Singin' in the Rain* [1952]), Buster Keaton (in *Steamboat Bill, Jr.* [1928]) and the dance hall scene from *Sweet Charity* (1969), each of which feature snatches of the appropriate music ("Funeral March of a Marionette" for Hitchcock, "Big Spender" for *Sweet Charity*, etc.). The spoofing even continues into the end credits this time as, following the collapse of the bed into the Seine, the cartoon Clouseau can be seen swimming about in the water, only for a giant, shark-toothed Panther to appear below him accompanied by John Williams' famous theme from *Jaws* (1975), which was about as up to date as a spoof could be at the time (after the following credit roll has ended, the Panther can finally be seen relaxing on the word "Fin").

Shot between 28 January and 4 July 1976, the film was budgeted at $4.5m. However, its original fourteen-week schedule ballooned following a series of health scares and dramas of varying description. When it was finally ready, the first edit ran a rather unwieldy two hours,

More Mancini magic. The LP release of *The Pink Panther Strikes Again* (1976) (UA/Amjo/Geoffrey 1964/RCA).

and was subsequently trimmed by seventeen minutes to better speed up the action, though it had been Edwards' original hope to send out a three hour movie akin to his comedy epic *The Great Race* (1965), an idea that was nixed by United Artists, who financed and released the film as a UA/Amjo/Geoffrey 1964 co-production (Lew Grade also had an uncredited financial stake in the production following the success of *Return*). "He's back again. Peter Sellers as Inspector Clouseau in his latest, greatest, most baffling case," exclaimed the narrator of the trailer, whose scenes involving the various assassins lead him to ponder, "Will this be the end of the world's greatest detective? You'll find out when the Pink Panther strikes again." In addition to the special Lom/Dreyfus trailer, Byron Kane also appeared as the Kissinger-like Secretary of State in another, warning audiences from the Oval Office, "My fellow Americans, our nation has endured many great crises, but today we face

The assassins assemble. Poster artwork featuring Peter Sellers in his hilarious Quasimodo disguise for *The Pink Panther Strikes Again* (1976) (UA/Amjo/Geoffrey 1964).

perhaps our greatest test. Inspector Jacques Clouseau has been declared to be the most dangerous man alive. If Clouseau is not found and eliminated, half the world may be destroyed. It is your duty to be on the lookout for him. Clouseau *must go* before it's too late," at which he steps

Chapter and verse. Frank Waldman's novelization of *The Pink Panther Strikes Again* (1976) (Ballantine/UA/Amjo/Geoffrey 1964).

7. Lightning Strikes Twice

aside to reveal the President (Dick Crockett) at his desk, after which the narrator encourages, "And *you* must go to see Peter Sellers as Inspector Clouseau in Blake Edwards' *The Pink Panther Strikes Again*, coming for Christmas."

The assassination plot was meanwhile highlighted in one of the film's posters, which wondered, "Why are the world's chief assassins after Inspector Clouseau?" to which it answered, "Why not? Everybody else is." It also described the film as being "The newest, pinkest Panther of all!" Another featured the Panther holding a weight over Clouseau, who is standing underneath examining it with a magnifying glass. Here the strapline ran, "The all-new adventures of the world's most bumbling detective." As before, an exhibitor's campaign book was released to help promote the film, while Frank Waldman again penned a novelization, this time published by Ballantine on 1 December 1976, the cover blurb for which exclaimed, "The most cunning klutz in police (or movie) history is back for more danger, more clever stupidity and more laughs than ever before!" There was also an eight-minute promotional short titled *Clouseau, the Greatest Fumbler in the World* (1976), which featured Sellers and Edwards, who are briefly interviewed, along with valuable behind the scenes footage shot during the filming of the drawbridge sequence. Behind the scenes footage was also featured in the 29 November 1976 episode of the long-running British movie program *Clapperboard* (1972–1982, TV).

The movie was released with a PG rating in some 600 theaters across America on 15 December 1976 and had its Royal Charity premiere on 16 December in London at the Odeon Leicester Square (where it went on to run for a staggering fifteen weeks), after which it went on general release in the UK with a U certificate on 17 December (this despite the suggestive bedroom scenes involving Clouseau and Olga). Awkward to the end, Sellers refused to attend the premiere as his girlfriend and future wife Lynne Frederick was not included on the guest list, which included Julie Andrews, Henry Mancini, Lew Grade, Herbert Lom, Lesley-Anne Down, Michael Robbins and Burt Kwouk. Despite the annoyance this caused, the royal guest of honor, Prince Charles, nevertheless admitted to having enjoyed the film. Again, the movie was an instant smash, and went on to earn $33,833,201 in the U.S. and Canada, the equivalent of 15,884,131 tickets sold, and came in at number twelve in the year's box office rankings, just behind Mel Brooks' *Silent Movie* (1976) and just ahead of Sellers' other release of the year, *Murder by Death* (1976). *Strikes Again* would eventually go on to earn $75m worldwide.

As before, the reviews were a mixed bunch, not that it mattered.

From Russia with love. Lesley-Anne Down as the delectable Olga in *The Pink Panther Strikes Again* **(1976) (UA/Amjo/Geoffrey 1964).**

The New York Times described Sellers and Lom as "a hilarious team" and also highlighted the film's "delight in old gags," while the *Chicago-Sun Times* found that "it has moments as good as anything Sellers and Edwards have ever done," but finally admitted that it was perhaps "time for them to move on." The one true dissenting voice came from Rex Reed who, writing in the *New York Daily News*, found the film to be "moronic" and described those who went to see it as being "sub-mental," which led to him being banned from future UA screenings.

In addition to its financial success, the film also went on to earn an Oscar nomination at the 49th Academy Awards for best song "Come to Me" which Tom Jones performed at the ceremony, which was broadcast live by ABC on 28 March 1977 (the winner proved to be "Evergreen" from *A Star Is Born* [1976]). The film was also nominated for two Golden Globes (for best comedy or musical and best actor in a comedy or musical for Sellers), while Edwards and Frank Waldman won the Writers Guild of America award for best comedy adapted from another medium. It also went on to win the 1977 *Evening Standard* British Film Award for best comedy.

7. Lightning Strikes Twice

Obviously, despite all the various dramas involved in its making, *Strikes Again* had clearly been a win-win situation for all concerned. But would Edwards and Sellers be encouraged to do it all again, despite the riches being offered for them to do so? Said Edwards of the situation, "Any time Sellers was successful, he would become a total monster and think it was the worst thing he'd ever done. You then had to wait until he'd done a couple of bad ones and was down on his luck and needed money before you knew another one was going to happen. And then I had to talk myself into it."[18] However, given the success of *Strikes Again*, it was obvious Edwards was going to have to give himself a "talking to" far sooner than he perhaps expected to.

8

Revenge Is Sweet

According to Blake Edwards, Peter Sellers "could be totally schizophrenic"[1] when it came to working on the Panthers. Yet the director admitted that once shooting got underway, "then usually we had a great time. We had such fun making those films."[2] However, it was during the making of *Revenge of the Pink Panther* (1978) that things finally came to an impasse. Said Herbert Lom of the situation, "He [Sellers] had difficulties with the director. They weren't on speaking terms for many months, so we had quite a difficult time on the set. Blake would send his secretary to Peter saying, 'Tell him to come down the stairs and sit at the table on the right.' Then Peter's secretary would come back and say, 'Mr. Sellers would prefer to stand by the stairs and not sit down in the scene.' All the while, we were standing there, looking at the ceiling. Luckily, they made it up, and I must say I helped them to become friends again."[3] Unfortunately, despite the truce, by the time filming was completed, the two agreed to go their separate ways again, only on this occasion it proved to be permanent.

As before, Edwards had to talk himself into making the film, despite the rewards it promised. "I was able to use a couple of those offers to get other things done. 'I'll do another Panther for you if you will do *10*,' say."[4] As for his working relationship with Sellers, he revealed, "He really alternately loved me and hated me. I would say he hated me more than he loved me."[5] This, it would seem, hailed back to the fact that as the writer, producer and director, Edwards was solely in charge, and had, with Maurice Richlin, originally created the character of Clouseau, which clearly rankled Sellers. As Edwards freely admitted, "He did things that were purely his authorship and not mine, which was fine by me,"[6] but when it came to the success of the series, "Sellers wanted to prove that it was him and the character and not me.... That is not to say that he didn't contribute a lot, you know."[7]

Recalled Julie Andrews of the negotiations for the new film, "Peter Sellers was acting up again, making unreasonable contractual demands, and the studio finally told Blake it was up to him to get Peter onboard."[8] So Blake and Julie headed off on holiday to the South of France, where Sellers and his fourth (and final) wife, Lynne Frederick, had bought a house, and it was while on vacation that Blake would meet with his belligerent star to thrash things out. Said Andrews, "Blake took daily meetings with Sellers and the situation with him became even more crazy. Peter was hustling all sides, telling Blake one thing and the producers another. Lawyers and managers flew in and became embroiled in the discussions.... He and Peter seemed destined to continue their 'merry dance'—part competitive, part love-hate, yet dependent on one another for so many reasons."[9] Noted Walter Mirisch of the Edwards-Sellers partnership, "I think that the careers of both of them illustrates the fact that they both realised what the other meant to his own talent, and they kept coming back to one another at various stages."[10] Consequently, in order to placate Sellers and acknowledge his contribution to the series, *Revenge* was made as a Sellers-Edwards Production (with Sellers' name listed first, note) in association with Jewel and UA. Observed Graham Stark of the situation on what proved to be the final film between director and star, "There's no doubt that he [Sellers] and Blake were getting tetchy together. I think it was wearing a bit thin. At the finish, the last film was a co-production, and after that he and Blake agreed never to work again together."[11]

In addition to the complex negotiations, there was also the matter of Sellers' declining health to consider. Revealed Walter Mirisch, "He [Sellers] had married a very young woman. Beautiful young woman. He had plastic surgery. And yet he was quite ill. He had a pacemaker. He had a lot of difficulty with his pacemaker. It was a difficult time of his life."[12] Said Edwards of the situation, "I can't tell you how many times, particularly towards the end, that we had to have Joe Dunne—his double, who doubled him perfectly—come in and do this thing."[13] Recalled Dunne, "He [Sellers] wasn't the healthiest guy in the world, so he wouldn't exert himself too much if he didn't have to. Which was good for me. I didn't mind doing that sort of stuff. I went all over the world with the guy. That was great."[14]

For the film, whose working title was *Curse of the Pink Panther*, a moniker Edwards would later re-use, the director had hoped to incorporate much of the material excised from *Strikes Again*, around which he intended to fashion a new plot. Sellers nixed the idea, which resulted in a new script, again penned by Edwards and Frank Waldman (from a story by Edwards), who were this time joined in their endeavors by TV writer Ron Clark, a regular contributor to *The Smothers Brothers Comedy Hour* (1967–1969, TV), whose recent movie work had taken in collaborations with Mel Brooks on *Silent Movie* (1976) and *High Anxiety* (1977). Again based at Shepperton Studios, the film's new storyline involved an underworld plot to kill Clouseau, and featured scenes in Paris and the South of France, as well as further afield in Hong Kong.

Said Graham Stark, "The Panther series had now become an awesome money-making machine, as each new film of the series took more money at the box office so, in 1978, it was off to yet another glamorous location—Hong Kong. *Revenge of the Pink Panther* was soon cast, as Blake was loyal to his own personal repertory company, and once more Herbert Lom, Burt Kwouk and myself were assembled."[15] Of his continued involvement in the series, Kwouk, who would be featured more heavily than usual this time, enthused, "When Peter was doing it I used to say, 'A new Pink Panther. Great. Let's do it.' I just said, 'Fix the deal and I'm in.'"[16] For Herbert Lom, the films were now starting to merge into one, but he still enjoyed being one of the regular participants. Admitted the actor, "I don't remember the titles of the films, all I remember is the wonderful part I was given and the wonderful role that Peter played. It was such a success."[17]

In addition to Lom, Kwouk and Stark, returning cast members this time included André Maranne as Chevalier and, from *Strikes Again*, Anthony Chinn, John Clive and George Leech, as well as Herb Tanney (who'd appeared in both *Return* and *Strikes Again*, and who also gets a name check here in an early scene ["Dr. Herb called"]), while stuntman Ed Parker (who'd been Edwards' martial arts trainer and had worked on several of his earlier films) got to play a small but key role (John Bluthal, who'd played the blind beggar in *Return*, is also credited, though his scenes appear to have been excised). Behind the cameras, the old gang included production designer Peter Mullins, editor Alan Jones (again assisted by Edwards' son Geoffrey), construction manager Tony Graysmark (who'd joined the team with *Return*), associate producer Derek Kavanagh (promoted from production supervisor on *Return* and *Strikes Again*), fellow associate producer Ken Wales (who'd worked with Edwards in this capacity on *Gunn* [1967], *The Party* [1968] and *Darling Lili* [1970], as well as a producer on *Wild Rovers* [1971] and *The Tamarind Seed* [1974]), second unit director Anthony Squire (who'd helmed the aerial sequences for *Darling Lili* [1970]), make-up man Harry Frampton, wardrobe supervisor Tiny Nicholls (billed as Nichols), script supervisor Pamela Davies, cinematographer Ernest Day (who, billed as Ernie Day, had been the camera operator on *Strikes Again*), and of course composer Henry Mancini. Newcomers who in turn would likewise go on to become regulars behind the scenes included assistant director Terry Marcel, sound mixer Roy Charman, sound editor Gordon Daniel

8. Revenge Is Sweet

Advance warning. Early promotional poster for *Revenge of the Pink Panther* (1978) (United Artists/Sellers-Edwards/Jewel).

(billed as Daniels) and personal assistant Francine Taylor, who would continue to perform this role for both Blake and his wife for many years to come (she'd previously worked as a secretary for Bond producer Harry Saltzman).

Cast-wise, the new faces included the former Mrs. Cary Grant, Dyan Cannon, best known for her performance as Alice in *Bob & Carol & Ted & Alice* (1969), which had earned her a best supporting actress Oscar nomination (Blake had already directed her ex in *Operation Petticoat* [1959]); Robert Webber (who'd go on to work with Edwards on *10* [1979] and *S.O.B.* [1981]); Robert Loggia (who'd also go on to work with Edwards on *S.O.B.* [1981], *That's Life!* [1986] and two further Panthers); Paul Stewart (who'd also be cast in *S.O.B.* [1981]); Tony Beckley; Alfie Bass; Ferdy Mayne; Sue Lloyd; Lon Satton; Elisabeth Welch; Valerie Leon; Adrienne Corri; Andrew Sachs; Julian Orchard; Michael Ward; Frank Williams; Henry McGee; Steve Plytas; Maria Charles (who'd go on to appear in Edwards' *Victor/Victoria* [1982]); and Rita Webb.

Filming on the $9m movie began in Paris on 2 November 1977, and would continue until 16 April 1978, with the unit moving to Hong Kong on 5 February 1978, where Edwards took advantage of the Chinese New Year, then back to France and Nice on 21 March. It was also during this period that Sellers made a guest appearance on *The Muppet Show* (1976–1981, TV), in which he was featured in a handful of sketches, including a cold opening in which he briefly appeared as Clouseau (in the skit, Scooter knocks on Sellers' dressing room door to let him know that it's fifteen seconds to curtain, at which it is revealed that Gonzo has been practicing his knife throwing act on the star who, standing against a pink wall as the Inspector, retorts with a panicked, "Fifteen seconds? I should live so long!", before dropping out of frame). Made by Lew Grade's ITC, the program aired in the UK on 1 January 1978 and in the U.S. on 25 February.

With its rather more serious background of drug smuggling, the story for *Revenge* sees crime boss Philippe Douvier, who is involved in a major narcotics operation emanating from Hong Kong known as the Gannet Transaction, attempting to reassert his authority with his New York counterparts. When one of his minions suggests he do this by eliminating Clouseau, he goes along with the idea. However, as before, all attempts to assassinate the Inspector end in disaster, until he gives a lift to an armed robber named Claude Russo, who carries out his crimes in full drag, and who steals Clouseau's car and clothes. When Russo is subsequently killed by the assassins, the world assumes that Clouseau has been murdered, only for the Inspector, who has been forced to wear Russo's outfit to cover his modesty, to be carted off to the same psychiatric hospital from which Dreyfus, having now fully recovered from his bout of megalomania, is about to be discharged.

Having escaped the hospital disguised as Dreyfus, who is subsequently reinstated in his old job and put in charge of discovering who killed Clouseau, the Inspector returns home, only to find that Cato has turned his flat into a "Chinese nooky factory" complete with a whip-yielding dominatrix (note that the brothel's door chimes play the opening notes from "Love Is a Many-Splendored Thing"). Taking advantage of the fact that everyone believes him to be dead, Clouseau decides to enter the criminal underworld to discover who wanted to assassinate him, and in doing so joins forces with the beautiful Simone, Douvier's former secretary and girlfriend, whom he inadvertently rescues from a nightclub when the crime boss attempts to have her bumped off for knowing too much. "Working under the covers," Clouseau thus heads for Hong Kong with Cato and Simone, who has provided him with information about the drugs operation, and, disguised as a Brando-esque godfather (complete with cotton wool in his cheeks which he inevitably chokes on), he attempts to expose the deal going down between Douvier and the New York boss Scallini, only for things to resolve themselves with a high speed car chase around the city culminating with an explosive finale in a fireworks factory. Having returned back home in triumph, Clouseau is decorated for a second time by the president, after which he and Simone take an evening walk together, seemingly set for a romantic future together.

After the zany antics of the previous installment, it's nice to see the series again rooted in reality (or rather what passes for it in the world of Clouseau), and while the laughs don't quite flow as quick and fast this time round thanks to the various machinations of the rather involved plot, there are certainly enough highlights and set pieces here to keep fans of the series chuckling away. As with *Strikes Again*, things get off to a slightly hesitant start with the setting up of the assassination scenario, after which follow the titles, thus making it some eleven minutes before Clouseau makes his first appearance. However, it's worth the wait, as what follows is one of Sellers' classic encounters with Graham Stark, who this time plays Dr. Auguste Balls, the provider of the Inspector's outrageous disguises (the role had previously been played by Harvey Korman in the scenes excised from *Strikes Again*). And it's while in Balls' emporium, trying on a Toulouse-Lautrec costume, that the assassins first attempt see off Clouseau by blowing him up with a hand delivered "beum" which, despite the devastation it causes fails to have the desired effect.

As predicted by Stark, filming the sequence resulted in the

Hats off. Peter Sellers prepares to film a scene with Clouseau wearing his Toulouse-Lautrec disguise in *Revenge of the Pink Panther* (1978) (United Artists/Sellers-Edwards/Jewel).

expected chaos, as he recalled. "The character I was to play was a *mittel*–European conman, crawler and supposed expert at disguises with the improbable name of Dr. Balls. As I read the script the thought of Peter and I playing the scene using that name, and trying not to laugh, loomed in my mind. However, you do not start a film telling the director he's got to change the name of your character."[18] Inevitably, Sellers quickly succumbed to the giggles when it came to shoot the sequence. Said Stark, "All my predictions about playing Dr. Balls came true as Peter, needless to say, started laughing as we tried to get through the scenes.... Peter had to leave the set he was laughing so much."[19]

Sellers also succumbed to the giggles during his scenes with Dyan Cannon in Simone's apartment, which was also compromised by other issues. Recalled Edwards, "That awful heart he had apparently affected his memory. If you gave him any kind of intricate physical moves in scenes in which he also had lines, he became literally incapable of doing both. I remember a scene in *The Revenge of the Pink Panther* in which I started rehearsing him on all kinds of funny moves that would have just been par for the course in the early Pink Panther movies; there was absolutely no way he was able to do it, so I stuck him up against a fireplace and kept his moves to a minimum. Under normal conditions, that scene would have taken no more than the morning and possibly part of the afternoon to shoot. It ended up taking two and a half days."[20] Elsewhere, a scene set in a night club had to be abandoned, in which Clouseau and Cato were set to appear wearing zoot suits and dreadlocks. Revealed Edwards, "Peter was then supposed to come out with a lot of what Clouseau thought was very hip black street lingo and, of course, screw it all up. Peter absolutely couldn't get it. That made him very angry and resulted in a very unpleasant day on the set."[21] Attempts to capture the scene the next day proved no better. Said Edwards, "What he did was awful…. We had to cut the entire sequence and replace it with a new one … in which we used a double. It was very sad."[22] Regarding this, Edwards admitted, "We got more and more away from Clouseau's character involvements and we put in more and more physical comedy so that we could use doubles for Peter."[23]

The issues didn't end there though, as Julie Andrews revealed. "Blake suddenly decided that the final scene of the film didn't work and needed to be replaced. With as much courage as inspiration, he came up with a new ending, and within two days he'd raised the necessary funds, brought most of the company back together, procured a soundstage at MGM and had a set built."[24]

Watching the film, you wouldn't know there had been so many problems, and its other highlights include Clouseau accidentally setting the Police Commissioner's office on fire with his still smoking costume following the explosion at the costume shop; the various scenes in which he keeps bumping into Dreyfus, who thinks he is dead ("Peek-a-boo?" he says when Dreyfus discovers him hiding in his closet at the clinic, prompting him to faint dead away); Clouseau walking into the crotch-level blades of a fan in his old apartment while reprimanding Cato for turning it into a brothel; Dreyfus barely being able to suppress his laughter when forced to read the eulogy at Clouseau's funeral; Clouseau disguised as a one-legged salty Swedish seadog whose blow-up parrot inevitably keeps deflating (how many takes did *that* need?); the attempts by Clouseau and Cato to break into the back entrance of the nightclub (Le Club Foot), only to end up crashing through the window of a nearby bakery ("At least you're not yellow anymore," observes Clouseau of Cato, who is covered in flour); Cato bumbling about Hong Kong in a disguise whose bottle bottom glasses prevent him from seeing

Parrot fashion. Peter Sellers (left) and Alfie Bass are featured in this French lobby card for *Revenge of the Pink Panther* **(1978).** *La malediction de la panthere rose* **actually translates as "The Curse of the Pink Panther," which was the film's working title, and which would officially be used later in the series (United Artists/Sellers-Edwards/Jewel).**

where he is going; and the explosive firework climax which sees Clouseau's godfather costume blown off to reveal his red all-in-one long johns bearing the name Balls (however, a brief exchange between Clouseau and Simone as they arrive at the hotel in Hong Kong wearing Chinese disguises pushes the series' casual racism envelope somewhat; expressing her concern at not being able to go through with the ruse, Clouseau encourages Simone to "Just think yellow and follow me").

Inevitably by this time, there are repetitions of certain gags. Dreyfus falling into the open grave when Clouseau appears disguised as a priest during his burial ceremony recalls Clouseau's graveside tumble in *Inspector Clouseau* (1968), while the car chase and firework climax are revamps of those in *The Pink Panther* (1963). Still, there are some good variations on established situations, among them the sequence in which Clouseau, believing he is about to have one his impromptu fights with Cato, inadvertently dispatch one of his would-be assassins, sending him out of the window, through a skylight and several floors of the

8. Revenge Is Sweet

building below (Sellers had already used the horn the Inspector blows in this scene in the opening of *The Party* [1968]). Even better is his subsequent fight with Cato, who saws through the floor Clouseau is standing on, at first prompting him to think he is breathing heavily before falling through to the apartment below (note that Clouseau's hat hovers for a moment before following him).

Given that this was his fifth time out as Clouseau, Sellers, despite what might have been going on behind the cameras, appears to be enjoying himself, particularly in those scenes involving the various disguises. Indeed, if he was losing interest in the role, "I wasn't aware of it,"[25] said Herbert Lom, who is, as usual, in good form as Dreyfus, particularly in the aforementioned eulogy scene. Others adding to the fun include Dyan Cannon (both glamorous and feisty as Simone), Robert Webber as the duplicitous Douvier, Tony Beckley as his sidekick Guy Algo, Douglas Wilmer as the hangdog Police Commissioner (Wilmer had previously played Henri LaFarge in *A Shot in the Dark* [1964]), Valerie Leon as Tanya the whip lady, Elisabeth Welch as Mrs. Wu (the madam of Cato's knocking shop, who exclaims, "And another round-eye bites the dust," as Clouseau succumbs to Tanya's ministrations),

Drag race. Sue Lloyd and Peter Sellers share a ride in *Revenge of the Pink Panther* (1978) (United Artists/Sellers-Edwards/Jewel).

Ed Parker as the seemingly indestructible assassin Mr. Chong, and Sue Lloyd who plays the dragged up Russo (which means she is a woman playing a man pretending to be a woman, a setup which may well have stuck in Edwards' mind when he came to make *Victor/Victoria* [1982]). In fact Clouseau has one of the film's best exchanges with Russo when he picks "her" up at a bus stop. "It's green," she observes. "Is it?" asks Clouseau. To which comes the retort, "The traffic light," at which Clouseau drives off.

Technically, the film is on firmer ground than *Strikes Again*, and is very ably shot by Ernie Day (in Panavision and Technicolor), though it must be said that neither Hong Kong nor the Excelsior Hotel look particularly glamorous. Peter Mullins' sets are certainly more eye-catching than before, notable among them Douvier's office (which features some striking bas relief wall art) and Simone's nicely appointed apartment (whose fireplace Clouseau inevitably singes himself on when he leans against it). As always, composer Henry Mancini provides much to catch the ear, including a funky, disco-style variation on his celebrated title theme, complete with electric guitar riffs, with the tenor sax again performed by Tony Coe. This time the credits see Clouseau and the Panther chase each other with guns and bombs of various sizes, with Clouseau inevitably coming off worse during each encounter. Back in the hands of DePatie-Freleng, they are fairly workmanlike compared to Richard Williams' dazzling efforts for the previous two installments, yet there are certainly laughs to be had as Clouseau is chased by a dog made up of the letters of Herbert Lom's surname and has a giant cannonball land on him during Dyan Cannon's credit. There's even a nod to nascent computer gaming, as Clouseau shoots at the Panther in a couple of brief arcade-like sequences. Designed by Arthur Leonardi and John Dunn, the sequence was produced by David H. DePatie and Friz Freleng and animated by staff cartoonists Warren Batchelder, Bob Bemiller, Tony Love, Walt Kubiak, Virgil Ross and Nelson Shin.

The score also features several pleasant easy listening source cues, among them "A Touch of Red" and "Almond Eyes" which play under the brothel scene, and "After the Shower" and "Simone" (both of which feature piano solos by Mancini) which can be heard in Simone's apartment. Elsewhere, there's the shanty-like "Thar She Blows" which accompanies Clouseau's antics as the salty Swedish sea dog, while things come to a lively conclusion with the Oriental burlesque "Hong Kong Fireworks." Mancini also provided a mock heraldic piece titled "The Silver Hornet" to accompany the emergence of Clouseau's souped up car from the garage, only for it to fall to pieces in the street (curiously, this cue was cut from the DVD release of the film, but later appeared on an extended CD of the score). There's also an amusing song for the night club scene, "Move 'Em Out," performed by Lon Satton, which reunited Mancini with lyricist Leslie Bricusse. Revealed Bricusse of their teaming up, "When I met Hank, which was in the sixties, he had Johnny Mercer as his lyricist, so he didn't need anyone else. But we became pals and I wrote a couple of songs with him during the Mercer era. I did *Two for the Road* and the film version of *Peter Gunn*. Then, after Johnny Mercer died, I started working with Hank more and more,"[26] all of which eventually led to their greatest success together, Edwards' musical *Victor/Victoria* (1982).

The soundtrack album, again recorded at the Music Center London and released by United Artists Records, also contained a bonus track, that of Sellers performing the Maurice Chevalier standard "Thank Heaven for Little Girls" which Clouseau sings in the film while dressed as Toulouse-Lautrec (note that Omar Sharif had also sung this very briefly in *Strikes Again*). Recalled Mancini, "That was Peter's idea. He did that completely on his own. I was back in the States. I wasn't even around when he did that…. I guess that tickled his fancy."[27]

As before, the expected elements were assembled to promote the film, whose poster this time featured the title chiseled out in stone against a blue background, with the cartoon Clouseau crushed under the "r" of the word Panther ("Just when you thought it was safe to go back to the movies," exclaimed one version in a variation on the tagline for *Jaws 2* [1978]). There was also an exhibitor's campaign book ("The Pink Panther's newest ... and funniest adventure!" claimed the cover) and a teaser trailer which spoofed the James Bond gun barrel logo, with Clouseau entering from the wrong side of the screen, struggling to get his gun from his holster, which falls to the floor, failing to get off a shot and then exiting in embarrassment (runs the commentary, "He's back! The man who recovered the world's most valuable diamond, dazzled the world's most beautiful women, survived the world's most deadly assassins and saved the world from total destruction. Now, he faces his most dangerous assignment. Peter Sellers in Blake Edwards' *Revenge of the Pink Panther.* Coming soon"). The official trailer, whose narration likewise referenced UA's most recent Bond hit *The Spy Who Loved Me* (1977), meanwhile queried, "Nobody does it better than guess who? Inspector André Clouseau, that's who," prior to which we are we also are invited "to hear a few short words from Inspector André Clouseau" who is wearing his Toulouse-Lautrec disguise, though who *André* Clouseau could be is anyone's guess (did no one notice the clanging mistake?). There were also two books, one of which featured the script

Three's a crowd. (From left) Burt Kwouk, Peter Sellers and Dyan Cannon in *Revenge of the Pink Panther* (1978) (United Artists/Sellers-Edwards/Jewel).

accompanied by stills from the movie care of New English Library and a "fotonovel" care of Fotonovel Publications featuring "Over 350 beautiful, fun-filled, full-color pictures directly from the hit film!" More importantly, as reported in the 5 July 1978 edition of *Variety*, some 300 members of the media, along with celebrities and guests, were flown out to the Kuilima Hyatt in Oahu, Hawaii, for a weekend junket at a cost of $300,000 to UA, with cameras on hand to record the event for a TV special titled *That's Panthertainment* (1978, TV), which aired in an hour-long slot on WFLD on 16 August 1978.

Executive produced by Tony Adams, the program was written and directed by Kenneth L. Kramer and Carolyn F. Russell for Premacy Productions, and features tantalizing clips from *Revenge* as well as its predecessors. Several of the cast and crew are also interviewed on camera, among them Sellers, Edwards, Lom and Mancini ("I'll tell you one thing. He never called to thank me for writing the theme,"[28] jokes the composer when asked about his feline friend). The program also contains shots of the guests enjoying the festivities, among them Julie Andrews, Sellers' wife Lynne Frederick and Steve Martin, who comments, "Peter

8. *Revenge Is Sweet*

Lights, camera, action! Blake Edwards (with folded arms) and his crew on location in Hong Kong while shooting a scene for *Revenge of the Pink Panther* (1978) (United Artists/Sellers-Edwards/Jewel).

Sellers has always been one of my idols.... He immortalized that role."[29] Of course, Martin (who is shown in a photograph with Sellers at the event) would later go on to play Clouseau himself. Says Dyan Cannon during one Q&A session, "Blake, I think, is probably the best director I've ever worked with,"[30] while of the new movie Sellers observes, "This, as far as I can see, as far as you can ever tell, is the best one we've ever made."[31] The program also features revealing behind the scenes material from *Revenge*, *Strikes Again* and *Return* (including the cut gag as Clouseau tries to get through the revolving hotel door with his ski equipment from the latter), as well as outtakes, goofs and gags as the cast and crew break up on set, among them the scene from *Revenge* in which Clouseau, dressed as the godfather, is in a lift in Hong Kong with the gangsters when one of them breaks wind. This clip and several of the other outtakes were also featured in the British program *It'll Be Alright on the Night 2* (1979, TV), which aired in the UK on 28 October 1979, and which also includes an interview with Sellers.

The film received it official world premiere in London at the Odeon Leicester Square on 13 July 1978 with Prince Charles in attendance. This time Sellers turned up, along with his wife Lynne. Unfortunately, they did so forty minutes too early, much to Sellers' chagrin, and so they stormed off until the appointed hour. The film opened to the public at the same theater the following day and went on to run there for nine weeks. It went on general release in the UK with an A certificate care of UA on 15 July. Its American release followed on 19 July 1978 at the Ziegfeld Theatre in New York and the Cinerama Dome in LA (over the entrance of which was strung a giant inflatable Pink Panther), after which it went out across the U.S. and Canada with a PG rating, again care of UA, bringing in a box office return of $37,337,746, which saw it ranked at number fourteen in the annual box office charts, with 15,956,301 tickets sold. Its eventual worldwide gross was $49,579,269.

Whip crack away! The always delectable Valerie Leon as Tanya in *Revenge of the Pink Panther* (1978) (United Artists/Sellers-Edwards/Jewel).

Even the reviews were a little more charitable this time round. Said *Variety*, "*Revenge of the Pink Panther* isn't the best of the continuing film series, but Blake Edwards and Peter Sellers on a slow day are still well ahead of most other comedic filmmakers," to which *The New York Times* added, "If you have the Clouseau habit ... there's very little that Mr. Edwards and Mr. Sellers could do that would make you find the movie disappointing." The review also mentioned "the inestimably funny Herbert Lom," and noted, "Most important of all, Dyan Cannon is around to play what might be called a flawed femme fatale." Clearly proud of her husband's efforts, Julie Andrews described the film as "the most surreal, the most mad of all the Panthers."[32] In addition to its box office success, the film also won Edwards the *Evening Standard* British Film Award for best comedy, while Mancini and Bricusse found themselves nominated for a Grammy for best original score written for a motion picture or television special.

Clearly, after this latest success, United Artists wanted the series to continue. But given that Edwards and Sellers had now agreed to go their separate ways, how was this even going to happen?

9

The Trail Goes Cold

After the successful release of *Revenge of the Pink Panther* (1978), Blake Edwards and Peter Sellers finally and absolutely went their own ways. The period that followed proved to be a busy one for both of them, resulting in the hit sex comedy *10* (1979) for Edwards, which he followed with his coruscating satire on Hollywood, *S.O.B.* (1981), and the much admired gender-bending musical *Victor/Victoria* (1982), which earned an Oscar for best original song score for Henry Mancini and Leslie Bricusse, along with six further nominations, among them best actress for Julie Andrews and best screenplay based on material from another medium for Edwards. Said the director of the movie, which also featured a Clouseau-like detective named Charles Bovin played by Herb Tanney (billed as Sherloque Tanney) and another classic cameo from Graham Stark (this time as a mordant waiter), "I think it's one of the best jobs of filmmaking I've done. Certainly as far as my writing career is concerned, it rates up there with a few of the best things that I've done."[1]

Meanwhile, Sellers went on to play three roles in an elaborate comic remake of *The Prisoner of Zenda* (1979), which not only features his wife Lynne Frederick, but also several of his former Panther co-stars, among them Elke Sommer, Catherine Schell and Graham Stark. Produced by Walter Mirisch and directed by Blake's former associate Richard Quine, the film, which also contains a charming Henry Mancini score, unfortunately tanked at the box office (Edwards had already done a potted version of the story as part of his epic comedy *The Great Race* [1965]). Sellers fared far better with his next outing, the acclaimed *Being There* (1979), in which he plays a simpleminded gardener who, after the death of his employer, finds himself moving in the rarified circles of Washington politics. The film earned Sellers his second best actor Oscar nomination (which he really should have won), and some of the best notices of his career ("Sellers hasn't been so terrific—or had such terrific material—in years," enthused the *LA Times*). It was then back to broader strokes with *The Fiendish Plot of Dr. Fu Manchu* (1980), which proved to be something of a disaster. Two directors (John Avildsen and Richard Quine) were fired during pre-production, and a third (Piers Haggard) during filming, with Sellers taking over for the last week or so. Executive produced by Lynne Frederick, the film sees Sellers play both Fu Manchu and his nemesis Nayland Smith of Scotland Yard (with Burt Kwouk appearing briefly as Fu's servant), but it's a ramshackle affair which *The Washington Post* described as "an indefensibly inept comedy." It also came in for criticism for its racist stereotypes. Thankfully, Sellers had another career saving Panther film up his sleeve to help reassert his standing at the box office.

Even between the release of each new entry in the series, the franchise remained a familiar presence in movie theaters around the world, thanks to a calculated re-release strategy which saw the films sent out by UA as double bills, either with themselves or other features, all of which helped to maintain Clouseau's profile (and bring in some extra change for little expenditure save for advertising and the shipping of prints). Subsequently, *The Pink Panther* (1963) was double billed with *A Shot in the Dark* (1964), while *The Return of the Pink Panther* (1975) was sent out separately with the original Panther as well as (at various points) *A Shot in the Dark* (1964), *The Pink Panther Strikes Again* (1976) and *Revenge of the Pink Panther* (1978). *Strikes Again* also did double duty with UA's *The Spy Who Loved Me* (1977), for which the tagline ran, "Nobody does it better than Bond and the Panther together!"

Given that Edwards had turned his back on the Panthers, it was now up to Sellers to maintain the franchise with the next installment, *Romance of the Pink Panther*. Scheduled to begin filming in September 1980 at the Studios de Boulogne in Paris, with a planned release date of summer 1981, the new film, which had an initial budget of $9m, was scripted by Sellers himself along with Jim Maloney, who'd worked as one of the writers on the Fu Manchu picture. Originally signed to direct was Sidney Poitier, despite Sellers' own hopes to helm the movie himself (at the time, Edwards, Sellers, Poitier and Maloney were all with the same agent Marty Baum at CAA, as were Dyan Cannon and Julie Andrews). However, when the script was delayed, Poitier pulled out and was replaced by Clive Donner, a rather more probable choice given that he had already worked with Sellers on *What's New Pussycat* (1965). Also onboard was Donner's wife Jocelyn Rickards, who was set to design the costumes, and producer Danton (Dan) Rissner, who had already been involved in the most recent Panthers as United Artists' Executive Vice President in Charge of European Production, while Lynne Frederick was again down as an executive producer. Billed as "A madcap comedy

Double trouble. Bond meets the Panther in this audience-pleasing double bill of *The Spy Who Loved Me* (1977) and *The Pink Panther Strikes Again* (1976) (UA/Eon/Danjaq [Bond]/ UA/Amjo/Geoffrey 1964 [Panther]).

of crime and fun," the movie would also have co-starred Herbert Lom, Burt Kwouk, André Maranne, Graham Stark and the Dutch-born comedian Max Geldray, whose association with Sellers went all the way back to *The Goon Show* (1951–1960) and such TV series as *A Show Called Fred* (1956, TV) and *Son of Fred* (1956, TV).

The story would have seen Clouseau, now working as a private detective, become romantically involved with the Countess Anastasia Puissance, an international arch criminal also known as Le Frog, to be played by Pamela Stephenson, then riding high from her appearance in the hit British sketch show *Not the Nine O'Clock News* (1979–1981, TV). Hoping to guide Anastasia back to a life of honesty, Clouseau at first joins her on a series of escapades, among them the theft of an albino gorilla from Barcelona Zoo, before finally taking her up the aisle, only for the nuptials to be wrecked by one of Cato's impromptu attacks at the church. Sellers was to receive $3m for the picture ($1m for the script, $2m to star), while Blake Edwards was to receive $3m *not* to direct it, according to Marty Baum's assistant at CAA, Adam Fields, who also revealed, "Peter would call, usually at five from either his home in Gstaad or Paris, and would want to talk to Marty for an hour and a half, which meant I couldn't go home. He was either quitting the business or quitting *Panther* and every day Marty had to talk him off the cliff, because so much was riding on the movie, not just for the agency in terms of money but also for the importance to United Artists."[2] But it was not to be, as Sellers suffered a heart attack and died on 24 July 1980. He was just 54, and it seemed that the whole world mourned his loss ("Sellers is dead," ran the stark front-page headline in Britain's *Daily Star*).

Said Henry Mancini of the proposed film, "I didn't know about that, and I would thank heavens that it wasn't done. Mr. Donner is a fine director. I don't know if the chemistry would have been there, but we'll never know. It may have been."[3] Observed Edwards, "They got some pretty good people to do it [*Romance*]. They just didn't understand that you can't let Sellers take the reins."[4]

Following the actor's death, United Artists had hoped to persuade Dudley Moore, the star of Edwards' *10* (1979), to take over the role of Clouseau, but he and Blake were already planning a spy spoof for Orion titled *The Ferret*, in which a jazz musician assumes his father's role as a special agent for the United Nations after he has gone missing. Written by Edwards, Maurice Richlin, Stanley Shapiro and Tom and Frank Waldman, the film unfortunately stalled, and didn't see the light of day until it eventually emerged as an hour-long pilot on NBC in 1984, with Steve Guttenberg now starring as the musician Sam Valenti and Robert Loggia as his father Sam Sr., with support provided by Clive Revill, Sam Wanamaker, Sandahl Bergman, Brian Dennehy and Edwards' daughter Jennifer. Executive produced by Edwards via Blake Edwards Entertainment, Centerpoint Productions and DePatie-Freleng Enterprises, the film was helmed by Blake's former assistant director Terry Marcel and was scored by Henry Mancini. Unfortunately, it didn't go to series, and the pilot has since slipped into obscurity. Regarding the Clouseau offer, Moore eventually agreed to appear as the character as a one-off, to bring the franchise to a close, but insisted that Edwards be the director, but Blake refused to film Sellers' script, and instead came up with his own ideas on how to continue the series (he and Moore instead went on to work together again on *Micki + Maude* [1984]).

It had always irked Edwards that so much material from *The Pink Panther Strikes Again* (1976) had ended up on the cutting room floor (as has been noted, Sellers had refused to incorporate it into *Revenge*). Consequently, he came up with the notion to use the excised footage to create a new Sellers/Clouseau film, which would act as a bridge to another character then taking over. The idea was to shoot the two projects back to back on a combined budget of $17m, with some of the same sets and actors appearing in both films. In the first movie, *Trail of the*

Pink Panther (1982), to which $6m of the combined budget was allotted, a television reporter named Marie Jouvet would attempt to discover the whereabouts of Clouseau, who has gone missing, and in the course of her investigations, she would meet with many of the Inspector's former associates, who would reminisce about his past. In the follow-up, *Curse of the Pink Panther* (1983), the Sureté uses a computer to find the second best detective in the world to track down Clouseau, but Dreyfus rigs the program and they instead get an NYPD sergeant named Clifton Sleigh, who turns out to be the worst. The hope was that *Trail* would be released in December 1982, with *Curse* set to follow in the summer of 1983.

Both screenplays were written at the same time by Edwards, Tom and Frank Waldman, and Edwards' son Geoffrey (all of whom are credited on *Trail*, with Edwards and his son credited for *Curse*), with *Trail* going before the cameras on 15 February 1982 at Pinewood (where the film would be based), with location work in Paris, Nice and several other European locations to follow. Among those returning to the fray cast-wise were Herbert Lom, Burt Kwouk and André Maranne in their usual roles of Dreyfus, Cato and Duval, along with Graham Stark, reviving the role of Hercule from *A Shot in the Dark* (1964), plus, from the original Panther, David Niven as Sir Charles Litton and Capucine

Paws for thought. Poster artwork for *Trail of the Pink Panther* (1982) (UA/Amjo/Lakeline/Titan Productions/Blake Edwards Entertainment).

(formerly Madame Clouseau) as Lady Simone Litton (there is no sign of Claudine, Sir Charles' wife in *Return*). Also onboard were Joanna Lumley, fresh from her success with *The New Avengers* (1976–1977, TV) and *Sapphire and Steel* (1979–1982, TV), as Marie Jouvet, Robert Loggia as a French godfather named Bruno Langois (Loggia had already appeared as Al Marchione in *Revenge of the Pink Panther* [1978]) and Richard Mulligan as Clouseau's father (the actor, who had scored a hit on TV with the comedy *Soap* [1977–1981, TV], would go on to appear in two more films for Edwards, for whom he had recently appeared in *S.O.B.* [1981]). They were also joined by Lucca Mezzofanti as Clouseau aged eight, Daniel Peacock as Clouseau at the age of eighteen, Peter Arne, Ronald Fraser, Marne Maitland and Madlena Nedeva (as the previously unseen Mme. Dreyfus).

Back behind the cameras were production designer Peter Mullins, editor Alan Jones (again assisted by Edwards' son Geoffrey), producer Tony Adams (now producing alongside Blake), associate producer Gerald T. Nutting (who'd joined Edwards' team with *S.O.B.* [1981]), second unit director Terry Marcel, stunt coordinator Joe Dunne (who again doubled for Sellers, along with John Taylor, who had worked with the star on the Fu Manchu film) and cinematographer Dick Bush (who had joined Edwards with *Victor/Victoria* [1982], and who here shoots in Panavision and Technicolor). Interestingly, the costumes were in the hands of Edwards' first wife Patricia (who'd also provided the wardrobe for *10* [1979]), while the film's assistant casting director was Lucy Boulting, the daughter of producer and director John Boulting, who had worked with Sellers on several films, among them *I'm Alright Jack* (1959).

The movie, which was made via United Artists, Amjo, Lakeline, Titan Productions and Blake Edwards Entertainment, opens with the theft of the Pink Panther (again) and the request that Clouseau be assigned the case (again), to which end he travels to London to interview the Phantom (who he believes to be responsible), after which he is sent to Lugash to continue his investigations, only to disappear on the way. It is now that Marie Jouvet takes up her own investigation, among those she interviews being Dreyfus, Hercule, the Phantom, his wife Simone (Clouseau's former spouse), Cato and the Inspector's aged father. Given that Clouseau's disappearance has meant that the criminal underworld has been able to better operate in his absence, she also finds herself told to cease her enquiries by Bruno Langois, the French godfather.

After having Clouseau call in for his fitting at Professor Balls' disguise emporium, during which Edwards got to use the footage featuring

Harvey Korman and Liz Smith as Balls and his wife Martha, the plot then has him travelling to London to question Sir Charles (even though the Phantom lives in the South of France), which enabled the director to finally use all the remaining excised sequences from *Strikes Again*, including scenes of Clouseau's plane journey, during which, heavily disguised in bandages and a leg cast, he has troublesome encounters with an overweight female passenger and a toilet cubicle, and his London hotel, where he finds himself hanging from his bedroom window after being inadvertently pushed out by the maid. Scenes of him setting fire to his office, arriving home at his apartment encumbered by his grocery shopping and attempting to get a taxi to the airport are also included, but by the 37-minute mark, all of this material has been used, after which Jouvet's investigation dominates the remainder of the proceedings, which are accompanied by flashbacks to the earlier films, among them Cato's fight with the Inspector from *Strikes Again*, Clouseau's attack on Mr. Chong from *Revenge*, his blackboard summary of the Gambrelli case from *Shot*, and the inn and car chase scenes from the original Panther.

Said Henry Mancini of the footage available for *Trail*, "Everybody knew that what we had in the can was what we had in the can, and that was all there was going to be to play with. It was a kind of strange feeling. Some people thought it shouldn't have been done. But the ideas as Blake started to map them out seemed to work very well."[5] Of shooting the two new films without Sellers, Burt Kwouk admitted "Yes, I felt a bit odd doing them, I must say. Not so odd that I couldn't function, but yes, it seemed odd."[6] Graham Stark agreed, commenting, "It was a spooky sensation, but I'm a realist. I'm an actor. It was bizarre in a way, but you've got to understand—it's nice to be asked, and Lumley, who I adored, was in *Trail*. And a lot of other nice people."[7] Said Herbert Lom of the situation, "I was sorry that we had to carry on, but I suppose when something is a phenomenal world success, everybody wants to carry on, and I suppose I said, 'Okay, I'll do my best.'"[8]

Unfortunately, although it's intriguing to finally see all the cut material from *Strikes Again*, it quickly becomes apparent *why* it was cut: it just isn't up to standard. Had it been included the first time round, the film would have been bloated and unwieldy, bogged down by irrelevancies that would have slowed the pace and weakened the impact of the good stuff. Undeniably, there are some amusing moments, the best of which involves Clouseau being constantly pushed out of his hotel window by the turn down maid, which climaxes with the receptionist and his switchboard being pulled through the wall by the phone cable on which the Inspector is dangling, but the sets look cheap, and many of the scenes frustrate as much as they tickle the funny bone. Indeed, the encounter with Professor Balls goes on *far* too long and features a rather tactless joke about one of the fake noses Clouseau tries on ("It's from our Streisand line," reveals Balls), and the scene in which he gets stuck in the toilet cubicle on the plane is agony to watch.

Sadly, the new material isn't much better. A running joke about Dreyfus's swimming pool being filled with jello (a dream) or having its cover on when he dives in falls flat on its face, and the scenes with Clouseau's aged parent are just plain embarrassing (these include a pointless topless shot featuring two young women crushing grapes on his vineyard and a re-run of the ancient housekeeper gag from *10* [1979], with the servant here corralled across the room by the family dog). The sequences showing Clouseau's younger years add little to the mix (he manages to blow up himself rather than a bridge full of Nazis during the war), and the interviews with his contemporaries are undeniably on the dull side, and while it's nice to see the likes of Burt Kwouk, Graham Stark, David Niven and Capucine again, they are given far too little of consequence to do (although he looks well enough, Niven was in the early stages of motor neuron disease at the time of filming, and had to be dubbed by celebrity impersonator Rich Little who, lest we forget, had also provided vocals for the Pink Panther in two of the early cartoon shorts). As for the scenes from the earlier films, they are little more than padding (surely a retrospective featuring clips, outtakes and comments from the cast and crew along the lines of *That's Entertainment* [1974] would have been a better option?).

Of the performances, Herbert Lom comes off best as the perpetually frustrated Dreyfus (keep an eye out for Julie Andrews as a charwoman as he exits the office of his psychiatrist before falling down the stairs). Unfortunately Lumley, though charming to look at, flounders as Jouvet (her cod French accent isn't exactly the best), and her investigation is clearly on a hiding to nothing, and the film ends with a rearview shot of Clouseau on a cliff, looking out to sea, only to be shat on by a bird ("Swine seagull"), thus leaving the plot waiting to be taken up by *Curse*. Of the patchwork effect of *Trail* Burt Kwouk noted, "What's interesting for me about that film is to watch myself progressively get older. It's full of clips from the early films. 'Gee,' I thought. 'Who is that good looking young fella?' As the years went by—two decades almost—I could see that Cato was a sizeable chunk of my adult life. Herbie Lom doesn't seem to get a bit older. I don't understand that!"[9]

Thankfully, Henry Mancini's score, recorded at The Music Centre in Wembley between 5 and 6 August 1982, does much to tie all the disparate elements together, the highlight being "The Easy Life in Paris," which accompanies the scene in which Jouvet interviews Hercule on his boat. "The Inspector Clouseau Theme" from *Strikes Again* also gets a re-working in "The Bagman." However, "The Easy Life in Paris" and the main title theme were the only cues to appear on the accompanying soundtrack LP released by Liberty, which otherwise featured music from the previous films, among them "The Greatest Gift" from *Return*, "Hong Kong Fireworks" from *Revenge* and "It Had Better Be Tonight" from the first film, as well as the main title from *A Shot in the Dark*, previously available only as a single (a CD featuring the entire score for *Trail* eventually appeared many years later; it should also be noted that, in addition to the various official soundtrack LPs, the Panther theme itself became a concert staple and also appeared on such TV specials as *Mancini and Friends* [1987, TV], as well as such albums as *Henry Mancini Plays the Great Screen Hits* [1981], *Mancini Plays Mancini* [1984] and *James Galway & Henry Mancini—In the Pink* [1984], while the "Inspector Clouseau Theme" from *Strikes Again* appeared on *Mancini's Angels* [1977] and *Premier Pops* [1988], the latter of which also included "Hong Kong Fireworks" from *Revenge*).

As for the main credits for *Trail* (which contain the dedication "To Peter ... the one and only Inspector Clouseau"), they were again written and directed Arthur Leonardi (as per *Revenge*), albeit this time via Marvel Productions. "Based on the David H. DePatie and Friz Freleng animated characters," as we are informed, they as usual feature the Panther and Clouseau in conflict with the expected bombs and guns. They are also depicted as Pac-man like characters, chomping away at each other and the scenery, while the cheekiest moment has Clouseau appear to urinate over Edwards' story credit, only for him to turn around and reveal that he is using a fire extinguisher. Perhaps the weakest of the title animations, they generally lack the invention of the previous films, save for an over-extended moment of would-be cleverness where the Panther makes use of a piece of fluff supposedly caught in the lens (a hair in the gate) to spin a cat's cradle with which to capture Clouseau. At least the end credits are accompanied by a selection of comic highlights from the previous films, among them many of the disasters, calamities and humiliations Clouseau has suffered down the years (the globe gags, the fights with Cato, the bombs, the parallels, etc.), while things come to a conclusion with a promotion for the follow-up ("Coming Soon *Curse of the Pink Panther*"). As for the poster, it featured Clouseau trailing the Panther's footprints with a magnifying glass, accompanied by the tag line, "There is only one Inspector Clouseau. His adventure continues..." along with a secondary line that claimed the film to be "The newest and funniest 'Panther' of them all." The narration for the movie's trailer meanwhile encouraged audiences to "Follow the trail of the world's greatest detective."

With filming for both movies completed by 15 June 1982, *Trail* went into post-production and was ready for release in December 1982 as intended, being distributed with a PG rating by UIP in the UK and MGM/UA in the U.S. on 3 and 17 December respectively. Unfortunately, despite the poster's the enticements, and a tribute program to the series titled *Bob Hope's Pink Panther Thanksgiving Gala* (1982, TV), which aired on NBC on 21 November 1982, and which featured Julie Andrews, Dudley Moore, Robert Preston and Robert Wagner, along with clips from *The Pink Panther, A Shot in the Dark, Strikes Again* and *Revenge*, audiences generally shunned the picture, which eventually went on to make $9,056,073 worldwide, of which it earned just $1,341,695 in the U.S. on its opening weekend across 800 theaters, which didn't bode well for the imminent release of the follow-up, which was waiting in the wings.

The New York Times reviewed the movie quite favorably, describing it as "an uproarious retrospective," though it did admit that "not all of the material is terrific." Rather more dubious was *Variety*, which called it "a thin, peculiar picture unsupported by the number of laughs one is accustomed to in this series," adding that it was "by a long way the slightest of the of the six Inspector Clouseau efforts" Sellers had appeared in. Said Graham Stark of the finished film, "I realised afterwards it was a gigantic mistake. It couldn't work."[10] If that weren't enough, Sellers' widow Lynne Frederick sued UA and Lakeline (after an eventual nineteen day hearing in London in 1985, a judge ruled that *Trail* breached the Performers' Protection Act and awarded her $1m in damages, soon after followed by an additional $475,000 in interest).

All of which brings us to *Curse of the Pink Panther* (1983), which as has been noted, was made back to back with *Trail* via UA, Titan, Jewel and Blake Edwards Entertainment. Said Graham Stark of the situation, "It was the old tradition of the show must go on."[11] Again based at Pinewood and featuring scenes shot in such destinations as New York, Valencia (taking advantage of the Las Fallas festival), Paris and the South of France, the film not only sees the Pink Panther diamond stolen (yet again), but also follows the catastrophic exploits of the dim-witted New York cop, Sergeant Clifton Sleigh, who has been assigned the task of tracking down the missing Clouseau. As the story progresses a number of familiar characters are featured, among them Sir Charles Litton (David Niven, who gets top billing and is again voiced by Rich Little), his wife Simone (Capucine) and his nephew George (Robert Wagner), who all end up in possession of the diamond, which may or may

Leap of faith. Poster artwork for *Curse of the Pink Panther* (1983) (UA/Titan/Jewel/Blake Edwards Entertainment).

not have been originally stolen by Clouseau. Also featured are Dreyfus (Herbert Lom), Cato (Burt Kwouk), Duval (André Maranne), Professor Balls (Harvey Korman) and the French godfather Bruno Langois (Robert Logia), all of whom appear in newly shot scenes. Also returning are Joanna Lumley, albeit somewhat confusingly as a different character named Countess Chandra, Graham Stark, this time as a bored waiter, and Peter Arne as Colonel Bufoni, as whom he'd appeared briefly in *Trail*.

As Sleigh, the film introduced Tess Wass to the screen fresh from his success in the hit sitcom *Soap* (1977–1981, TV), in which he'd co-starred with Richard Mulligan (Clouseau's father from *Trail*), although Edwards had originally approached both Dudley Moore (again) and John Ritter for the role, for which Rowan Atkinson had also been considered, though rejected by MGM (he'd go on to play the equally blundersome Johnny English in a series of films beginning in 2003). The supporting cast includes the likes of Leslie Ash, Michael Elphick, Bill Nighy, Danny Schiller (returning to the role of Balls' assistant Cunny, whom he'd already played in *Revenge* and *Trail* [using the cut scenes from *Strikes Again*, which means he played the character with both Graham Stark *and* Harvey Korman]), Steve Franken (the drunken waiter from *The Party* [1968] who'd also appeared in Sellers' final film *The Fiendish Plot of Dr. Fu Manchu* [1980]), Mollie Maureen (who'd appeared in *Return* as the old lady whose apartment is bombed), Herb Tanney (billed as Sidi Bin Tanney), Emma Walton Hamilton (Julie Andrews' daughter with her first husband Tony Walton), Ed Parker (making a re-appearance as the deadly Mr. Chong from *Revenge*), Patricia (Patti) Davis (the daughter of Nancy and Ronald Reagan, Davis being her mother's maiden name) and Denise Crosby (granddaughter of Bing, again as Bruno Langois' moll, whom she had played in *Trail* following a brief appearance in *10* [1979], and who would go on to become the second of Geoffrey Edwards' three wives). James Bond legend Roger Moore also appears as a character we are led to believe is Clouseau, who has undergone a change of identity (Moore, who is billed as Turk Thrust II in reference to Bryan Forbes' credit for *A Shot in the Dark* [1964], filmed his scenes immediately following the completion of his latest Bond opus *Octopussy* [1983]).

Incredibly, Wass was signed to appear in a total of six Panther films, the plan being to retire the original running cast of characters (Dreyfus, Duval, Cato, Balls, etc.) from the series following this introductory escapade, with Pat Corley (later known as Phil in *Murphy Brown* [1988–1998, TV]), here playing Lieutenant Palmyra, taking over the frustrated authority figure as Sleigh's boss, whose assistant is a hip young black officer named Charlie, here played by Joe Morton (soon to find fame as the lead in *The Brother from Another Planet* [1984]). Edwards' assistant director Terry Marcel was set to take over the directorial reigns with the next episode, with Tony Adams producing from a script by

Geoffrey Edwards and Sam Bernard, the intention being that a new Panther would appear every three years. All big plans, but they all came to naught when *Curse* crashed and burned at the box office.

Recalled Roger Moore of his involvement with the film, "In *The Curse of the Pink Panther*, Clouseau is tracked down, in the final reel, to some mountain-top lair guarded by Joanna Lumley. There, having stolen the Pink Panther diamond and with his head bandaged after the plastic surgery that gave him a new identity, I was to be revealed as the new look of post-surgery Clouseau. Blake said they could film at Pinewood at the tail end of *Octopussy*. I figured it would be a five-day engagement, and as they were offering $100,000 a day, it seemed pretty attractive. However, the buggers worked me from morning till night and filmed it all in just one day. I enjoyed hamming it up and attempting the funny French accent. I don't think the film received much of a release though, and that was that."[12]

"You know, François, I have a horrible feeling we're seeing history repeat itself," says Dreyfus from his hospital bed after Sleigh has tripped across the room upon their first meeting, crashing into the Chief Inspector's desk and sending him backwards out of the window to land in an ornamental pond below. Indeed, the film is very much a repeat of

Blast off. Dreyfus (Herbert Lom) aims and fires at the bumbling Clifton Sleigh in *Curse of the Pink Panther* (1983) (UA/Titan/Jewel/Blake Edwards Entertainment).

9. The Trail Goes Cold   155

the established recipe, with the rather tedious plot punctuated at regular intervals with elaborate stunts, chases and pratfalls, best among them Sleigh opening his umbrella as he exits an airport only to be blown away by the force of the storm outside, and the now wheelchair-bound Dreyfus's attempt to blow up his new nemesis with a rocket launcher, only to be propelled backwards over the edge of a cliff and into the sea. Some of the dialogue even manages a little of the old sparkle. "Is that Sleigh as in kill?" queries Dreyfus of the Sergeant's surname, to which comes the reply, "No, it's Sleigh as in one-horse open." Unfortunately, these are but momentary distractions, the rest of the film being a rather tired rehash of former glories, with Moore's appearance as the "new" Clouseau adding little to the proceedings. Indeed, a scene in which he removes an ice bucket that has become stuck on Sleigh's head only for it to end up rammed on his own is a real squirmer to sit through. As for his French accent, one could hardly call it consistent, but he at least seems to be having fun.

Elsewhere, Lom is in fine form as Dreyfus, suffering through all the indignities that Edwards can throw at him, but as in the previous outing, his fellow co-stars are given far too little to do, so that despite the glamorous locations, the film is a somewhat patchy affair that somehow lacks pace, despite the work of Edwards' favorite editor, Ralph E. Winters, officially back with the series for the first time since *A Shot in the Dark* (1964), though he had worked on several other Edwards productions in the interim (including some uncredited work on *Trail*). As for Wass's performance as Sleigh, he proves to be affable enough, but, as written, his character is more of a supporting player than a leading man, and while he bumbles and fumbles his way through the action with enthusiasm, including an extended sequence in which he finds himself paragliding over the French coast, he in no way comparable to Sellers, whose presence is sorely missed.

As always, Henry Mancini's tuneful score, which was recorded at The Music Centre in Wembley between 12 and 13 September 1982, does much to hold things together, though this time there would be no album release (a CD would eventually appear some years later). As always, the Panther theme itself gets a make-over during the credits, which are again written and directed by Arthur Leonardi via Marvel, and animated by such old hands as Virgil Ross and Warren Batchelder. This time, the super computer Dreyfus uses to select Sleigh is the focus of the action, and Mancini peppers his theme with synth embellishments to represent its inner workings (note that in the film, Geoffrey Edwards provides the voice of Aldous, the super computer). There's also a "Clifton Sleigh Theme" for the new man on the block, and like "The Inspector

Clouseau Theme" from *Strikes Again* (which was revived for *Trail*), it's a rather melancholy affair, and is reminiscent of the composer's "Cat and Mouse" theme from *Victor/Victoria* (1982). The score also references Mancini's earlier hit, "Moon River."

The trailer for the film concentrated on the introduction of its new leading man ("Introducing Ted Wass as Detective Sergeant Clifton Sleigh in Blake Edwards' *Curse of the Pink Panther*," heralded the narrator), while the poster featured the character mid-air, holding onto the strings of a parachute for dear life ("He's been bombed, blasted and plugged in the parachute.... Is this any way to welcome the World's Greatest Detective?" ponders the tag line). The film was released with a PG rating in the U.S. by MGM/UA on 12 August 1983 and by UIP in the UK on 30 November 1983 and went on to earn a paltry worldwide take of just $4,491,986. Generally speaking, the reviews were poor. "The most tedious of the whole series," sniped the *Monthly Film Bulletin*, while *Sight and Sound* described it as "another bout of film-making as grave robbing." Elsewhere, *The New York Times* found that the film had "very little reason to exist," though on a positive note, the *LA Times* described it as "simple, unadulterated fun." As with *Trail*, the film was subject to a lawsuit, with Edwards himself this time filing against MGM/UA for insufficiently promoting it. In turn, MGM/UA filed against Edwards for alleged budget overruns, to which Edwards responded by filing for libel (the various claims and counter claims were eventually settled out of court in 1988). All in all, it was a sad way for the series to end. But it turned out there was still life in the old Panther yet...

In 1989, a television pilot was made by CBS for a proposed half-hour series with the title *The New Pink Panther*, in which a young TV reporter teams up with the animated Pink Panther to solve a series of arson attacks, among them one in the movie theater where he is watching a Pink Panther cartoon, during which the Panther steps off the screen to rescue him. In part inspired by the recent success of *Who Framed Roger Rabbit* (1988), the program, which was scripted by Bill Dial and Gina Goldman, was directed by TV veteran Gary Nelson, whose features included *Freaky Friday* (1976) and *The Black Hole* (1979). It starred Charlie Schlatter as the reporter, with support provided by Teri Hatcher, Tim Stack and Lisa Waltz. Unfortunately, a regime change at the studio meant that the pilot never even made it to air, and the series was subsequently scrapped (note that *Roger Rabbit* won a special achievement Oscar for its animator, Richard Williams, who had provided the dazzling title sequences for *Return* and *Strikes Again*). Recalled Charlie Schlatter of the junked pilot, "It was really, really funny. I have to say, that's like one of the few things in my life that I look back at and go,

God, I wish that was given a fair chance, you know, because it was such a sweet show. There was so much heart in it, too."[13] Interestingly, the same year, Blake Edwards instigated plans to bring the franchise back to the big screen, though it would eventually be ten years after the release of *Curse* that *Son of the Pink Panther* (1993) finally made it into theaters.

Despite their differences over the release of *Curse*, MGM/UA, which co-owned the rights to the Panther franchise with Edwards, encouraged the director to pursue his plans for *Son*, but the project came to a temporary halt when the Italian financier Giancarlo Parretti acquired the studio, which consequently became MGM-Pathé, against whom Edwards filed a suit for reneging on the offer to finance the latest installment. Things were back on track, however, when Alan Ladd, Jr., regained control of the company, leaving the way clear for Edwards to proceed as planned.

As the title indicates, the story this time involves the exploits of Clouseau's illegitimate son, Jacques Gambrelli, the result of the Inspector's liaison with Maria Gambrelli, and a search was launched to find a suitable actor to play the role. Among those Edwards had hoped to snag for the part were Kevin Kline, Rowan Atkinson and Gérard Depardieu. Tim Curry had also been a consideration, and his likeness even appeared in some early concept artwork, while Bronson Pinchot also expressed interest in the role. The director finally settled on the Italian comic actor Roberto Benigni, then little known in America, whose most recent film was the mob comedy *Johnny Stecchino* (1991), which had broken box office records in Italy. To support Benigni, several of the old guard were brought back, including Herbert Lom as Dreyfus, Burt Kwouk as Cato and Graham Stark (who'd since appeared for Edwards in *Blind Date* [1987]) as Dr. Balls (note that the previous year, Lom had played "Komisar Dreyfus" in a forty-minute TV show titled *Sherlock Holmes v panskem klubu aneb Komisar Dreyfus zasahuje* [1992, TV, rough translation *Sherlock Holmes in the Gentleman's Club, or Commissioner Dreyfus Intervenes*], which he made in his home country of Czechoslovakia).

The film also saw the return of Claudia Cardinale to the series for the first time since *The Pink Panther* (1963), although here she is somewhat confusingly cast as Maria Gambrelli, the role previously played by Elke Sommer in *A Shot in the Dark* (1964). Also onboard were Robert Davi, Debrah Farentino (who married the third of her four husbands, Panther producer Tony Adams, during production), Anton Rodgers, Henry Goodman, Nadim Sawalha, Herb Tanney (billed as Sputare Tanney), Edwards' daughter Jennifer Edwards (who'd already appeared in several of her father's non–Panther films) and Liz Smith (returning as

Dr. Balls' wife, a role she'd already played in *Trail* [in clips from taken *Strikes Again*] and *Curse*). Familiar faces behind the cameras included producer Tony Adams, cinematographer Dick Bush, production designer Peter Mullins, construction manager Tony Graysmark, stunt coordinator Joe Dunne and composer Henry Mancini, with Edwards' son Geoffrey this time working as the second unit director.

Based at Pinewood and made via UA, International Traders, Zaman and Filmauro (which was run by Aurelio De Laurentiis, nephew of the legendary Dino De Laurentiis), shooting on the $28m production ($13.8 of which came from Filmauro) began in Nice on 8 June 1992, with location work subsequently taking place in Monaco, Italy and Jordan. The plot was based on a story by Edwards, which he subsequently scripted with Steve and Madeline Sunshine, who had worked as both writers and executive producers on episodes of the sitcom *Julie* (1992, TV) which had starred Edwards' wife Julie Andrews, and which he had directed. An abduction scenario, it sees the kidnapping of Princess Yasmin of Lugash (Farentino) by a group of terrorists led by Hans Zarba (Davi), whose motive is to persuade her father to abdicate, thus making way for her stepmother's lover, a disgraced general, to claim the throne. Given that the kidnapping took place off the coast of Nice in the territorial waters of France, Dreyfus is assigned the case, in which a bumbling local gendarme called Jacques Gambrelli becomes involved, having spotted the Princess in the kidnappers' van. Zarba makes plans to have

Relative values. (From left) Herbert Lom, Claudia Cardinale and Roberto Benigni in a scene from *Son of the Pink Panther* (1993) (UA/International Traders/Zaman/Filmauro).

the young copper killed, but he is saved by Dreyfus, who returns him home safely to his mother, who he realizes is the beautiful suspect in the murder case he worked on almost thirty years earlier, and who reveals that the boy's father is in fact Jacques Clouseau.

After an explosion at the house instigated by the terrorists in which Dreyfus is injured, Gambrelli decides to take on the case himself and rescue the Princess. However, when Zarba moves her to a safe house in Lugash, Gambrelli consults with his father's old friends and, with disguises provided by Dr. Balls, he and Cato travel to Lugash to rescue the Princess, who they discover is being kept locked up in a castle. Having staged a daring rescue with the aid of the military, Gambrelli is hailed a hero, and receives a promotion, allowing him to become an inspector in the Sureté like his father. In the meantime, Dreyfus and Gambrelli's mother have fallen in love and become engaged, and at the wedding reception, Maria reveals that in addition to a new stepson, Dreyfus will also have a stepdaughter, the equally blundersome Jacqueline (played by Benigni's wife Nicoletta Braschi), given that she had borne Clouseau twins! The film concludes with Gambrelli receiving a special medal from Princess Yasmin and her grateful father, but the ceremony ends in chaos thanks to his inherited clumsiness, proving him to be very much the son of Clouseau ("He's just like his father," says Maria at one point).

Filming was completed by 12 September 1992, with the work in the heat of Jordan having proved particularly difficult for the company. Post-production was a fairly straightforward affair, with the editing of the picture in the hands of Robert Pergament, who'd been promoted from working as an assistant editor under Ralph E. Winters on several films for Edwards before becoming his preferred cutter with *A Fine Mess* (1986). It was during this period that a scene featuring Clouseau's ghost, played by Andy Scourfield, was deleted from the film, along with a scene featuring a character called Marcel Langois, played by Tony Kirwood (though both remain listed in the end credits). The main titles were also filmed by Geoffrey Edwards via Desert Music Pictures at this time. Made at a cost of $1m, the sequence, which offers a high tech blend of animation, computer graphics and live action, was an update of the old formula and sees the Pink Panther and Jacques Gambrelli come to blows in a studio where the Panther is trying to record the film's theme tune, which was given another update care of Henry Mancini, who can be seen at the top of the sequence handing his baton to the Panther. Said the composer, "We're going to be doing the Pink Panther theme in a very unusual way—Bobby McFerrin is going to do an *a cappella* version of it, and they are going to animate the titles to that!"[14] The "Don't Worry, Be

Happy" vocalist is also featured in the sequence himself, which was produced by Jeffrey Tinnell, with animation provided by Chris Hummel and Darlie Brewster.

In the run up to scoring the movie, Mancini felt that it had potential, commenting, "The script is very good, the film has a great cast, and I'm obviously looking forward to working on the music. Leslie Bricusse and I have already written one song called 'God Bless Clouseau.'"[15] In fact, Mancini retained his enthusiasm for the series right to the end, especially as it allowed him to carry on with his own particular brand of scoring, which at the time was somewhat out of vogue. Said the composer, "Now we have the crash and bash syndrome with all of the action pictures, and sometimes in those pictures you really don't know where the music starts and the sound effects end! It's a style—not particularly *my* style—but it's a style!"[16] Here, the score, which was released on CD by Milan and recorded by the National Philharmonic Orchestra at the Air Studios in London between 18 and 21 January 1993, features a number of cues comparable to his best work for the series, among them the energetic "The Bike Chase," the ethereal "The Dreamy Princess" (with its floaty flutes and harp *glissandi*), the darkly comical "Rendezvous with Cato" and the touchingly romantic "Mama and Dreyfus," as well as such "local color" pieces as "Belly Up" and "Belly Down." It concludes with a more traditional version of the Panther theme, with the tenor sax solo this time performed by Phil Todd (note that "God Bless Clouseau" is listed as "Clouseau's Anthem" in the film's end credits).

The film was released with a PG rating by MGM/UA in the U.S. on 27 August 1993 and by UIP in the UK on 26 December 1993. "Clumsy has a color all its own," exclaimed one of the posters, which featured Benigni being held up by the Panther (using his finger as a gun), while the trailer revealed, "He's got the same legendary courage, the same powers of deduction, the same taste for adventure. The French have a word for a man like this." Unfortunately, the movie failed to revive the franchise, and took a paltry $2.4m in the U.S. and Canada, where audiences proved indifferent to its existence, perhaps because Clouseau's thunder had recently been stolen by the comic exploits, both verbal and physical, of another bumbling cop, Frank Drebin (Leslie Nielsen), in *The Naked Gun* (1988) and its sequels. However, it proved to be a runaway hit in Italy, where it made an astonishing $18m. Outside his home country, though, audiences failed to warm to Benigni, who was nominated for a Razzie as "worst new star," though he would eventually go on to win a best actor Oscar for his performance in *Life Is Beautiful* (1997), which he also co-wrote and directed, earning additional Oscar nominations for best screenplay and director.

9. The Trail Goes Cold

Commented the *LA Times*, "Blake Edwards hasn't exactly rung in a new era by casting Italian superstar comic Roberto Benigni in the title role.... He's frenetic in a charmless, groggy way. His squiggly mimetic movements don't add up to a character, just a conceit." It

The son also rises. Poster artwork featuring Roberto Benigni for *Son of the Pink Panther* (1993) (UA/International Traders/Zaman/Filmauro).

went on to conclude, "Edwards actually sets the stage at the end for a sequel. Is there anybody out there who would want to see it? More to the point, would Edwards want to *make* it? His work here is so spiritless that the idea of his doing a sequel is positively harrowing. Either that or it's the best joke in the movie." *Variety* was more upbeat about the new star, commenting, "Benigni's the major asset, but his vast talents are underutilized." However, the review came to a similar conclusion to that of the *LA Times*, noting, "It may be a good idea to put the Pink Panther to rest."

To be fair, the film looks reasonably good thanks to the lensing of Dick Bush (shooting in Panavision and Agfa/DeLuxe), and the comic highlights are well enough staged by Edwards. Performance-wise, Benigni undeniably has a certain rough-around-the-edges charm, and clearly devotes a good deal of manic energy to the proceedings, while it's nice to see the old guard back doing their familiar shtick one last time, with a romantic payoff for Lom's Dreyfus (albeit with the burden of not one but *two* of Clouseau's offspring!). Otherwise, the film is definitely a rehash of former glories. Observed Burt Kwouk of Benigni's take on the role, "Peter was a much more subtle Clouseau than Roberto, who is a much more physical actor. Also, Peter's crazy accent, because he was an actor who spoke perfect English, was much funnier than Benigni's, who naturally has an accent. The best funny foreign accents are done by people who speak English perfectly!"[17] Said Graham Stark of the comic, "I loved him. I thought he was delightful, but again I come back to this cliché, the memory is too powerful. Peter was so good that I don't think anyone can now take over. But I was a great fan of Benigni's."[18]

Of the film's poor performance, Herbert Lom revealed that he was "Very disappointed. But it was no surprise to me. I knew it while we were making it."[19] Admitted Blake Edwards, "It wasn't a good Panther. Benigni was great, but it wasn't the Panther. It just wasn't his. He didn't speak English very well and I certainly don't speak good Italian, and unless you have that contact.... I had that admiration for him, and he for me, but unless you have that twinned, joined at the cortex sense of humor, it somehow just doesn't work."[20] Indeed, when asked had the film been a success if he would have done any more Panthers with Benigni, Edwards replied, "I doubt it."[21] As a consequence, Edwards finally decided to call it a day with the series, albeit with a caveat. "I've signed off on them. If they do any more, it'll be the studio. However, I have held on to the rights to do it on the stage, because I have some ideas for that. Now might be the time to do that. I may just get very commercial and have a good time!"[22] Instead, he brought his hit musical *Victor/Victoria*

Treading the boards. Cover artwork for the stage version of *The Pink Panther Strikes Again* (1981) (William Gleason/The Dramatic Publishing Company/UA/Amjo/Geoffrey 1964).

(1982) to the Broadway stage in 1995, again starring his wife Julie Andrews, which he also filmed for video.

Son ultimately proved to be Edwards' last big screen movie, despite plans to make a project titled *Luck* with Kevin Kline, whom he'd hoped to cast as Jacques Gambrelli. Yet as late as 2002 he was still talking up the possibility of a stage Panther, though it should be noted that a play version of *The Pink Panther Strikes Again* had already been penned in 1981 by William Gleason for college and community theater groups to perform (the 85 page script was published by The Dramatic Publishing Company). Said Edwards of his own plans, "The Pink Panther, bless his greedy little heart, has provided me with a comfortable life.... Now we're gonna do a musical. We've got a book, we've got a score, looks like we've got the money,"[23] he told Larry King during a TV interview. Sadly, it was not to be. And even if it had gone ahead, it would have been without his most frequent collaborator, Henry Mancini, who'd passed away in 1994, thus making *Son* his own final movie (the score for the show that Edwards referred to was by Mancini's old collaborator Leslie Bricusse, who had provided lyrics for *Revenge* and *Son* as well as *Victor/Victoria* [1982]). Said Edwards of his association with Mancini on the film series, "It was a marriage made in heaven. It also helped that he had that kind of humor, too."[24] Said lyricist Leslie Bricusse of him, "Very few movie composers are great melody writers, and Hank was prime among them. John Williams, John Barry and Burt Bacharach share this gift,"[25] to which he added of Mancini's best known tunes, "You smile as they start, like the opening of the 'Pink Panther Theme'—it couldn't be anybody else."[26]

As for Edwards' remembrance of his hot and cold association with his friend and adversary Peter Sellers while working on the Panthers, he commented, "He was crazy. And out of this craziness blossomed this genius,"[27] to which he added of the star's behavior, "You couldn't like him. You might feel sorry for him, or like something he'd done, but to truly like the man? He was not a likeable man. And there were times when it almost bordered on being evil."[28] That said, good times were clearly had during the making of the movies, given the almost constant laughter on set. Admitted Edwards, "The outtakes are to die for. They really are. It's the best entertainment you'll ever have."[29] Meanwhile, of his most famous and lucrative creation, the Pink Panther itself, he observed, "I have a great fondness for the Panther, obviously. It made me independently wealthy for one thing, which ain't a bad reason. But more than that, it was a major turning point in my career."[30]

Indeed, the Panther *was* a valuable property, and though Edwards himself had now stepped away from the franchise, there were others keen to take it forward in a new direction…

10

Panther Resurrectus

As early as 1996, just three years after the release of *Son of the Pink Panther* (1993), plans were already in motion to reboot the franchise. Among those who were considered for the role of Clouseau were A-list comedy stars Robin Williams and Jim Carrey, both of whom seemed entirely credible suggestions. Unfortunately, the plans fizzled, though Carrey, a big Edwards fan, did go on to present the director with his 2004 honorary Oscar in recognition of his body of work as a writer, director and producer (during the presentation, Carrey impersonated Sellers as Hrundi V. Bakshi and Clouseau, and heaped praise on the director, describing *A Shot in the Dark* [1964] as "the perfect comedy,"[1] while Edwards made his entrance sporting a leg cast and riding a supercharged wheelchair across stage and crashing through a Styrofoam wall, grabbing his Oscar from Carrey as he passed him by—he was 82 at the time).

Sellers himself meanwhile continued to intrigue audiences and comedy historians alike, resulting in such tributes and documentaries as *Sellers' Best?* (1992, TV), in which Graham Stark, Bryan Forbes and Spike Milligan were among the talking heads recalling their much-missed friend, and *The Peter Sellers Story* (1995, TV), an all-encompassing three-part study care of the BBC's *Arena* strand, whose episodes (*Southsea to Shepperton*, *Jack to Jacques* and *I Am Not a Funny Man*) followed his career in detail, from his early years through to the Panthers and beyond, and featured interviews with Blake Edwards, Herbert Lom, Burt Kwouk, David Lodge, Graham Stark, Elke Sommer, Lesley-Anne Down and Robert Wagner, along with plenty of clips and behind the scenes footage, including material shot during the making of *The Return of the Pink Panther* (the three segments were later edited together into *The Peter Sellers Story: As He Filmed It* [2000, TV]).

In 2000, there were further rumblings regarding a reboot when Kevin Spacey was offered the role of Clouseau by MGM, but he turned it down, while in 2001 it appeared that Mike Myers had been sought to fill Sellers' shoes in a film potentially titled *Birth of the Pink Panther* with Ivan Reitman set to produce and direct. However, at this stage, there was only one confirmed casting choice, that of Herbert Lom, who was set to reprise Dreyfus for the eighth time. Said the actor of the situation, "A script has been written and filming is planned for later this year in Hollywood. They've offered me my old part and I've given the nod. In fact I've been nodding ever since."² The screenplay is said to have involved the theft of the Panther diamond by a heavily indebted fashion designer, but the film failed to appear, despite reports from *Variety* of a potential Christmas 2002 release care of MGM (as with *The New Pink Panther*, there was a suggestion, care of the *Calgary Sun*, that the animated Panther would be a part of the main action as well as the credits, while *Variety* reported Myers' fee to be an estimated $20m).

However, Clouseau *did* return to the screen in 2004, albeit not in a revival of the series. The film in question was the biopic *The Life and Death of Peter Sellers* (2004), in which the tortured comedy star is portrayed by the Oscar-winning Australian character actor Geoffrey Rush (Steve Coogan, Sacha Baron Cohen, Kevin Spacey and Robin Williams had also been considered for the role). Based upon the acclaimed biography by Roger Lewis and made by HBO and the BBC in association with The DeMann Entertainment Company and Company Pictures, it follows Sellers' rise to stardom via *The Goon Show* (1951–1960) and his early films before going on to cover his introduction to Edwards on *The Pink Panther* (1963) and their fractious working relationship thereafter.

Sadly, though a fairly extravagant production, both the script by Christopher Markus and Stephen McFeely and the direction by Stephen Hopkins include a number of distracting indulgences and affectations, while the factual narrative regarding the Panthers isn't always adhered to (for example, *Strikes Again* is shown as being the comeback Panther rather than *Return*, while a rant by Sellers against Edwards at the premiere of *Strikes Again* is pure fiction given that Sellers wasn't even there for it; the alternate BBC edit meanwhile makes it appear that the salty Swedish sea dog character is a part of *Strikes Again* rather than the later *Revenge*). A starry affair, the film also features Emily Watson as Sellers' first wife Anne, Miriam Margolyes as his mother Peg, Peter Vaughan as his father Bill, Sonia Aquino as Sophia Loren, Stanley Tucci as Stanley Kubrick, Charlize Theron as Sellers' second wife Britt Ekland, Stephen Fry as his advisor Maurice Woodruff, Henry Goodman as his agent Dennis Selinger, Nigel Havers as David Niven, Tom Wu as Burt Kwouk and John Lithgow as Blake Edwards.

Key scenes from many of Sellers' films are featured in the movie, and though a great deal of time and effort clearly went into the production, it's an often misguided and depressing affair, yet following its TV premiere in the U.S. on HBO on 5 December 2004, it went on to earn sixteen Emmy nominations, of which it won nine, among them best actor, director and script. Released theatrically elsewhere, it also appeared at a number of major film festivals, including Cannes, Edinburgh and Aspen ("Never judge a man by his cover," ran one of taglines, while another claimed, "Life is being someone else"). However, not everyone was smitten with the end results. "An adventurously conceived biopic of the late comic actor that, in the end, just doesn't convince," noted *Variety*, while *Sight and Sound* observed, "Director Hopkins, it seems, has minimal faith in his audience; time and again, his film doesn't just nudge us, but rams an elbow into our ribs while chortling fruitily in our ears." However, Blake Edwards is said to have been particularly impressed by Rush's performance, claiming that he thought he was watching the real Sellers in some shots.

The movie certainly helped to revive memories of Sellers and Clouseau, as did the 2004 release of *The Pink Panther Film Collection*, a DVD box set featuring *The Pink Panther, A Shot in the Dark, Strikes Again,*

Best Sellers. Geoffrey Rush is featured in the poster for *The Life and Death of Peter Sellers* **(2004) (HBO/BBC Films/The DeMann Entertainment Company/Company Pictures).**

Revenge and *Trail*, along with such bonuses as two new documentaries, *The Pink Panther Story* (2003) and *Behind the Feline—The Cartoon Phenomenon* (2003), both of which featured interviews with Blake Edwards and various other Panther personnel (Edwards also provided a commentary for the first film). TV also continued to be fascinated by Sellers, resulting in such programs as *The Unknown Peter Sellers* (2000, TV), another career overview which was also included as a bonus in the Panther box set, *The Paranormal Peter Sellers* (2002, TV), which explored his fascination with the occult and spiritualism, *Legends: Peter Sellers* (2002, TV), *Living Famously* (2003, TV), *Behind the Laughter* (2003, TV), *Somebody's Daughter, Somebody's Son* (2004, TV) and the Italian *Profondo Rosa—La vera storia della Pantera Rosa* (2004, TV [*Deep Pink—The True Story of the Pink Panther*]), another retrospective, this time hosted by Burt Kwouk, all of which helped to set the stage for the official return of the franchise, which finally occurred with *The Pink Panther* (2006), in which the character of Clouseau is played by Sellers fan Steve Martin, who, lest we forget, had attended the Hawaiian junket to launch *Revenge* (Chris Tucker was an alternate consideration for the role).

Written by Len Blum and Martin himself from a story by Blum and Michael Saltzman, the film, originally to have been titled *Birth of the Pink Panther* (as per the proposed Mike Myers reboot), was produced by Robert Simonds and helmed by Shawn Levy, both of whom had previously worked with the star on the 2003 remake of the 1950 comedy *Cheaper by the Dozen* (Martin seemed to have a penchant for remakes, having already appeared in *Father of the Bride* [1991] and its sequel, *Sgt. Bilko* [1996] and *The Out-of-Towners* [1999] among others). Budgeted at an astonishing $80m (more than all the other Panthers combined), the new Panther was made via MGM, Columbia and Robert Simonds Productions, as well as uncredited involvement from International Production Company and The Montecito Picture Company (the latter run by Tom Pollock and Ivan Reitman [who had been involved with the proposed Mike Myers reboot]), and began shooting on 10 May 2004 on locations in France, Italy and the Czech Republic, as well as on the back lot at Universal.

This time, the plot sees Clouseau assigned by Chief Inspector Charles Dreyfus to investigate the death of the French football coach Yves Glaunt following a game between France and China, during which his priceless ring bearing the fabled Pink Panther diamond also goes missing. Dreyfus's intention is that Clouseau be a distraction for the press while his own crack team, led by Gilbert Ponton, a far more clued up gendarme, solve the case and earn him a much desired Legion d'honneur, while at the same time keeping an eye on the bumbling Inspector ("Together we are going to catch a killer," vows Clouseau to Ponton upon their first meeting). Suspects include the coach's glamorous pop star girlfriend Xania (faint echoes of the Gambrelli case from *Shot*) and her former boyfriend, a player named Bizu, who had blamed Glaunt for stealing the singer from him, and though things don't always go Clouseau's way, he finally wins the day, proving Dreyfus's assertion that the Chinese envoy Dr. Pang was responsible for the crime to be wrong, and that the real culprit is Yuri, the football team's trainer, who had felt that his contribution to their success had been ignored. Meanwhile, the diamond is discovered to have been sewn into Xania's purse after it had been given to her by Glaunt as an engagement ring, all of which leads to Clouseau himself being awarded the Legion d'honneur in recognition for his services, much to the annoyance of the perpetually frustrated Dreyfus, who finds himself in hospital after his suit gets caught in the Inspector's car door, his bed ending up in the Seine following a visit by Clouseau, during which its brake is accidentally let off, allowing it to roll down a corridor and crash through a window ("Oh, that breeze feels good," observes Clouseau as he regards the wreckage with Ponton and Nicole).

The film at least acknowledges its forbears: "Based on the Pink Panther films of Blake Edwards," state the animated opening titles designed and supervised by Bob Kurtz, which see the Panther and Clouseau in familiar battle (Kurtz had worked as a writer on some of the Pink Panther shorts in the sixties, as well as episodes of *The Pink Panther Show* [1969–1970, TV]), while the end credits note that the Panther and Clouseau characters are "shown through an arrangement with Mirisch-Geoffrey-DePatie-Freleng" (Maurice Richlin also receives a name check alongside Edwards). Otherwise, save for an amusing gag in which Clouseau attempts to park his micro car only to trash two others in the process (despite there being plenty of space), the movie is a somewhat lackluster affair that simply warms over old conceits and situations to rather tedious effect (a variation on the old globe gag now sees it roll out of Clouseau's office and into the street where it crashes into a bunch of cyclists). That said, Martin is clearly committed to bringing Clouseau to life, but at the end of the day he is (like Arkin and Moore before him) simply a pale carbon copy of Sellers, albeit more manic, and the silly accent and forced acts of clumsiness irritate more often than they amuse, as there is no real rationale to any of them (a scene in which the Inspector receives a voice lesson so as to be able to speak with an American accent for a trip to New York by constantly repeating the phrase "I would like to buy a hamburger" is truly painful to endure, as is a sequence in which he attempts to retrieve a Viagra pill from the u-bend of a hotel sink, which sees him crashing through to the reception area below following the inevitable flood).

The fact that Martin is playing opposite Jean Reno as Ponton, a real French actor with a real French accent, doesn't help matters, and while Kevin Kline (a former consideration for Jacques Gambrelli in *Son*) has some fun as the pompous Dreyfus, one misses the gravitas (and nervous blinking) that Herbert Lom previously brought to the role (potentially, Lom could still have played the part, given that he was still working at the time). Sadly, there is no sign of Cato, and instead Clouseau attacks Ponton, who is always far too quick for him, though it should be noted that an early consideration was to cast Jackie Chan as Cato, only for him to be replaced by Ponton so as to avoid any accusations of political incorrectness. Others involved in the film include Beyoncé Knowles as Xania (the singer also performs the film's hit number-one theme song "Check on It"), Emily Mortimer as Clouseau's pretty secretary Nicole (with whom he falls in love), Roger Rees as Glaunt's former business partner Raymond Laroque, Kristin Chenoweth as the football club's P.R. rep and an uncredited (and speechless) Jason Statham as Glaunt, along with the likes of Henry Czerny, William Abadie and Clive Owen (also uncredited) as a Bond-like British secret agent named Nigel Boswell who crosses paths with Clouseau (it had been hoped that Pierce Brosnan would play this cameo role, aka 006, but his contract with Eon forbade him to appear as a tuxedoed spy until at least five years after his final Bond film *Die Another Day* [2002]).

Looking like a TV movie of the period writ large, the movie, which lacks the visual panache that Edwards brought to the early films in the series, is un-ambitiously presented by director Levy and his cinematographer Jonathan Brown (who'd photographed *Cheaper by the Dozen* for him, and who here shoots in Panavision and Technicolor), while the score by Christophe Beck (another *Cheaper* veteran) is little more than musical hubris occasionally enlivened by quotes from Henry Mancini's Panther theme, which at least helps to remind us that we are watching an actual Clouseau film, though there's nothing remotely equivalent to "Summer in Gstaad" or "Hong Kong Fireworks" or even "The Bike Chase" here, thus showing how valuable Mancini's contribution had been (David Newman had originally been sought to score the film, whose soundtrack, played by The Hollywood Studio Symphony, was subsequently released on CD by Varese Sarabande, albeit minus the hit song by Knowles ["This album does not contain a Beyoncé Knowles recording," warned the back cover]).

Promoted with a poster featuring Clouseau and a shadow of the

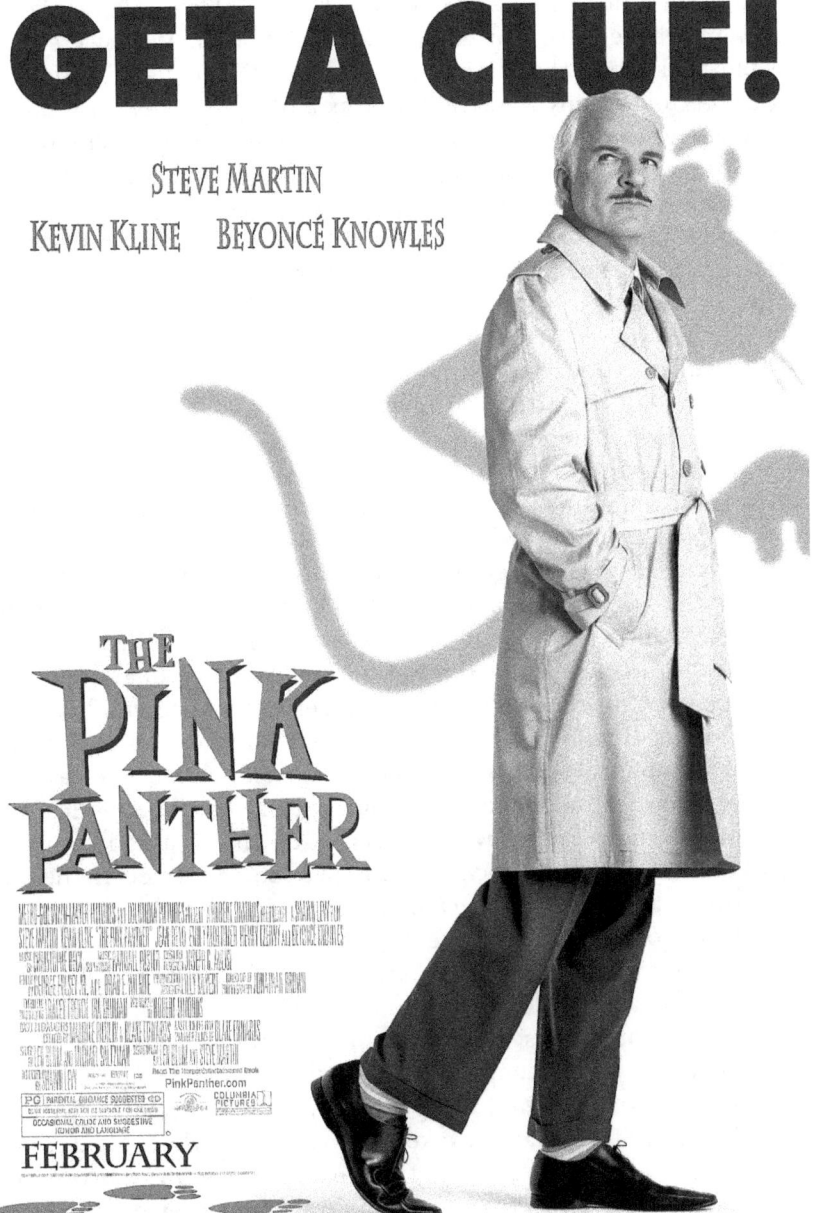

Déjà view. Steve Martin is featured in the poster for the reboot of *The Pink Panther* (2006) (MGM/Columbia/Robert Simonds Productions/International Production Company/The Montecito Production Company).

Panther, and bearing the tag line "Get a clue!" the film was released with a PG certificate in the U.S. on 10 February 2006 by Columbia and by Twentieth Century–Fox in the UK on 17 March. These were actually put-backs from the original release date of 5 August 2005 following concerns by Sony that the film was a little raunchy for a family audience, resulting in some last minute re-editing and re-shooting at a cost of some $5m (according to the *LA Times*, the original cut was "was peppered with references to oral sex and erectile dysfunction" and the film's trailer features a scene not in the film in which Clouseau uses a glass cutter device he has purloined from 006 to break into a pharmacy [presumably to get some Viagra in the original version]). Generally, the reviews weren't good. "Quite why anyone would follow Peter Sellers' cultish Clouseau is a mystery, although if anyone was going to try, it was Steve Martin," observed *Time Out*, before adding that he "merges his own persona with a Sellers imitation with only some success." It also found that "some of Clouseau's trademark blunders may amuse those unfamiliar with the originals, but in a modern movie with a contemporary actor, the national stereotypes and farcical humour appear dated," which is perhaps why *The Guardian* was prompted to describe the film as a "laughless francophopbic comedy." Elsewhere, *Sight and Sound* called it "flat and spiritless," while *Variety* found it to be "a hit and largely miss exercise—a glass about three-quarters empty or one-quarter full, depending on one's eagerness to succumb." The film also found itself nominated for two Razzies: worst supporting actress (Kristin Chenoweth) and worst re-make or rip-off. Audiences disagreed, however, and the film opened in the number-one spot in America, and went on to achieve a worldwide gross of $164.1m, coming in at number 24 on the annual movie chart, selling 12,553,660 tickets in the U.S. and Canada, thus scuppering *Time Out*'s hope that "with any luck this retread will not see any further sequels perpetrated."

Hence the sloppy seconds that are *The Pink Panther 2* (2009), which was again produced by Robert Simonds via MGM, Columbia and Robert Simonds Productions, along with an uncredited 21 Laps Entertainment. This time the screenplay (working titles *The Next Pink Panther* and *The Pink Panther Deux*) was penned by Scott Neustadter, Michael H. Weber and Steve Martin, taken from a story by Neustadter and Weber (with additional contributions by Lowell Ganz and Babaloo Mandel), while the director was Harald Zwart, best known for the teen spy comedy *Agent Cody Banks* (2003), with Shawn Levy (who'd helmed the first film) now onboard as an executive producer. Re-joining Martin from the previous cast are Jean Reno as Ponton and Emily Mortimer as Nicole, and due to a prior commitment elsewhere for Kevin Kline, the role of Dreyfus is this time played by John Cleese, who had previously appeared with Martin in the remake of *The Out-of-Towners* (1999).

As for the plot, it sees Clouseau and Ponton join an international team of investigators who are in pursuit of The Tornado, a notorious thief who has been stealing valuable artifacts from around the world, among them the Magna Carta, the Shroud of Turin, the Imperial Sword of Japan and (inevitably) the Pink Panther diamond, which is now apparently "the sacred symbol of France" (not Lugash) and no longer in the possession of the absent Xania, given that Beyoncé Knowles decided not to return for the follow-up (Spice Girl Emma Bunton was considered for a replacement character named Milly Baxter, but the role was finally excised from the script when she became pregnant). The Tornado is eventually revealed to be Sonia Solandres, an Indian criminologist who has joined the investigative team where she is able to manipulate events from the inside. But Clouseau is on her tail, and having finally brought her to justice, marries his girlfriend Nicole in a ceremony officiated by Dreyfus, which ends in the expected chaos.

Shot between 20 August and 2 November 2007, the film, which was budgeted at $70m, makes use of locations in Paris as well as closer to home in Boston and New Jersey, and is a far starrier affair than its predecessor. Among the new cast are Andy Garcia and Alfred Molina as part of the dream team of investigators; Aishwarya Rai Bachchan as The Tornado, who leaves a calling card at each crime scene (just as the Phantom left a monogrammed glove); Jeremy Irons as Avellaneda, a fence in collusion with The Tornado; Geoffrey Palmer as Commissioner Joubert; and Lily Tomlin as an etiquette teacher tasked with curtailing Clouseau's prejudices ("You are the most small-minded nitwit I have ever encountered," she tells him).

Again "Based on the Pink Panther films of Blake Edwards," the movie is a slightly more elaborate affair than its predecessor (even the opening credits designed by Karin Fong via Imaginary Forces, which feature great works of art, are better), though there is little that doesn't seem forced, and it inevitably repeats a few old gags (Clouseau this time finds himself precariously balanced on top of a globe while trying to break into Avellaneda's mansion, while his two young nephews who he calls his "little piglets" take on the mantle of Cato with surprise karate attacks; even the hamburger gag rears its head again). As before, it is presented with that blandly framed TV look of the period by director Zwart and his *Agent Cody Banks* cinematographer Denis Crossan (shooting in Panavision and DeLuxe), and is accompanied by another unremarkable score by Christophe Beck (which was issued on CD by Kraft-Engel Management).

Released with a PG certificate in the U.S. by Columbia on 6 February 2009 and in the UK by MGM on 13 February 2009, the film was promoted with a poster featuring Clouseau, a shadow of the Panther and a giant 2 covered in paw prints ("Inspect the unexpected," ran the tagline), but audiences this time proved indifferent, and though the film opened at number four in America with a take of $11.6m, it only managed a worldwide gross of $76,025,134, which, given its outlay, clearly wasn't

Two for the road. Steve Martin is featured in the poster for *The Pink Panther 2* (2009) (MGM/Columbia/Robert Simonds Productions/International Production Company/21 Laps Entertainment).

strong enough to sustain the series. The reviews didn't help, with *Variety* noting of the film's title sequence, "the enduring inspirations of the late composer Henry Mancini and animators Friz Freleng and David DePatie provide more consistent enjoyment than the miss-but-sometimes-hit merriment generated by the living participants." It also described Harald Zwart to be "a director to be remembered for a film that must be forgotten, *Agent Cody Banks*," and found that the "production values are pretty basic." Said the *LA Times*, "It is all about excess and extremes with any shred, sliver or speck of nuance as elusive as the Pink Panther diamond and apparently Jeremy Irons' self-esteem." It also found it to be "a series of short comedy sketches strung together rather haphazardly

HENRY MANCINI

January 17, 1992

Dear Howard:

You were very kind to send me your article which appeared in "What's On In London." I really appreciate your professionalism. The quotes were spot on.

I hope we can do it again.

Kindest regards,

Henry Mancini

Grace note. Letter from Henry Mancini to the author (Henry Mancini/ Howard Maxford).

trying to masquerade as a movie." *The Guardian*, which awarded the film just one star, meanwhile observed, "Steve Martin is back doing the fur-nay ack-saynt (now increasingly eun-fur-nay); and with this film he's very much channeling the spirit of the final Panther movies from the original series, when Peter Sellers had nothing to offer but despair." Like its predecessor, the film also found itself nominated for two Razzies: worst actor (Steve Martin) and worst remake, rip-off or sequel (a rip-off of a sequel to a remake).

Consequently, the Martin era came to a close. But Clouseau and the Panther are valuable commodities, and it seems highly unlikely that they will be allowed to slink away into the shadows. Indeed, on 19 November 2020 it was revealed by Deadline Hollywood that MGM had a new Panther movie in the works, while on 17 May 2023 *Variety* announced that Eddie Murphy was set to star as Clouseau, who is helped in his investigations by the animated Pink Panther (which again recalls the plotline of the unaired TV pilot *The New Pink Panther*). With script duties in the hands of Chris Bremner (*Bad Boys for Life* [2020], *Bad Boys: Ride or Die* [2024]), the film is set to be made via MGM, Geoffrey, Rideback and RGH Entertainment, with Dan Lin, Julie Andrews, Jonathan Eirich and Lawrence Mirisch (son of Walter) among the producers. David Silverman, known for his work as a producer and director on *The Simpsons* (1989–, TV), was originally slated to helm, given the initial intention to focus solely on the adventures of the animated Panther. However, when the concept was revised, the baton was handed to Jeff Fowler, whose success with live action-animation hybrids already includes the hugely successful *Sonic the Hedgehog* (2020) and its sequels.

It's certainly an intriguing way forward, and helps to prove that you can't keep a good panther down ... especially if he's a pink one.

"Well, until we meet again and the case is sol-ved." Inspector Clouseau, *The Pink Panther Strikes Again* (1976).

Filmography (Movies, Theatrical Cartoons, TV Shows, Computer Games)

The Pink Panther

1963, 115m, Technirama, Technicolor, cert A (UK)
Production companies: Mirisch/G-E Productions
Distributors: United Artists (U.S./UK)
Technical credits: Director: Blake Edwards. Screenplay: Blake Edwards, Maurice Richlin. Producer: Martin Jurow. Executive producer: Walter Mirisch. Associate producer: Dick Crockett. Cinematographer: Philip Lathrop. Music: Henry Mancini. Lyrics: Johnny Mercer, Franco Migliacci. Art director: Fernando Carrere. Editor: Ralph E. Winters. Costumes: Yves Saint-Laurent. Animation: David H. DePatie, Friz Freleng. Choreographer: Hermes Pan. Dialogue coach: James Lanphier. Stunts: Dick Crockett, Nosher Powell, Virgilio Ponto. Production supervisor: Jack McEdward. Second unit director: Owen Crump. Continuity: Betty Abbott.

Cast: David Niven (Sir Charles Lytton), Peter Sellers (Inspector Jacques Clouseau), Capucine (Simone Clouseau), Claudia Cardinale (Princess Dala), Robert Wagner (George Lytton), Brenda de Banzie (Angela Dunning), Colin Gordon (Tucker), James Lanphier (Saloud), Guy Thomajan (Artoff), John Le Mesurier (Defense Barrister), Michael Trubshawe (Felix Townes), Martin Miller (Pierre Luigi), Meri Wells (Monica Fawn), Riccardo Billi (Aristotle Sarajos), Fran Jeffries (Singer), Francesco Tensi (Lord Cravenwood)

A Shot in the Dark

1964, 102m, Panavision, DeLuxe, cert A (UK)
Production company: Mirisch
Distributors: United Artists (U.S./UK)
Technical credits: Director: Blake Edwards. Screenplay: Blake Edwards, William Peter Blatty. Producer: Blake Edwards. Executive producer: Walter Mirisch. Associate producer: Cecil F. Ford. Cinematographer: Christopher Challis. Music: Henry Mancini. Lyrics: Robert Wells. Production designer: Michael Stringer. Editors: Ralph E. Winters, Bert Bates. Costumes: Margaret Furse. Animation: David H. DePatie, Friz Freleng. Camera operator: Austin Dempster. Second unit photography: Skeets Kelly. Continuity: Connie Wills.

Cast: Peter Sellers (Inspector Jacques Clouseau), Elke Sommer (Maria Gambrelli), George Sanders (Benjamin Ballon), Herbert Lom (Chief Inspector Charles

Dreyfus), Graham Stark (Hercule LaJoy), Tracy Reed (Dominique Ballon), Burt Kwouk (Kato), Moira Redmond (Simone), Maurice Kaufmann (Pierre), Douglas Wilmer (Henri LaFarge), Vanda Godsell (Madame LaFarge), Ann Lynn (Dudu), David Lodge (Georges), Martin Benson (Maurice), André Maranne (François Chevalier), Reginald Beckwith (Receptionist [nudist camp]), Bryan Forbes (Attendant [billed as Turk Thrust]), Tutte Lemkow (Kazak Dancer), Rose Hill (Soprano), Jack Melford (Psychoanalyst)

Inspector Clouseau

1968, 96m, Panavision, DeLuxe, cert U (UK)
Production company: Mirisch
Distributors: United Artists (U.S./UK)

Technical credits: Director: Bud Yorkin. Screenplay: Tom Waldman, Frank Waldman. Producer: Lewis J. Rachmil. Cinematographer: Arthur Ibbetson. Music: Ken Thorne. Production designer: Michael Stringer. Editor: John Victor Smith. Costumes: Dinah Greet. Animation: David H. DePatie, Friz Freleng. Second unit director: Michael Frewin. Second unit photography: Skeets Kelly. Continuity: Ann Skinner.

Cast: Alan Arkin (Inspector Jacques Clouseau), Frank Finlay (Superintendent Weaver), Patrick Cargill (Commissioner Sir Charles Braithwaite), Delia Boccardo (Lisa Morell), Beryl Reid (Mrs. Weaver), Clive Francis (Clyde Hargreaves), Richard Pearson (Shockley), Susan Engel (Carmichael), Michael Ripper (Steven Frey), John Bindon (Bull Parker), Tutte Lemkow (Frenchie LeBec), Geoffrey Bayldon (Gutch), Katya Wyeth (Meg [billed as Kathja Wyeth]), Anthony Ainley (Bomber LeBec), George Pravda (Wolf), Eric Pohlmann (Bergesch), Leon Lissek (Taxi driver), Marjie Lawrence (Peggy), Ken Campbell (Reporter)

The Return of the Pink Panther

1975, 113m, Panavision, DeLuxe, cert G (U.S.), U (UK)
Production companies: ITC/Jewel/Pimlico
Distributors: United Artists (U.S./UK)

Technical credits: Director: Blake Edwards. Screenplay: Blake Edwards, Frank Waldman. Producer: Blake Edwards. Executive producer: Lew Grade. Associate producer: Tony Adams. Cinematographer: Geoffrey Unsworth. Music: Henry Mancini. Lyrics: Hal David. Production designer: Peter Mullins. Editor: Tom Priestley. Costumes: Bridget Sellers. Animation: Richard Williams. Stunts: Dick Crockett, Joe Dunne. Continuity: Connie Willis.

Cast: Peter Sellers (Inspector Jacques Clouseau), Christopher Plummer (Sir Charles Litton), Herbert Lom (Chief Inspector Charles Dreyfus), Catherine Schell (Lady Claudine Litton), Graham Stark (Pepi), Burt Kwouk (Cato Fong), David Lodge (Mac), Peter Arne (Colonel Sharki), Peter Jeffrey (General Wadafi), Eric Pohlmann (Fat Man), Grégoire Aslan (Lugash Chief of Police), André Maranne (François Chevalier), Victor Spinetti (Concierge), John Bluthal (Blind beggar), Peter Jones (Psychiatrist), Herb Tanney (Nice Chief of Police [billed as Serge Tanney]), Nadim Sawalha (Museum guide), Mollie Maureen (Old lady [billed as Molly Maureen]), Mike Grady (Bellboy), Claire Davenport (Masseuse)

The Pink Panther Strikes Again

1976, 103m, Panavision, DeLuxe, cert PG (U.S.), U (UK)
Production companies: UA/Amjo/Geoffrey 1964
Distributor: United Artists (U.S./UK)

Technical credits: Director: Blake Edwards. Screenplay: Blake Edwards, Frank Waldman. Producer: Blake Edwards. Associate producer: Tony Adams. Cinematographer: Harry Waxman. Music: Henry Mancini. Lyrics: Don Black. Production designer: Peter Mullins. Editor: Alan Jones. Costumes: Tiny Nicholls, Bridget Sellers. Animation: Richard Williams. Camera operator: Ernie Day. Stunts: Dick Crockett, John Sullivan. Continuity: Pamela Davies.

Cast: Peter Sellers (Chief Inspector Jacques Clouseau), Herbert Lom (Charles Dreyfus), Lesley-Anne Down (Olga), Burt Kwouk (Cato Fong), Graham Stark (Hotel clerk), Colin Blakely (Drummond), Leonard Rossiter (Quinlan), Dudley Sutton (McClaren), André Maranne (François Chevalier), Dick Crockett (President), Byron Kane (Secretary of State), John Sullivan (Jean Tournier), Richard Vernon (Professor Fassbender), Briony McRoberts (Margo Fassbender), Robert Beatty (Admiral), Hal Galili (Danny Salvo), Phil Brown (Senator), Michael Robbins (Ainsley Jarvis), Norman Mitchell (Mr. Bullock), Vanda Godsell (Mrs. Leverlilly), Patsy Smart (Mrs. Japonica), Tony Sympson (Mr. Shork), George Leech (Mr. Stutterstutt), Deep Roy (Assassin [billed as Roy Deep]), Geoffrey Bayldon (Dr. Duval), Anthony Chinn (Assassin), John Clive (Chuck), Joan Rhodes (Daphne), Damaris Hayman (Fiona), Herb Tanney (Assassin [billed as Sado Tanney]), Omar Sharif (Assassin)

Revenge of the Pink Panther

1978, 99m, Panavision, Technicolor, cert PG (U.S.), A (UK)
Production companies: Jewel/Sellers-Edwards
Distributor: United Artists
Technical credits: Director: Blake Edwards. Screenplay: Blake Edwards, Frank Waldman, Ron Clark. Story: Blake Edwards. Producer: Blake Edwards. Executive producer: Tony Adams. Associate producers: Derek Kavanagh, Ken Wales. Cinematographer: Ernest (Ernie) Day. Music: Henry Mancini. Lyrics: Leslie Bricusse. Production designer: Peter Mullins. Editor: Alan Jones. Costumes: Tiny Nicholls (billed as Tiny Nichols). Animation: David H. DePatie, Friz Freleng. Stunts: Dick Crockett, Joe Dunne. Continuity: Pamela Davies.

Cast: Peter Sellers (Chief Inspector Jacques Clouseau), Herbert Lom (Chief Inspector Charles Dreyfus), Dyan Cannon (Simone Legree), Robert Webber (Philippe Douvier), Graham Stark (Dr. Auguste Balls), Burt Kwouk (Cato Fong), Robert Loggia (Al Marchione), Tony Beckley (Guy Algo), Paul Stewart (Julio Scallini), André Maranne (François Chevalier), Alfie Bass (Fernet), Sue Lloyd (Claude Russo), Douglas Wilmer (Police Commissioner), Danny Schiller (Cunny), Ferdy Mayne (Dr. Paul Laprone), Lon Satton (Singer), Elisabeth Welch (Mrs. Wu), Valerie Leon (Tanya), Anthony Chinn (Doorman), Adrienne Corri (Therese Douvier), Steve Plytas (Board member), John Clive (Aide), Henry McGee (Officer Bardot), Andrews Sachs (Hercule Poirot), Julian Orchard (Hospital clerk), Michael Ward (Estate agent), Maria Charles (Viewing client), Frank Williams (Viewing client), Rita Webb (Lady at window), John Bluthal (Cemetery guard), Ed Parker (Mr. Chong), Herb Tanney (Hong Kong Police Chief)

Trail of the Pink Panther

1982, 96m, Panavision, Technicolor, cert a PG (U.S./UK)
Production companies: UA/Blake Edwards Entertainment/Lakeline/Titan/Amjo
Distributors: MGM/UA (U.S.), UIP (UK)
Technical credits: Director: Blake Edwards. Screenplay: Blake Edwards, Frank Waldman, Tom Waldman, Geoffrey Edwards. Producers: Blake Edwards,

Tony Adams. Executive producer: Jonathan D. Krane. Associate producer: Gerald T. Nutting. Cinematographer: Dick Bush. Music: Henry Mancini. Production designer: Peter Mullins. Editor: Alan Jones. Costumes: Patricia Edwards, Tiny Nicholls. Animation: DePatie-Freleng. Second unit director: Terry Marcel. Stunts: Joe Dunne. Continuity: Elaine Schreyeck.

Cast: Peter Sellers (Chief Inspector Jacques Clouseau [archive footage]), David Niven (Sir Charles Litton), Herbert Lom (Chief Inspector Charles Dreyfus), Capucine (Lady Simone Litton), Graham Stark (Hercule LaJoy), Burt Kwouk (Cato Fong), Richard Mulligan (Clouseau's father), Joanna Lumley (Marie Jouvet), André Maranne (François Chevalier), Robert Loggia (Bruno Langois), Peter Arne (Colonel Bufoni), Ronald Fraser (Dr. Longet), Marne Maitland (Deputy Commissioner Lasorde), Denise Crosby (Bruno's moll), William Hootkins (Taxi driver), Daniel Peacock (Clouseau aged 18), Lucca Mezzofanti (Clouseau aged 8), Madlena Nedeva (Madame Dreyfus), Arthur Howard (Bruno's butler), Claire Davenport (Maid), Kathleen St. John (Nanna), Harold Berens (Hotel clerk), Julie Andrews (Charwoman)

Curse of the Pink Panther

1983, 109m, Panavision, Technicolor, cert a PG (U.S./UK)
Production companies: UA/ Blake Edwards Entertainment/Lakeline
Distributors: MGM/UA (U.S.), UIP (UK)

Technical credits: Director: Blake Edwards. Screenplay: Blake Edwards, Geoffrey Edwards. Producers: Blake Edwards, Tony Adams. Executive producer: Jonathan D. Krane. Associate producer: Gerald T. Nutting. Cinematographer: Dick Bush. Music: Henry Mancini. Production designer: Peter Mullins. Editors: Ralph E. Winters, Bob Hathaway. Costumes: Patricia Edwards, Tiny Nicholls. Animation: Arthur Leonardi. Stunts: Joe Dunne. Continuity: Elaine Schreyeck.

Cast: David Niven (Sir Charles Litton), Ted Wass (Sergeant Clifton Sleigh), Robert Wagner (George Litton), Capucine (Lady Simone Litton), Herbert Lom (Chief Inspector Charles Dreyfus), Joanna Lumley (Countess Chandra), Burt Kwouk (Cato Fong), Graham Stark (Bored waiter), Robert Loggia (Bruno Langois), Harvey Korman (Professor Auguste Balls), Roger Moore (Chief Inspector Jacques Clouseau [billed as Turk Thrust II]), Leslie Ash (Juleta Shane), André Maranne (François Chevalier), Peter Arne (General Bufoni), Steve Franken (Harvey Hamilcard III), Denise Crosby (Bruno's moll), Ed Parker (Mr. Chong), Patti Davis (Michelle Chauvin [billed as Patricia Davis]), Emma Walton Hamilton (Angry hooker), William Hootkins (Taxi driver), Mollie Maureen (Rich old lady), Harold Kasket (President Sandover Haleesh), Liz Smith (Martha Balls), Danny Schiller (Cunny), Donald Sumpter (Dave), Bill Nighy (Doctor), Arthur Howard (Bruno's butler), Herb Tanney (Secret policeman [billed as Sidi Bin Tanney]), Geoffrey Beevers (Concierge), Sean Caffrey (Doorman)

Son of the Pink Panther

1993, 93m, Panavision, Agfa [printed by DeLuxe], cert PG
Production companies: UA/Filmauro/International Traders/Zaman
Distributors: MGM/UA (U.S.), UIP (UK)

Technical credits: Director: Blake Edwards. Screenplay: Blake Edwards, Madeline Sunshine, Steve Sunshine. Producer: Tony Adams. Executive producer: Nigel Wooll. Cinematographer: Dick Bush. Music: Henry Mancini. Lyrics: Leslie Bricusse. Production designer: Peter Mullins. Editor: Robert Pergament. Costumes: Annie Crawford. Animation: Jeffrey Tinnell, Chris Hummel, Darlie Brewster. Stunts: Joe Dunne. Continuity: Nikki Clapp.

Cast: Roberto Benigni (Gendarme Jacques Gambrelli), Herbert Lom (Police Commissioner Charles Dreyfus), Claudia Cardinale (Maria Gambrelli), Burt Kwouk (Cato Fong), Graham Stark (Dr. Balls), Robert Davi (Hans Zarba), Debrah Farentino (Princess Yasmin), Shabana Azmi (Queen), Jennifer Edwards (Yussa), Mike Starr (Hanif), Mark Schneider (Arnon), Anton Rodgers (Chief Lazar), Kenny Spalding (Garth), Oliver Cotton (King Haroak), Aharon Impalé (General Jaffar), Henry Goodman (Anchorman), Herb Tanney (Jean Claude [billed as Sputare Tanney]), Liz Smith (Martha Balls), Nadim Sawalha (Lugash agent), Nicoletta Braschi (Jacqueline Gambrelli)

The Pink Panther

2006, 93m, Panavision, Technicolor, cert PG

Production companies: MGM/Columbia/Robert Simonds Productions/International Production Company/The Montecito Picture Company

Distributors: Columbia (U.S.), Twentieth Century–Fox (UK)

Technical credits: Director: Harald Zwart. Screenplay: Len Blum, Steve Martin. Story: Len Blum, Michael Saltzman. Producer: Robert Simonds. Executive producers: Ira Shuman, Tracey Trench. Cinematographer: Jonathan Brown. Music: Christophe Beck. Production designer: Lilly Kilvert. Editors: George Folsey, Jr., Brad Wilhite. Costumes: Joseph G. Aulisi. Animation: Bob Kurtz. Stunts: George Aguilar. Continuity: Diane Durant.

Cast: Steve Martin (Inspector Jacques Clouseau), Jean Reno (Gendarme Gilbert Ponton), Kevin Kline (Chief Inspector Charles Dreyfus), Emily Mortimer (Nicole Durant), Kristin Chenoweth (Cheri), Henry Czerny (Yuri), Beyoncé Knowles (Xania), William Abadie (Bizu), Philip Goodwin (Deputy Chief Renard), Scott Adkins (Jacquard), Henri Garcin (President), Radu Spinghel (Huang), Clive Owen (Nigel Boswell, Agent 006), Jason Statham (Yves Glaunt)

The Pink Panther 2

2006, 92m, Panavision, DeLuxe, cert PG

Distributors: Columbia (U.S.), MGM (UK)

Technical credits: Harald Zwart. Screenplay: Scott Neustadter, Michael Weber, Steve Martin (and Lowell Ganz, Babaloo Mandel). Story: Scott Neustadter, Michael Weber. Producer: Robert Simonds. Executive producers: Shawn Levy, Ira Shuman. Cinematographer: Denis Crossan. Music: Christophe Beck. Production designer: Rusty Smith. Editor: Julia Wong. Costumes: Joseph G. Aulisi. Animation: Karin Fong. Stunts: Ernie Orsatti. Continuity: Kelly Cronin.

Cast: Steve Martin (Inspector Jacques Clouseau), Jean Reno (Gendarme Gilbert Ponton), John Cleese (Chief Inspector Charles Dreyfus), Emily Mortimer (Nicole), Alfred Molina (Pepperidge), Andy Garcia (Vincenzo), Jeremy Irons (Avellaneda), Lily Tomlin (Mrs. Berenger), Johnny Hallyday (Milliken), Yuki Matsuzaki (Kenji), Aishwarya Rai Bachchan (Sonia), Geoffrey Palmer (Joubert), Philip Goodwin (Renard), Armel Bellec (Louis), Jack Met (Antoine [billed as Jack Metzger]), Evgeniy Lazarev (The Pope [billed as Eugene Lazarev])

Filmography

Theatrical Cartoons

The Pink Panther

The Pink Phink (18 December 1964 [Oscar winner, best animated short])
Pink Pajamas (25 December 1964)
We Give Pink Stamps (12 February 1965)
Dial "P" for Pink (17 March 1965)
Sink Pink (12 April 1965)
Pickled Pink (12 May 1965)
Pinkfinger (13 May 1965)
Shocking Pink (13 May 1965)
Pink Ice (10 June 1965)
The Pink Tail Fly (25 August 1965)
Pink Panzer (15 September 1965)
An Ounce of Pink (20 October 1965)
Reel Pink (16 November 1965)
Bully for Pink (14 December 1965)
Pink Punch (21 February 1966)
Pink Pistons (16 March 1966)
Vitamin Pink (6 April 1966)
The Pink Blueprint (25 May 1966 [Oscar nomination, best cartoon short])
Pink, Plunk, Plink (25 May 1966)
Smile Pretty, Say Pink (29 May 1966)
Pink-A-Boo (26 June 1966)
Genie with the Light Pink Fur (14 September 1966)
Super Pink (12 October 1966)
Rock a Bye Pinky (23 December 1966)
Pinknic (6 January 1967)
Pink Panic (11 January 1966)
Pink Posies (26 April 1967)
Pink of the Litter (17 May 1967)
In the Pink (18 May 1967)
Jet Pink (13 June 1967)
Pink Paradise (24 June 1967)
Pinto Pink (19 July 1967)
Congratulations It's Pink (27 October 1967)
Prefabricated Pink (22 November 1967)
The Hand Is Pinker Than the Eye (20 December 1967)
Pink Outs (27 December 1967)
Sky Blue Pink (3 January 1968)
Pinkadilly Circus (21 February 1968)
Psychedelic Pink (13 March 1968)
Come on In! The Water's Pink (10 April 1968)
Put-Put, Pink (14 April 1968)
G.I. Pink (1 May 1968)
Lucky Pink (7 May 1968)
The Pink Quarterback (22 May 1968)
Twinkle, Twinkle, Little Pink (30 June 1968)
Pink Valiant (10 July 1968)
The Pink Pill (31 July 1968)
Prehistoric Pink (7 August 1968)
Pink in the Clink (18 September 1968)
Little Beaux Pink (2 October 1968)
Tickled Pink (6 October 1968)
Pink Sphinx (23 October 1968)
Pink Is a Many Splintered Thing (20 November 1968)
The Pink Package Plot (11 December 1968)
Pinkome Tax (20 December 1968)
Pink-A-Rella (8 January 1969)
Pink Pest Control (12 February 1969)
Think Before You Pink (19 March 1969)
Slink Pink (2 April 1969)
In the Pink of the Night (18 May 1969)
Pink on the Cob (29 May 1969)
Extinct Pink (20 June 1969)
A Fly in the Pink (23 June 1971)
Pink Blue Plate (18 July 1971)
Pink Tuba-Dore (4 August 1971)
Pink Pranks (28 August 1971)
The Pink Flea (15 September 1971)
Psst Pink (15 September 1971)
Gong with the Pink (20 October 1971)
Pink-In (20 October 1971)
Pink 8 Ball (6 February 1972)
Pink Aye (16 May 1974)
Pink Da Vinci (23 June 1975)
Trail of the Lonesome Pink (27 June 1974)
Pink Streaker (27 June 1975)
Salmon Pink (25 July 1975)
Forty Pink Winks (8 August 1975)
Pink Plasma (8 August 1975)
Pink Elephant (20 October 1975)
Keep Our Forests Pink (20 November 1975)
Bobolink Pink (30 December 1975)
It's Pink, But Is It Mink? (30 December 1975)
Pink Campaign (30 December 1975)
The Scarlet Pinkernel (30 December 1975)

Mystic Pink (6 January 1976)
The Pink of Arabee (13 March 1976 [reissued as *The Pink of Bagdad* in 1978])
The Pink Pro (12 April 1976)
Pink Piper (30 April 1976)
Pinky Doodle (28 April 1976 [reissued as *Yankee Doodle Pink* in 1978])
Sherlock Pink (29 June 1976)
Rocky Pink (July 1976 [reissued as *Pet Pink Pebbles* in 1978])
Therapeutic Pink (1 April 1977)
Pink Pictures (21 October 1978)
Pink Arcade (25 October 1978)
Pink Lemonade (4 November 1978)
Pink Trumpet (4 November 1978)
Sprinkle Me Pink (11 November 1978)
Dietetic Pink (11 November 1978)
Pink Lightning (17 November 1978)
Cat and the Pinkstalk (18 November 1978)
Pink Daddy (18 November 1978)
Pink S.W.A.T. (22 November 1978)
Pink and Shovel (25 November 1978)
Pink U.F.O. (26 November 1978)
Pinkologist (2 December 1978)
Yankee Doodle Pink (2 December 1978 [reissue of *Pinky Doodle*])
Pink Press (9 December 1978)
Pet Pink Pebbles (9 December 1978 [reissue of *Rocky Pink*])
The Pink of Bagdad (9 December 1978 [reissue of *The Pink of Arabee*])
Pink in the Drink (20 December 1978)
Pink Bananas (22 December 1978)
Pinktails for Two (22 December 1978)
Pink Z-Z-Z (23 December 1978)
Star Pink (23 December 1978)
Pink Breakfast (1 February 1979)
Pink Quackers (4 April 1979)
Toro Pink (4 April 1979)
String Along Pink (12 April 1979)
Pink in the Woods (27 April 1979)
Pink Pull (15 June 1979)
Spark Plug Pink (28 June 1979)
Doctor Pink (16 November 1979)
Pink Suds (19 December 1979)
Supermarket Pink (1 February 1980)

The Inspector

The Great De Gaulle Stone Operation (21 December 1965)
Reaux, Reaux, Reaux Your Boat (1 February 1966)
Napoleon Blown-Aparte (2 February 1966)
Cirrhosis of the Louvre (9 March 1966)
Plastered in Paris (5 April 1966)
Cock-A-Doodle Deux Deux (15 June 1966)
Ape Suzette (24 June 1966)
The Pique Poquette of Paris (25 August 1966)
Sicque! Sicque! Sicque! (23 September 1966)
That's No Lady—That's Notre Dame! (26 October 1966)
Sacré Bleu Cross (1 February 1967)
Le Quiet Squad (17 May 1967)
Bomb Voyage (22 May 1967)
Le Pig-Al Patrol (24 May 1967)
Le Bowser Bagger (30 May 1967)
Le Escape Goat (29 June 1967)
Le Cop on Le Rocks (3 July 1967)
Crow De Guerre (16 August 1967)
Canadian Can-Can (20 September 1967)
Tour de Farce (25 October 1967)
The Shooting of Caribou Lou (20 December 1967)
London Derrière (7 February 1968)
Les Miserobots (21 March 1968)
Transylvania Mania (26 March 1968)
Bear De Guerre (26 April 1968)
Cherche le Phantom (13 June 1968)
Le Great Dane Robbery (7 July 1968)
Le Ball and Chain Gang (24 July 1968)
La Feet's Defeat (24 July 1968)
French Freud (22 January 1969)
Pierre and Cottage Cheese (26 February 1969)
Carte Blanched (14 May 1969)

TV Shows

The Pink Panther Show (1969–1971)
The New Pink Panther Show (1971–1974)
The Pink Panther and Friends (1974–1976)

The Pink Panther Laugh-and-a-Half Hour-and-a-Half Show (1976–1977)
Think Pink Panther (1977–1978)
The All New Pink Panther Show (1978–1979)
The Pink Panther Show (1980)
Pink Panther and Sons (1984)
The Pink Panther (1993–1995)
Pink Panther and Pals (2010)

Computer Games

Pink Goes to Hollywood (1993)
The Pink Panther: Passport to Peril (1996)
The Pink Panther: Hokus Pokus Pink (1997)
Pink Panther: Pinkadelic Pursuit (2002)

Chapter Notes

Introduction

1. Author interview, 1991, previously unpublished material.
2. Author interview, 1999, previously unpublished material.
3. Author interview, 1999, previously unpublished material.
4. Author interview, 1999, previously unpublished material.
5. Author interview, 1999, previously unpublished material.
6. Author interview, 1999, previously unpublished material.

Chapter 1

1. Author interview, 1999, previously unpublished material.
2. *The Pink Panther*, DVD commentary, MGM Home Entertainment, 2004.
3. *The Pink Panther*, DVD commentary, MGM Home Entertainment, 2004.
4. Author interview, previously quoted in *What's On in London*, November 20, 1991, p. 16.
5. Author interview, previously quoted in *Gold*, Vol. 1, No. 6, 1992, p. 67, includes previously unpublished material.
6. 34th *Academy Awards*, AMPAS/ABC, 9 April 1962.
7. Author interview, previously quoted in *What's On in London*, November 20, 1991, p. 17.

Chapter 2

1. Author interview, 1999, previously unpublished material.
2. *The Pink Panther*, DVD commentary, MGM Home Entertainment, 2004.
3. Author interview, 1999, previously unpublished material.
4. Author interview, 1999, previously unpublished material.
5. Author interview, 1999, previously unpublished material.
6. *Film '76*, BBC 9 January 1976, also featured in *Talking Pictures: Great British Comedies*, BBC, 31 October 2015.
7. Author interview, 1999, previously unpublished material.
8. Author interview, 1999, previously unpublished material.
9. Author interview, 1999, previously unpublished material.
10. Author interview, previously quoted in *Film Review*, #581, May 1999, p. 82, includes previously unpublished material.
11. Author interview, previously quoted in *Film Review*, #581, May 1999, p. 82.
12. *Film '76*, BBC 9 January 1976, also featured in *Talking Pictures: Great British Comedies*, BBC, 31 October 2015.
13. Author interview, 1999, previously unpublished material.
14. Roger Lewis, *The Life and Death of Peter Sellers* (Arrow, 1995), p. 838.
15. *The Pink Panther*, DVD commentary, MGM Home Entertainment, 2004.
16. *The Pink Panther*, DVD commentary, MGM Home Entertainment, 2004.
17. *The Pink Panther*, DVD commentary, MGM Home Entertainment, 2004.
18. *The Pink Panther Story*, MGM Home Entertainment, 2003.
19. *The Pink Panther Story*, MGM Home Entertainment, 2003.
20. *The Pink Panther Story*, MGM Home Entertainment, 2003.

21. *The Pink Panther Story*, MGM Home Entertainment, 2003.
22. *Film Review*, #581, May 1999, p. 82.
23. Author interview, 1999, previously unpublished material.
24. *The Pink Panther*, DVD commentary, MGM Home Entertainment, 2004.
25. *Film '76*, BBC 9 January 1976, also featured in *Talking Pictures: Great British Comedies*, BBC, 31 October 2015.
26. Author interview, 1999, previously unpublished material.
27. *Film '76*, BBC 9 January 1976, also featured in *Talking Pictures: Great British Comedies*, BBC, 31 October 2015.
28. *The Pink Panther*, DVD commentary, MGM Home Entertainment, 2004.
29. *The Pink Panther Story*, MGM Home Entertainment, 2003.
30. *The Pink Panther*, DVD commentary, MGM Home Entertainment, 2004.
31. *The Pink Panther Story*, MGM Home Entertainment, 2003.
32. *The Pink Panther*, DVD commentary, MGM Home Entertainment, 2004.
33. *The Pink Panther*, DVD commentary, MGM Home Entertainment, 2004.
34. *The Pink Panther*, DVD commentary, MGM Home Entertainment, 2004.
35. *The Pink Panther*, DVD commentary, MGM Home Entertainment, 2004.
36. Henry Mancini, *Did They Mention the Music?* (Cooper Square Press, 2001), p. 62.
37. Author interview, previously quoted in *What's On in London*, November 20, 1991, p. 17.
38. Author interview, 1991, previously unpublished material.
39. Author interview, 1991, previously unpublished material.
40. Author interview, 1991, previously unpublished material.
41. Author interview, 1999, previously unpublished material.
42. Author interview, 1991, previously unpublished material.
43. Peter Sellers, *The Pink Panther* soundtrack LP liner notes, RCA/BMG, 1963.
44. *The Pink Panther*, DVD commentary, MGM, 2004.
45. *Behind the Feline: The Cartoon Phenomenon*, MGM Home Entertainment, 2003.
46. *Behind the Feline: The Cartoon Phenomenon*, MGM Home Entertainment, 2003.
47. *Behind the Feline: The Cartoon Phenomenon*, MGM Home Entertainment, 2003.
48. Author interview, previously quoted in *Film Review*, #581, May 1999, p. 82, includes previously unpublished material.
49. *The Pink Panther Story*, MGM Home Entertainment, 2003.
50. Author interview, previously quoted in *Film Review*, #581, May 1999, p. 82.

Chapter 3

1. *Behind the Feline: The Cartoon Phenomenon*, MGM Home Entertainment, 2003.
2. *Behind the Feline: The Cartoon Phenomenon*, MGM Home Entertainment, 2003.
3. *Behind the Feline: The Cartoon Phenomenon*, MGM Home Entertainment, 2003.
4. *The Pink Panther*, DVD commentary, MGM Home Entertainment, 2004.
5. *The Pink Panther*, DVD commentary, MGM Home Entertainment, 2004.

Chapter 4

1. *The Pink Panther Story*, MGM Home Entertainment, 2003.
2. Author interview, previously quoted in *Film Review*, #581, May 1999, pp. 82–83, includes previously unpublished material.
3. *The Pink Panther*, DVD commentary, MGM Home Entertainment, 2004.
4. Author interview, previously quoted in *Film Review*, #581, May 1999, p. 83, includes previously unpublished material.
5. Author interview, previously quoted in *Film Review*, #581, May 1999, p. 83.
6. Author interview, previously quoted in *Film Review*, #581, May 1999, p. 83.
7. Author interview, previously quoted in *Film Review*, #581, May 1999, pp. 83–84.
8. Author interview, previously

quoted in *Film Review*, #581, May 1999, p. 83.
9. Author interview, previously quoted in *Film Review*, #581, May 1999, p. 83.
10. Author interview, 1999, previously unpublished material.
11. Author interview, 1999, previously unpublished material.
12. Author interview, 1999, previously unpublished material.
13. Author interview, 1999, previously unpublished material.
14. Author interview, 1999, previously unpublished material.
15. Author interview, 1999, previously unpublished material.
16. Author interview, 1999, previously unpublished material.
17. Author interview, 1999, previously unpublished material.
18. Author interview, previously quoted in *Film Review*, #581, May 1999, p. 84
19. Author interview, previously quoted in *Film Review*, #581, May 1999, p. 83.
20. Author interview, previously quoted in *Film Review*, #581, May 1999, p. 83.
21. Author interview, 1999, previously unpublished material.
22. Author interview, 1999, previously unpublished material.
23. Author interview, 1999, previously unpublished material.
24. Author interview, 1999, previously unpublished material.
25. Author interview, 1999, previously unpublished material.
26. Author interview, 1999, previously unpublished material.
27. *Sight and Sound*, Spring 1964, p. 57.
28. *Sight and Sound*, Spring 1964, p. 57.
29. Author interview, 1991, previously unpublished material.
30. Author interview, previously quoted in *What's On in London*, November 20, 1991, p. 17.
31. Author interview, previously quoted in *What's On in London*, November 20, 1991, p. 17.
32. Author interview, 1991, previously unpublished material.
33. Author interview, previously quoted in *What's On in London*, November 20, 1991, p. 17, includes previously unpublished material.
34. *The Pink Panther Story*, MGM Home Entertainment, 2003.
35. *Inside the Party*, MGM Home Entertainment, 2004.

Chapter 5

1. *Inside the Party*, MGM Home Entertainment, 2004.
2. *The Pink Panther Story*, MGM Home Entertainment, 2003.
3. Author interview, 1991, previously unpublished material.
4. Author interview, 1999, previously unpublished material.
5. Bobbie Wygant interview, NBC/KXAS-TV (formerly WBAP-TV), 1968.
6. Bobbie Wygant interview, NBC/KXAS-TV (formerly WBAP-TV), 1968.
7. Bobbie Wygant interview, NBC/KXAS-TV (formerly WBAP-TV), 1968.
8. Author interview, 1999, previously unpublished material.
9. Author interview, 1999, previously unpublished material.
10. Author interview, 1991, previously unpublished material.
11. Author interview, 1999, previously unpublished material.
12. *The Pink Panther Story*, MGM Home Entertainment, 2003.

Chapter 6

1. Author interview, 1991, previously unpublished material.
2. Roger Lewis, *The Life and Death of Peter Sellers* (Arrow, 1995), p. 965.
3. *The Pink Panther Story*, MGM Home Entertainment, 2003.
4. Author interview, 1999, previously unpublished material.
5. Author interview, previously quoted in *Film Review*, #581, May 1999, p. 84
6. Author interview, 1999, previously unpublished material.
7. Author interview, 1999, previously unpublished material.
8. Author interview, 1999, previously unpublished material.

9. Author interview, previously quoted in *Film Review*, #581, May 1999, p. 84, includes previously unpublished material.
10. Author interview, 1999, previously unpublished material.
11. Author interview, 1999, previously unpublished material.
12. Author interview, 1999, previously unpublished material.
13. Author interview, 1999, previously unpublished material.
14. Graham Stark, *Stark Naked* (Right Publishing, 2017), p. 145.
15. Author interview, 1999, previously unpublished material.
16. Author interview, 1999, previously unpublished material.
17. Author interview, 1999, previously unpublished material.
18. Author interview, previously quoted in *Film Review*, #581, May 1999, p. 84, includes previously unpublished material.
19. Author interview, 1999, previously unpublished material.
20. Author interview, 1999, previously unpublished material.
21. Author interview, previously quoted in *Film Review*, #581, May 1999, p. 85, includes previously unpublished material.
22. Author interview, 1991, previously unpublished material.
23. Author interview, 1991, previously unpublished material.
24. Graham Stark, *Stark Naked* (Right Publishing, 2017), p. 146
25. Julie Andrews, *Home Work: A Memoir of My Hollywood Years* (Weidenfeld & Nicolson, 2019), p. 206.
26. Author interview, 1999, previously unpublished material.
27. Author interview, 1999, previously unpublished material.
28. Julie Andrews, *Home Work: A Memoir of My Hollywood Years* (Weidenfeld & Nicolson, 2019), p. 215.
29. Julie Andrews, *Home Work: A Memoir of My Hollywood Years* (Weidenfeld & Nicolson, 2019), p. 213.
30. Graham Stark, *Stark Naked* (Right Publishing, 2017), p. 151.
31. Author interview, 1999, previously unpublished material.
32. Author interview, 1999, previously unpublished material.
33. Author interview, 1999, previously unpublished material.
34. Author interview, 1991, previously unpublished material.

Chapter 7

1. *Inside the Party*, MGM Home Entertainment, 2004.
2. *The Pink Panther*, DVD commentary, MGM Home Entertainment, 2004.
3. Author interview, 1999, previously unpublished material.
4. Author interview, 1999, previously unpublished material.
5. Author interview, 1999, previously unpublished material.
6. Author interview, 1999, previously unpublished material.
7. *Arena: The Peter Sellers Story*, episode 3, *I Am Not a Funny Man*, BBC, 25 February 1995.
8. Author interview, 1999, previously unpublished material.
9. Author interview, 1999, previously unpublished material.
10. Author interview, previously quoted in *Film Review*, #581, May 1999, p. 85, includes previously unpublished material.
11. Author interview, 1999, previously unpublished material.
12. Author interview, 1991, previously unpublished material.
13. *Cinema Retro*, Vol. 2, #6, 2006, p. 44.
14. *Cinema Retro*, Vol. 2, #6, 2006, p. 44.
15. Graham Stark, *Stark Naked* (Right Publishing, 2017), p. 151.
16. Don Black, *The Sanest Guy in the Room* (Constable, 2020), p. 212.
17. Author interview, 1991, previously unpublished material.
18. Author interview, previously quoted in *Film Review*, #581, May 1999, p. 85.

Chapter 8

1. Author interview, previously quoted in *Film Review*, #581, May 1999, p. 85.
2. Author interview, 1999, previously unpublished material.

3. Author interview, 1999, previously unpublished material.
4. *The Pink Panther*, DVD commentary, MGM Home Entertainment, 2004.
5. *The Pink Panther*, DVD commentary, MGM Home Entertainment, 2004.
6. Author interview, 1999, previously unpublished material.
7. Author interview, 1999, previously unpublished material.
8. Julie Andrews, *Home Work: A Memoir of My Hollywood Years* (Weidenfeld & Nicolson, 2019), p. 229.
9. Julie Andrews, *Home Work: A Memoir of My Hollywood Years* (Weidenfeld & Nicolson, 2019), p. 230.
10. *Inside the Party*, MGM Home Entertainment, 2004.
11. Author interview, 1999, previously unpublished material.
12. *The Pink Panther Story*, MGM Home Entertainment, 2003.
13. *The Pink Panther Story*, MGM Home Entertainment, 2003.
14. *The Pink Panther Story*, MGM Home Entertainment, 2003.
15. Graham Stark, *Stark Naked* (Right Publishing, 2017), p. 162.
16. Author interview, 1999, previously unpublished material.
17. Graham Stark, *Stark Naked* (Right Publishing, 2017), p. 162.
18. Author interview, 1999, previously unpublished material.
19. Graham Stark, *Stark Naked* (Right Publishing, 2017), pp. 162–163.
20. Roger Lewis, *The Life and Death of Peter Sellers* (Arrow, 1995), p. 635.
21. Roger Lewis, *The Life and Death of Peter Sellers* (Arrow, 1995), p. 791.
22. Roger Lewis, *The Life and Death of Peter Sellers* (Arrow, 1995), p. 791.
23. Roger Lewis, *The Life and Death of Peter Sellers* (Arrow, 1995), p. 635.
24. Julie Andrews, *Home Work–A Memoir of My Hollywood Years* (Weidenfeld & Nicolson, 2019), p. 246,
25. Author interview, 1999, previously unpublished material.
26. Author interview, previously quoted in *Film Review*, #564, March 1999, p. 83.
27. Author interview, 1991, previously unpublished material.
28. *That's Panthertainment*, MGM Home Entertainment/Premacy Productions, 1978.
29. *That's Panthertainment*, MGM Home Entertainment/Premacy Productions, 1978.
30. *That's Panthertainment*, MGM Home Entertainment/Premacy Productions, 1978.
31. *That's Panthertainment*, MGM Home Entertainment/Premacy Productions, 1978.
32. Julie Andrews, *Home Work: A Memoir of My Hollywood Years* (Weidenfeld & Nicolson, 2019), p. 247.

Chapter 9

1. Author interview, previously quoted in *Film Review*, #564, March 1999, p. 85.
2. Andrew James Miller, *Power House: The Untold Story of Hollywood's Creative Artists Agency* (Custom House, 2016), p. 71.
3. Author interview, 1991, previously unpublished material.
4. Author interview, 1999, previously unpublished material.
5. Author interview, 1991, previously unpublished material.
6. Author interview, 1999, previously unpublished material.
7. Author interview, 1999, previously unpublished material.
8. Author interview, 1999, previously unpublished material.
9. Roger Lewis, *The Life and Death of Peter Sellers* (Arrow, 1995), p. 427.
10. Author interview, 1999, previously unpublished material.
11. Author interview, 1999, previously unpublished material.
12. Roger Moore, *My Word Is My Bond* (Michael O'Mara, 2008), p. 250.
13. IndustryPodcast.org, 2023.
14. Author interview, previously quoted in *Gold*, Vol. 1, No. 6, 1992, p. 67.
15. Author interview, previously quoted in *Gold*, Vol. 1, No. 6, 1992, p. 67.
16. Author interview, previously quoted in *What's On in London*, November 20, 1991, p. 17.
17. Author interview, previously quoted in *Film Review*, #581, May 1999, p. 85.

18. Author interview, 1999, previously unpublished material.
19. Author interview, 1999, previously unpublished material.
20. Author interview, 1999, previously unpublished material.
21. Author interview, 1999, previously unpublished material.
22. Author interview, previously quoted in *Film Review*, #581, May 1999, p. 85.
23. *Larry King Live*, CNN, 2002.
24. Author interview, previously quoted in *Film Review*, #564, March 1999, p. 82.
25. John Caps, *Henry Mancini: Reinventing Film Music* (University of Illinois Press, 2012), p. 241.
26. John Caps, *Henry Mancini: Reinventing Film Music* (University of Illinois Press, 2012), p. 241.
27. *Larry King Live*, CNN, 2002.
28. *Larry King Live*, CNN, 2002.
29. *Larry King Live*, CNN, 2002.
30. *The Pink Panther*, DVD commentary, MGM Home Entertainment, 2004.

Chapter 10

1. *76th Academy Awards*, AMPAS/ABC/Dakota Pictures/Revolution Studios, 29 February 2004.
2. *Daily Mail*, 24 July 2001.

Bibliography

Books

Andrews, Julie. *Home Work: A Memoir of My Hollywood Years*. London: Weidenfeld & Nicolson, 2019.
Black, Don. *The Sanest Guy in the Room*. London: Constable, 2020.
Caps, John. *Henry Mancini: Reinventing Film Music*. Urbana: University of Illinois Press, 2012
Forbes, Bryan. *A Divided Life*. London: Heinemann, 1992.
Lewis, Roger. *The Life and Death of Peter Sellers*. London: Arrow, 1995.
McFarlane, Brian. *An Autobiography of British Cinema*. London: Methuen, 1997.
Mancini, Henry. *Did They Mention the Music?* Lanham: Cooper Square Press, 2001.
Miller, James Andrew. *Power House: The Untold Story of Hollywood's Creative Artists Agency*. New York: Custom House, 2016.
Niven, David. *Bring on the Empty Horses*. London: Putnam, 1975.
Niven, David. *The Moon's a Balloon*. London: Hamish Hamilton, 1971.
Stark, Graham. *Stark Naked*. Bristol: Right Publishing, 2017.

Newspapers and Periodicals

Calgary Sun
Chicago Sun-Times
Chicago Tribune
Cinema Retro
Daily Mail
Daily Variety
007 Magazine
Evening Standard (London Evening Standard)
Film Review
Films and Filming
Gold
The Guardian
The Hollywood Reporter
Kinematograph Weekly (Kine Weekly)
LA Times
Mad
Monthly Film Bulletin (MFB)
New York Daily News (Daily News)
The New York Times
The New Yorker
Playbill
Punch

Replay
Sight and Sound
Spotlight
Starburst
The Telegraph
Time
Time Out
Variety
The Washington Post
What's On in London

DVD/Blu-ray Documentaries and Commentaries

Behind the Feline: The Cartoon Phenomenon (MGM Home Entertainment, 2003)
Inside the Party (MGM Home Entertainment, 2004)
The Pink Panther (MGM Home Entertainment, 2004 [commentary])
The Pink Panther Story (MGM Home Entertainment, 2003)
The Unknown Peter Sellers (Crew Neck Productions/Adler Media, 2000)

TV Programs

Film '76 (BBC, 9 January 1976)
Talking Pictures: Great British Comedies (BBC, 31 October 2015)
34th Academy Awards (AMPAS/ABC, 9 April 1962)

Websites

AFI
BFI
Deadline Hollywood
IMDb
IndustryPodcast.org
The Numbers
Wikipedia

Index

Numbers in ***bold italics*** indicate pages with illustrations

Abbott and Costello Meet the Mummy 10
After the Fox 76
All Ashore 8
The All New Pink Panther Show 50
The Ant and the Aardvark 50
The Apartment 16
Ape Suzette 48, 183
Arabesque 69
Arena 165, 188

Bachelor in Paradise 13
Bad Boys for Life 176
Bad Boys: Ride or Die 176
Le Ball and Chain Gang 183
Bear De Guerre 183
Beau Brummell 18
Behind the Feline—The Cartoon Phenomenon 168, 186, 192
Behind the Laughter 168
Being There 142
The Benny Goodman Story 10
The Best Years of Our Lives 6
Birth of the Pink Panther 166, 168
Blind Date 157
The Blues Brothers 11
Bob & Carol & Ted & Alice 130
Bob Hope's Pink Panther Thanksgiving Gala 151
Bobolink Pink 182
The Bomb 8
Bomb Voyage 48
Boston Terrier 76
Le Bowser Bagger 183
Breakfast at Tiffany's 3, ***13***, 15
Bully for Pink 182

Canadian Can-Can 183
The Carey Treatment 87

Carol for Another Christmas 75
Carry On Spying 99
Carte Blanched 48, 183
The Case of the Mukkinese Battle Horn 22
Casino Royale 76, 78, 102
Cat and the Pinkstalk 183
Charade 3, 68
Cheaper by the Dozen 168, 170
Cherche le Phantom 183
A Christmas Carol 102
Cirrhosis of the Louvre 183
City Detective 8
Clapperboard 123
Cleopatra 5, 17, 33
Clouseau, the Greatest Fumbler in the World 123
Cock-a-Doodle Deux Deux 183
Come Blow Your Horn 78
Come On In! The Water's Pink 182
Congratulations It's Pink 182
Le Cop on Le Rocks 183
Crazy People 22
The Creature from the Black Lagoon 10
Crow De Guerre 183
Cruisin' Down the River 8
Curse of the Pink Panther 127, ***134***, 146, 149, 150, 151, ***152***, 154, ***154***, 156, 157, 158, 180

Dante 12
Darling Lili 87, 99, 128
Days of Wine and Roses 14, 15, 19
Death on the Nile 2
Deep Pink—The True Story of the Pink Panther 168
Deliverance 91
Detective's Holiday 15
Dial "P" for Pink 48, 182

193

Index

Diamonds Are Forever 119
The Dick Powell Show 76
Die Another Day 170
Dietetic Pink 183
Divorce American Style 78, 81
Doctor Pink 183
Dr. Strangelove 42, 109
Don't Raise the Bridge, Lower the River 82–83
Down Among the Z Men 22, 55
Drive a Crooked Road 8
Duck Soup 33

Le Escape Goat 183
The Exorcist 55
Experiment in Terror 14, 15
Extinct Pink 182

Father of the Bride 168
The Ferret 145
The Fiendish Plot of Dr. Fu Manchu 76, 93, 143, 153
Film '76 105, 185, 186, 192
Five Miles to Midnight 52
A Fly in the Pink 182
Foreign Correspondent 34
Forty Pink Winks 182
Four Star Playhouse 8, 12, 15, 17
Freaky Friday 156
French Freud 183
Frenzy 69
Full of Life 9

Genie with a Light Pink Fur 182
The Ghost in the Noonday Sun 88
G.I. Pink 182
The Glenn Miller Story 10
Goldfinger 42, 46
Gong with the Pink 182
Good Neighbor Sam 55
The Goon Show 22, 144, 166
Goonreel 22
Le Great Dane Robbery 183
The Great De Gaulle Stone Operation 48, 183
The Great Escape 17
The Great Race 3, 75, 120, 142
The Great St. Trinian's Train Robbery 81
The Great Waldo Pepper 91
The Grip of Fear 14
Gunn 76, 128
A Guy Named Joe 6

The Hand Is Pinker Than the Eye 182
Hatari! 3

Hawaii 77
He Laughed Last 9
Heavens Above! 19
Helen of Troy 17
Henry Mancini Plays the Great Screen Hits 150
Herb Alpert & the Tijuana Brass Double Feature 46
He's Also a Great Giggler 100
High Anxiety 128
High Time 12, 76
Hoffman 88

I Am Not a Funny Man 165, 188
The Idiot Weekly, Price 2d 22
L'Idiote 52
I'm Alright Jack 19, 22, 147
In the Pink 48, 182
In the Pink of the Night 182
The Inn of the Sixth Happiness 57
Inspector Clouseau Strikes Again 109
Irma la Douce 55
It Came from Outer Space 10
It'll Be Alright on the Night 2 139
It's Pink, But Is It Mink? 182

Jack to Jacques 165
Jacoby's Vacation 77
James Galway & Henry Mancini—In the Pink 150
Jaws 2 137
Jet Pink 182
John Goldfarb, Please Come Home 55
Johnny Stecchino 157
Julie 158
The Julie Andrews Hour 87, 89
Julie: My Favorite Things 116
The Junior Crazy Gang 22

Keep Our Forests Pink 182
Kings of the Sun 77
Kiss Me, Stupid 75
Knockout 8

The Ladykillers 57, 91
La Feet's Defeat 48, 183
Land of the Pharaohs 52
Leather Gloves 8
Legends: Peter Sellers 168
The Life and Death of Peter Sellers 166, 167, 185, 187, 189, 191
Little Beaux Pink 182
Living Famously 168
Lolita 19
London Derriere 48, 183
Loser Take All 8

Index

Lost in Alaska 10
Lucky Pink 182

The Magnificent Seven 16
La malediction de la panthere rose *134*
The Maltese Falcon 94
Man Afraid 10
The Man from the Diner's Club 55
Mancini and Friends 150
The Mancini Generation 91
Mancini Plays Mancini 150
Mancini's Angels 150
Marshal of Reno 6
Mary Poppins 38, 42
The Men 42
Micki + Maude 145
Mike Hammer! 8, 14
The Millionairess 53, 54, 55, 76
Les Miserobots 183
Mister Cory 9
Mr. Lucky 12, *12*, 15
Mr. Topaze 35, 56, 78
More Music from Peter Gunn 11, 36
The Mouse That Roared 19
The Muppet Show 130
Murder by Death 90
Murphy Brown 153
My Fair Lady 42
My Sister Eileen 8
Mysterious Island 56
Mystic Pink 183

The Naked Gun 160
The Naked Truth 22, 58
Napoleon Blown-Aparte 183
Nero 17
Never Let Go 66
Never Steal Anything Small 9
Never Too Late 78
The Next Pink Panther 172
The New Avengers 147
The New Pink Panther 156, 166, 176
The New Pink Panther Show 49
New to You 21
Not the Nine O'Clock News 144
The Notorious Landlady 9

Octopussy 153
One More Time 83
Operation Mad Ball 9
Operation Petticoat 12, 15, 130
An Ounce of Pink 182
The Out-of-Towners 168, 173

Paper Tiger 90
Paradise Postponed 82

The Paranormal Peter Sellers 168
The Party 3, 76, *77*, 87, 96, 128, 135, 153, 187, 188, 189, 192
Penny Points to Paradise 22
The Pepsi-Cola Playhouse 8
The Perfect Furlough 12, 19
The Persuaders! 89
Pet Pink Pebbles 183
Peter Gunn 9, 10, *11*, 12, 15, 68, 77, 137
Peter Sellers og hans verden 105
The Peter Sellers Story 165, 188
The Peter Sellers Story: As He Filmed It 165
The Phantom of the Opera 117
Pickled Pink 182
Pierre and Cottage Cheese 183
Le Pig-Al Patrol 183
Pink-A-Boo 182
Pink-A-Rella 182
Pink and Shovel 183
Pink Arcade 183
Pink Aye 48, 182
Pink Bananas 183
Pink Blue Plate 182
The Pink Blueprint 46, 49, 182
Pink Breakfast 183
Pink Campaign 182
Pink Da Vinci 182
Pink Daddy 183
Pink 8 Ball 48, 182
Pink Elephant 182
The Pink Flea 182
Pink Goes to Hollywood 184
Pink Ice 46, 182
Pink-In 182
Pink in the Clink 182
Pink in the Drink 183
Pink in the Woods 183
Pink Is a Many Splintered Thing 182
Pink Lemonade 183
Pink Lightning 183
The Pink of Arabee 183
The Pink of Bagdad 183
Pink of the Litter 182
Pink on the Cob 182
Pink Outs 182
The Pink Package Plot 182
Pink Pajamas 46, 182
Pink Panic 182
The Pink Panther 1, 4, 5, 14, 16, *17*, 18, 23, *23*, *26*, *28*, *31*, *32*, *33*, *34*, *36*, *37*, 38, *39*, 40, *41*, *43*, 44, 45, *47*, 52, 53, 71, 74, 76, 85, 90, 134, 143, 151, 157, 166, 167, 168, *171*, 177, 185, 186, 188, 189, 190
The Pink Panther and Friends 183
Pink Panther and Pals 184

Index

Pink Panther and Sons 184
The Pink Panther Deux 172
The Pink Panther Film Collection 167
The Pink Panther: Hokus Pokus Pink 184
The Pink Panther Laugh-and-a-Half Hour-and-a-Half Show 50, 184
The Pink Panther: Passport to Peril 184
Pink Panther: Pinkadelic Pursuit 184
The Pink Panther Show 48, **49**, 50
The Pink Panther Story 185, 186, 187, 189
The Pink Panther Strikes Again 1, 109, 110, **110**, 111, **111**, **113**, 116, **116**, **118**, **119**, **121**, **122**, 123, **124**, 125, 127, 128, 131, 136, 139, 143, **144**, 145, 148, 150, 151, 153, 156, 158, 163, **163**, 166, 167, 176, 178
The Pink Panther 2 172, 181
Pink Panzer 46, 182
Pink Paradise 182
Pink Pest Control 182
Pink Pictures 48, 183
The Pink Phink 44, 46, **47**, 182
Pink Pictures 48, 183
The Pink Pill 182
Pink, Plunk, Plink 17, 182
Pink Piper 183
Pink Pistons 182
Pink Plasma 182
Pink Posies 182
Pink Pranks 182
Pink Press 183
The Pink Pro 183
Pink Pull 183
Pink Punch 182
Pink Quackers 183
The Pink Quarterback 182
Pink Sphinx 182
Pink Streaker 182
Pink Suds 183
Pink S.W.A.T. 183
The Pink Tail Fly 46, 49, 182
Pink Trumpet 183
Pink Tuba-Dore 182
Pink U.F.O. 183
Pink Valiant 182
Pink Z-Z-Z 183
Pinkadilly Circus 182
Pinkfinger 46, 182
Pinknic 182
Pinkologist 183
Pinkome Tax 182
Pinktails for Two 183
Pinky Doodle 183
Pinto Pink 182

The Pique Poquette of Paris 183
Plastered in Paris 183
Prefabricated Pink 182
Prehistoric Pink 182
Premier Pops 150
The Prince and the Pauper 114
The Prize 55
Profondo Rosa—La vera storia della Pantera Rosa 168
Psst Pink 182
Psychedelic Pink 182
Pulp 91
Put-Put Pink 182

Le Quiet Squad 183
Quo Vadis 18

Rachel and the Stranger 89
Rage to Live 77
Rainbow 'Round My Shoulder 8
Reaux, Reaux, Reaux Your Boat 48, 183
Reel Pink 182
The Return of the Pink Panther 1, 3, 88, **89**, 91, **95**, **98**, 99, 100, **101**, 102, 103, **104**, 105, **106**, 107, **107**, 109, 110, 115, 116, 118, 120, 128, 139, 143, 147, 150, 153, 156, 165, 166, 178
Revenge of the Pink Panther 2, 126, 127, 128, **129**, 130, **132**, 133, **134**, **135**, 137, 138, **138**, 139, **139**, 140, 140, 142, 143, 145, 147, 148, 150, 151, 153, 164, 166, 168, 179
Revudeville 21
Richard Diamond 8
Richard Diamond, Private Detective 7
Robbery 81
Rock a Bye Pinky 182
Rocky Pink 183
Romance of the Pink Panther 143, 145
The Running Jumping & Standing Still Film 22
The Russians Are Coming, the Russians Are Coming 78

Sacré Bleu Cross 183
Salmon Pink 182
Salome 5
Salt and Pepper 82
Salute to Sir Lew—The Master Showman 88
San Ferry Ann 56
Santa Claus: The Movie 69
Sapphire and Steel 147
The Scarlet Pinkernel 182
Sellers' Best? 165
Sgt. Bilko 168

Sherlock Holmes in the Gentleman's Club, or Commissioner Dreyfus Intervenes 157
Sherlock Holmes v panskem klubu aneb Komisar Dreyfus zasahuje 157
Sherlock Pink 48, 183
Shocking Pink 182
The Shooting of Caribou Lou 183
A Shot in the Dark 48, 52, **53**, 54, **56**, 57, **58**, **62**, **63**, 65, **65**, 66, **67**, 69, **70**, **72**, 73, 73, 74, 75, 77, 82, 85, 86, 90, 95, 97, 107, 117, 135, 143, 146, 148, 150, 151, 153, 155, 157, 165, 167, 169, 177
A Show Called Fred 22, 55, 144
Show Time 21
Sicque! Sicque! Sicque! 183
Silent Movie 123, 128
Silver Streak 69
The Simpsons 176
Singin' in the Rain 119
Sink Pink 46, 182
633 Squadron 54, 77
Sky Blue Pink 182
Slink Pink 182
The Smallest Show on Earth 22
Smile Pretty, Say Pink 182
The Smothers Brothers Comedy Hour 127
Soap 147, 153
S.O.B. 130, 142, 147
Soft Beds, Hard Battles 88, 177
Soldier in the Rain 15
The Solid Gold Cadillac 9
Some Like It Hot 16
Somebody's Daughter, Somebody's Son 168
Son of Fred 22
Sound Off 8
Southsea to Shepperton 165
Spark Plug Pink 183
Spartacus 18, 56
Sprinkle Me Pink 183
The Spy Who Loved Me 137, 143, **144**
Stampede 6
The Star and the Story 8
Star Pink 48
Star Wars 38
Starlight Hour 21
Steamboat Bill, Jr. 119
Strangler of the Swamp 6
Strictly for Pleasure 12
String Along Pink 48, 183
Super Pink 182
Supermarket Pink 183
Sweet Charity 119
Switch 2

10 3, 142, 145
The Terror of the Tongs 57
That's No Lady—That's Notre Dame! 183
That's Panthertainment 138, 189
Therapeutic Pink 48, 183
They Were Expendable 6
The Thief Who Came to Dinner 91
Think Before You Pink 182
Think Pink Panther 50, 184
This Happy Feeling 9
Those Magnificent Men in Their Flying Machines 35
Thunderball 48, 99
Tickled Pink 182
Tom and Jerry: The Movie 2
Tom Thumb 22
Tony Rome 40
Too Many Chefs 69
Topkapi 18, 42
Toro Pink 183
A Touch of Evil 10
Tour de Farce 183
Trail of the Lonesome Pink 182
Trail of the Pink Panther 1, 145, 146, **146**, 148, 149, 150, 151, 153, 155, 156, 158, 168, 179
Transylvania Mania 183
Twinkle Twinkle Little Pink 182
Two for the Road 137
Two Way Stretch 58

The Unknown Peter Sellers 168
Up the Creek 22, 58
Upstairs, Downstairs 117

Variety Band Box 21
Vertigo 53
Victor/Victoria 3, 4, 113, 117, 130, 136, 137, 142, 147, 156, 162, 164
The Victors 66
Visa to Canton 57
Vitamin Pink 182
Voodoo 77

Wait Until Dark 69
A Walk on the Wild Side 27
We Give Pink Stamps 46, 182
West Side Story 16
What's New Pussycat 55, 75, 102, 116
Where Does It Hurt? 88
Where the Americas Meet 108
Who Framed Roger Rabbit 102, 156
Who Is Killing the Great Chefs of Europe? 69
Witness for the Prosecution 52

Index

The Wizard of Oz 14
A Woman There Was 5
Workers' Playtime 21
The World of Henry Orient 43
The World of Peter Sellers 105

The Wrong Arm of the Law 55
The Wrong Box 60, 76

Yankee Doodle Pink 183
Yellow Submarine 71